BOAT GIRL

A Memoir of Youth, Love & Fiberglass

Melanie Neale

Published 2012 by Beating Windward Press LLC

For contact information, please visit:
www.BeatingWindward.com

First Edition
ISBN: 978-0-9838252-2-7

For Dad

Author's note: *I want to thank my mentor, Dan Wakefield, for helping me conceptualize this book in 2003 at a small writer's conference in Seaside, Florida. I also want to thank my friend, Matt Peters, for bringing it back to life in 2012 and my husband for his steadfast humor and support throughout the whole messy process.*

This story would not exist without my parents—two brave people who had the courage to live an unconventional life and give my sister and me the greatest gifts a parent can give: open minds and adventurous souls. For that, and for many other things, I want to thank them.

Melanie Neale

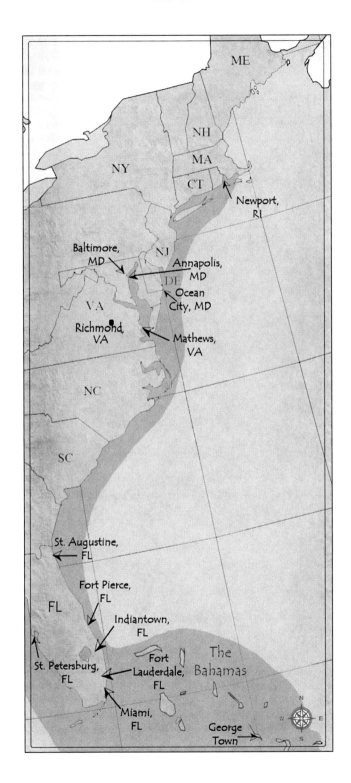

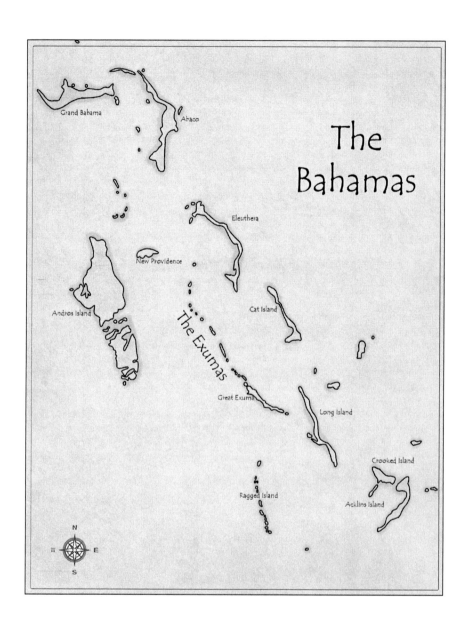

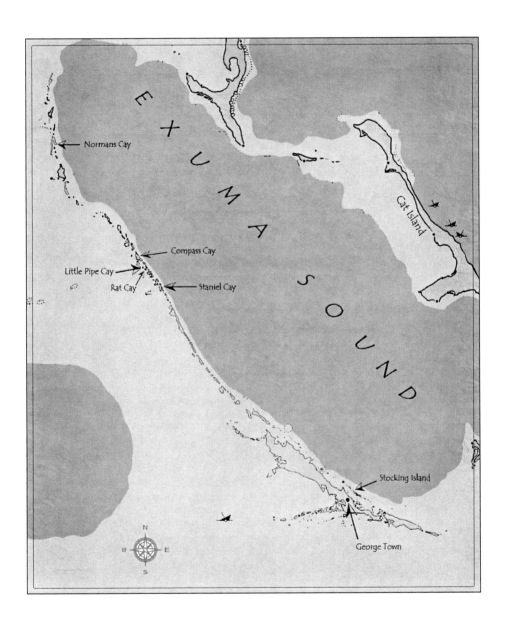

Melanie Neale

Fiberglass, Flesh and Bone

1979

Age 1

An airplane banked over St. Petersburg, Florida, and the Gulf of Mexico, flat and green, spread out under my parents and me. It was 1979 and my mom held me in her belly. She was sick from her pregnancy and from the plane ride, but I felt healthy and rested and light inside her. We visited the Gulfstar sailboat factory as soon as we got off the plane, my dad in cutoffs and a T-shirt. He'd left his suit and tie back in Virginia. My mom was granola-healthy, skin like polished bronze, her baby-belly leading the way. I couldn't see any of this, but I smelled raw fiberglass and uncured polyester resin, sharp and piney, through the membranes in her skin. The factory workers stopped as we entered the building, glancing briefly at our family before either looking at the ground or resuming their work. My dad had come to make their lives hell.

The boat had to be perfect. Dad had flown down before, entering the yard unannounced, checking to be sure that the hull was thick enough and the layout met his specifications. The workers, mostly retired carpenters and builders, must have resented him. He was half their age, a hotshot lawyer from the Tidewater area of Virginia who represented the labor unions and had made enough money doing so that by his early thirties he was able to commission a brand new sailboat. My dad: tangled brown hair a little longer than most lawyers', wire-framed glasses sitting on his wide nose, the veins in his neck constantly pulsing as he gritted his teeth, always right, and always ready to argue.

The boat was *Chez Nous*, hull # 20, with a modified cruising keel, heavy rudder, big Perkins diesel, Onan generator, sloop rigged, a slight stern overhang and a heavy bowsprit. Inside, the forward cabin was to be the kids' room and had a large V-berth and a hanging locker. There was a head across from the galley, and steps lead up to a main salon with a big teak table in the center, and a chart table and navigation station next to the companionway. Aft of the main salon, more steps lead down into my parents' room, with a queen-size bed and another hanging locker and its own private head.

I was born on August 7, 1979, somehow knowing all this. I fell in love with the 47' fiberglass sailboat the day I came aboard from the hospital.

I

Two years passed and I recognized my sister, Carolyn, the same way I recognized *Chez Nous*. I saw her lined up with the other babies in the hospital in Newport News, VA, small and red and screaming, and I knew she was made of the same stuff as me: fiberglass, flesh and bone, made to my dad's specifications. She was the final building block of our family—the completion of what my dad had been working so hard to create.

In the early days, we sailed the Chesapeake Bay on the weekends or whenever Dad had some time off. Work took him all over the country and there was talk of a promising political career. But the time on the boat is all I remember. We trolled a fishing line and hooked bluefish, which Mom reeled in and pried from the hook with delicate fingers. Once a fish bit her thumb and held on so tight that Dad had to pull the bony mouth open with steel pliers.

We glided up alongside the oyster boats that dredged the bay for the rough-shelled bivalves and loaded bucketfuls of them onto the stern of *Chez Nous*. Dad set me up on a shelf behind the cockpit and opened the oysters with a dull knife, holding them so that his fingers gripped the edges as he slipped the knife between the two shells and pushed them gently apart. He cut the muscle that attached the creature to its shell and poured hot sauce from a glass bottle onto the trembling and wet meat. Some oysters went onto a saltine cracker, but most went straight into his mouth with just a dab of hot sauce. I ate them too, sucking them down even before I had a full set of teeth. You didn't need teeth to eat raw oysters.

Mom sat at the helm and Carolyn rested in a basket wedged between floating cushions, secure so that it wouldn't slide as we tacked up and down the bay, heeling as the gusts came. When Monday came and Dad went back to work, Mom toted Carolyn and me to the sitter's house so that she could resume her teaching job. Both of my parents were trying to think of a way that they could make our weekend lifestyle permanent.

Chez Nous at anchor in the Bahamas.

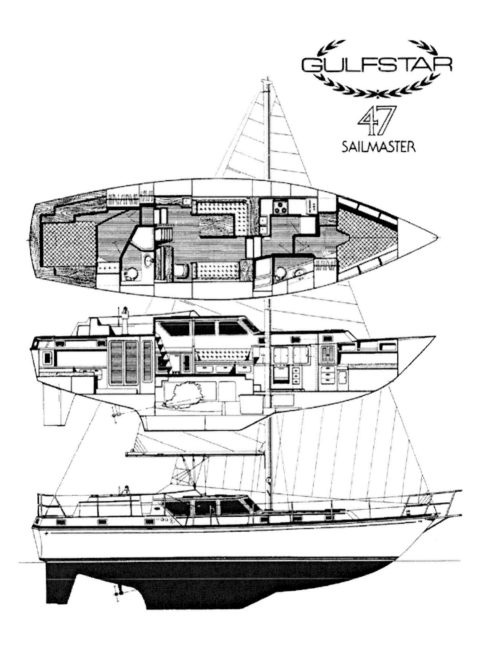

BOOK 1

Migrations

Melanie Neale

Trade and Barter

Virginia, Summer • 1984

Age 4

Grandmom Margaret helped my mom set up a picnic on the hood of my parents' blue Oldsmobile. Heat simmered off the dirt road and the car, and sweat pooled between my grandmother's breasts and soaked her tight T-shirt. Her breasts were brown and patchy with sun spots, and her fingers were long. I watched her unpack a cool stainless-steel thermos and twist the lid off. She tilted her head back and her throat moved as she drank, then she lit a Virginia Slim and leaned back against the Oldsmobile. I wondered how she could touch the car without burning her skin. Perhaps the years and years of sun that she and my grandfather had exposed themselves to while cruising the Bahamas had burnt the nerves on her skin to the point where she couldn't feel hot or cold. I sat on a blanket thrown over a patch of dry grass next to the car and marveled over her skin and breathed in the sweet cigarette smoke.

"You didn't pack a martini lunch, did you?" Mom picked up her mother's thermos and drank, frowned, and handed it back.

"It's after noon," Grandmom Margaret checked her wrist where a watch would have been if she'd been wearing one.

"It's still too early for martinis." Mom turned the thermos upside-down as if she were about to dump the contents into the red Virginia dirt, but the lid was screwed on tight. "I thought you'd brought drinks for the kids."

"I did," she said. She grabbed two diet colas off the backseat of her Thunderbird, which was parked next to the Olds. The cans were warm and had silver flecks of dirt sticking to them.

Mom shook her head, probably imagining how much caffeine and chemicals were inside the cans. She tossed them back into the Thunderbird. "The girls will just have to wait until we get home to get something to drink," she said. I eyed the soda cans, and ran a dry tongue over the roof my mouth. Mom had brought along a bag of sesame-seed and honey candy, and I unwrapped one and licked the honey off my fingers. It melted faster than I could eat it in the heat.

Grandmom Margaret downed her martini and closed her eyes, leaning her head back so that sunlight spread across her face. She coughed and pulled another long cigarette from the pack in her purse.

"You and Tommy really going to go cruising?" she asked my mom. "Raise those kids on the boat?"

"We're planning on it," Mom said. "Why?"

"Just watch the girls," she said. "Boat life might not be good for them. Might be a little rough—they're going to turn out to be completely unrefined."

"There are worse things in life than being unrefined," Mom said as she opened a Ziploc bag of carrot sticks and chewed one. Mom, Carolyn and I watched Grandmom Margaret draw from the cigarette, sucking her cheekbones in until they were hollow and skeletal. I pictured myself smoking Virginia Slims when I got older.

"I raised you okay, didn't I?" she said once she'd exhaled.

We all turned to watch my dad and Granddad crunch through the brush next to the road. Dad carried a machete. They'd been surveying the piece of waterfront land my parents had just bought—right next to my grandparents. Their plan was to build a dock on the land and keep *Chez Nous* there during the summers, when our family returned from the Bahamas. The Wittigs, who were my mother's parents, did the same thing—they kept their small cruising trawler docked at a rickety pier stretching into a creek off the Corrotoman River. They were slowly building a house on the land, doing all the work themselves. During the summers, they worked on their house and on the boat and gardened and hosted their five daughters and all the grandkids that came from having five daughters on their little slice of Virginia waterfront. In the fall, they untied their dock lines and headed south on the Intracoastal Waterway, a series of rivers and canals and creeks and estuaries that ran from Norfolk, VA all the way down to the tip of Florida and then continued back up Florida's West Coast. They crossed the Gulf Stream from Miami or Fort Lauderdale, depending on the weather, and spent several months in the Bahamas. My grandmother had beautiful shells in her house and on her boat, which she said she had collected during hours of walking the Bahamian beaches at low tide.

"We waited until we retired to do it," Grandmom Margaret said, exhaling as she spoke.

"You mean until Dad retired," Mom said.

"I had plenty of work to do raising five kids."

Mom was the oldest of the five. She and her sisters had been raised in Portsmouth, Virginia. They lived adjacent to her father's veterinary practice, and she helped her father out in the office, tending to customers and caring for the animals that they boarded. She also took care of her sisters. She cooked for them on the occasional nights when her mother didn't feel like cooking.

Tuna casseroles, Ritz crackers, Saltines and milk. During the summers, Dr. Dog, as everyone called my grandfather, would take a few weeks off and the family would cruise the Chesapeake Bay aboard their trawler, the *Sevenwytts*. The Wittig girls wore bikinis and flirted with the boys at the marinas. They swam in the muddy brown water of the Chesapeake, careful to avoid jellyfish, and lay out in the sun until their skin was copper and their hair was bright blond. My mom varnished the boat's mahogany and scrubbed the decks, keeping it beautiful and shipshape.

The Wittig girls all went to college to find husbands, and all succeeded. My mother met my father her senior year at Mary Washington College, where she studied Fine Art. He was lifeguarding at a private club in Richmond that my mother visited with a sorority sister, and was a law student at the University of Richmond. He was handsome, confident, and came from a good family. He was a catch. He asked my mother out and she agreed to a date. They were engaged a month after they met, and married in six months.

Over jugs of cheap wine in their small Richmond apartment, they would talk about their plans. They wanted to buy a boat and sail away—get away from the city and the rat race. They knew they needed money so my dad worked hard in his law practice and my mom taught high school art. They moved to Newport News, Virginia, which was a little bit closer to the water. They bought a small sailboat, a Tartan 27, and spent the weekends aboard, sailing in good and bad weather. Dad's law practice grew and they bought another sailboat, a Gulfstar 41. This one was big enough and comfortable enough for both of them to stay aboard for long periods of time, but they still didn't think it was big enough for a family. They kept it docked behind the brick waterfront house that they bought in a small town near Newport News.

At the Annapolis Sailboat Show in 1978, they stopped at the Gulfstar booth and picked up a brochure for the new Gulfstar 47. "A cruising sailboat for the discriminating yachtsman who demands quality, comfort and performance," the ad said. "This is the boat," my mom told my dad. With money that Dad had earned from a recent case, they put a down payment on *Chez Nous* at the show. "This is the boat we've been waiting for," Mom told him. "We can buy the boat now and go cruising as soon as we can afford it. In the meanwhile, we can move aboard."

Grandmom Margaret had finished her pack of cigarettes and had her eyes half-shut. She leaned against the hot metal of the Thunderbird. "Just make sure you all are careful over there," she said.

My mom played pat-a-cake with Carolyn, who squealed and clapped. I pulled a small deer tick off my leg and flicked it into the grass. The property was alive with ticks and chiggers, and even though we'd all sprayed ourselves with Off we still had to be diligent.

Grandmom Margaret continued. "The worst of the drug smuggling is over but there is still a lot of action in the Bahamas. If you get in with the wrong people, it could mean your boat gets seized. Or worse."

"We don't plan on getting mixed up with those types of people," Mom said.

"You know what they say about plans. You just have to be careful. That's all. Careful of the weather. The sharks. Getting sick. There are doctors over there but you may not want to go to them. Your father's a vet, but people still call him all the time for medical advice when we're over there. You have to have something you're good at—something you can use to trade and barter. If you have medical skills, you can help someone out and in return maybe they can fix your engine or repair something on your boat."

Trade and barter. It sounded so simple and so wonderful. I traded with Carolyn all the time—my half-finished cup of hot chocolate for her full one, convincing her that the marshmallows would make her sick, or my one cookie for her two. Mom seemed to like the idea too—she sat back and her eyes focused on something in the distance that didn't really exist. She looked like that when she was thinking. Her eyes drifted over our heads and focused on anything that was convenient—a wall, a tree, a cloud. She did it a lot at the dinner table, when my dad was talking and Carolyn and I were silently eating. It was a look of peace and focus—of concentrating on a dream and trying to connect it to the real world.

"Take plenty of supplies with you," Grandmom Margaret said. "Things that are hard to get or that are expensive over there. Like cigarettes or beer, or candy. You can trade the Bahamians cigarettes for fresh fish or conch."

"We're going to catch all of our fish and conch," Mom said.

The heat made me tired, and I lay down in the grass and folded my hands beneath my head. I drifted off to the Bahamas, where I was sure we would find tropical beaches lined with palm trees and strewn with colorful shells: pink conch shells, majestic tritons, cream-colored cowries. I would gather them and make jewelry out of them, hanging long shell necklaces around my neck. Maybe I would trade my jewelry for something more useful. I wondered what the Bahamians would have that I would want.

Northerly

Virginia • Fall 1984

Age 5

"I don't know if it's such a good idea to bring the guns with us," Mom said. We sat around the teak table in the boat's salon, the October wind from a strong northerly whipping the main halyard against the mast. Mom stood to clear dinner from the table as Dad cleaned one of his guns. Carolyn had her head to the base of the mast, listening to the thwacking sound from the halyard vibrate down through the aluminum where the mast came though the deck and into the cabin. She'd cried when I told her the sound was really a ghost trapped inside the mast, but she listened anyway.

"I've been doing some research," Dad said. "We just have to play by the rules—you know, declare all our weapons when we check in with customs, tell them how many bullets we have on board." Dad came from a long line of Virginia good-old-boys who thought you were irresponsible if you didn't own at least two guns for protecting your family.

"What happens if you don't?" Mom fidgeted with the cassette player that sat up over the chart table. The Judy Collins tape had started squealing again. She pulled it out and I watched as the thin ribbons of shiny tape streamed behind it, stuck in the player like the bubble gum I'd gotten stuck in my hair earlier that week. Mom groaned and wound them back into the tape, turning the wheels of the cassette with the eraser end of a #2 pencil. I hoped the tape wasn't shot, because I liked listening to Judy Collins.

"They can confiscate your boat." Dad ran an oily rag over his rifle until I could see my reflection in the metal from all the way across the cabin.

"I just wish there was a better way," Mom said. "We're going down there to get the kids away from guns and violence." She sighed as she popped Judy Collins back into the tape deck and I climbed onto the chair at the chart table and leaned my head toward the speakers so I could hear it a little better.

"Look, Mel," Dad said, "did you know that there are still pirates out there?"

Mom didn't say anything. She knew he was right. She had read all the books and magazines on cruising the islands, and knew that it was prudent to have a way of protecting your family from the many things that could go wrong.

"Pirates," Dad continued. "They just drive go-fast boats instead of sailing ships, and they smuggle cocaine instead of gold coins."

"Now you're going to scare the kids," Mom said.

I thought about it—pirates. I hoped we'd run into some greasy long-haired guy with an eye patch and a macaw, who'd take a liking to me and kidnap me on his pirate ship. I'd be good at being a pirate, even though I was only five. I was a fast learner. Judy Collins sang, "Someday soon, I'm going with him. Someday soon…"

"They can't be ignorant of what the real world is like," Dad said. "There are lots of bad people out there."

He always said he knew a lot about bad people because he'd been a lawyer for more than ten years and he'd seen a lot of them. He liked to tell us about the time he'd had to defend a serial killer. It was a court appointed case. He said the serial killer had been sitting there in the courtroom, eyeing a member of jury who fit the profile of the type that the killer preferred. The killer had salivated and smacked his lips, and had not been shy about his desires. We were never sure whether this story was made-up. Bad people were kind of like mean dogs, Dad said—they could look cute and trustworthy, but then could turn and bite your hand. You had to be careful and approach everyone with caution.

"There are plenty of good people out there too," Mom liked to tell him. "Like you." Mom believed in him wholeheartedly, and in the idealism that had guided him to practicing law. Dad returned his guns to the padlocked cabinet he'd had custom built for them in the stern. Mom pulled Carolyn away from the mast, holding her by the waist.

"I want to hear the ghosts!" Carolyn clung to the mast with both hands.

"There aren't any ghosts," Mom said.

"Melanie said there were!" Carolyn's eyes widened as the halyard banged extra hard against the mast outside, and the whole boat shook with a gust of wind.

"Carolyn, that's the wind," Mom said. Carolyn started to cry, so Mom took her up to the V-berth to put her to bed. Dad and I sat in the main cabin, me at the chart table and Dad on the settee, scraping the grease out from under his fingernails. The wind howled like a pack of hounds running down the Chesapeake Bay.

"It's time to head south, Melanie," Dad said. "That wind's getting a little too cold. I've been in the Chesapeake for too many winters now. Are you ready?"

"Yeah," I said. I was tired of sitting at the dock in Virginia, looking at the same marsh every day. I'd seen a muskrat earlier that afternoon, ducking into a hole under the crumbling dock down at the north end of Narrows Marina. Dad had told me that it was probably hiding from the cold. Narrows was a run-down marina that sat precariously between two rivers on the Chesapeake Bay. There was a playground with a jungle gym covered in chipped paint and squeaky swings and a sandbox, and big pine trees that shook in the fall when the cold fronts started coming through. My parents had bought the property off the Corrotoman River, next to the Wittigs, but we were staying in the marina until our dock was finished. "When are we leaving?" I asked.

"Soon as your mom's ready, and soon as your grandparents will let us go," he said. The Neale grandparents were protesting—saying that Carolyn and I were going to be malnourished if Mom and Dad went through with their insane plan. June, who was my dad's mother, had a hard enough time with the fact that Mom made us eat whole wheat bread and sesame seed candy.

"I'm ready," I said, even though I was tired and wanted to follow my sister up to the V-berth. Dad leaned his head back on the settee and we both listened to the wind, sharing the knowledge that there really were ghosts in it, just like there really were bad people and pirates out there in the rest of the world. The mast shook again, the wind vibrating though the boat and under me until I felt it moving up through the soles of my feet. A chill ran the length of my spine and my arm hairs stood on end, the way you're supposed to feel when someone walks over your grave. There was something alive in the wind. It sent waves of electricity through the boat's fiberglass and teak and the big Perkins engine. *You're taking me someplace completely new, aren't you?* I thought. I closed my eyes and felt *Chez Nous* shudder under my feet.

Grandmom June called us a week before we planned to head south and told Dad that we couldn't leave. "I'm afraid your father might be close to having a heart attack," she said. He'd had his first bypass surgery right before I was born, and lived with the constant fear that his heart would simply stop working.

"How is he feeling?" Dad asked.

"Well, he is feeling fine. But I just know that he is going to get sick again."

"We're still going south," Dad said. "But we'll spend a few days with you and C.T. before we leave."

C.T. stood for Carroll Thomas, Jr. Dad was Carroll Thomas the Third. C.T. had a huge belly, and he drank lots of bourbon. He was bald and always joked about needing to get his hair cut. My dad referred to him by his initials and not by "Dad" or "Father," which I always thought was a little strange, but it was just the way things were so I didn't question it too much.

We docked the boat on the Pamunkey River in West Point, a small and sobering town outside of Richmond. It was where my dad had grown up—a town with a paper mill and train tracks that cut along the river. It had a quaint downtown, two independent grocery stores, and was supported by the paper mill. Dad's childhood had been spent exploring the marsh of the two rivers that met there, the Pamunkey and the Mattaponi. Together, they merged into the York River. He said that he was unpopular in school because he had the right answers when the teachers asked and because he was skinny, so he disappeared sometimes for days in one of his skiffs. The water was much more of a home to him than the house that he shared with his parents and his two younger brothers.

"You know, you can move off the boat and stay with me," Grandmom June said as soon as Carolyn and I were in the house with her and Mom and Dad were out of earshot. I sat on the floor, legs splayed out on the stain-proof carpet. She'd fixed me a big bowl of vanilla ice cream with butterscotch sauce, and I swirled my spoon around in the caramel sea.

"You can go to a regular school and be around other kids. You don't want to be over there in the Bahamas. Did you know that everyone is black over there?" Grandmom June wrinkled her nose and, with a white and delicate hand, pushed a carefully set curl back over her ear. She had a black housekeeper who came in once a week and vacuumed and cleaned the large house. She also had been one of the first white citizens of West Point, VA, to stand up for integration in the local schools. Her house had two stories, large rooms, and antique furniture, and she baked cakes and hid the insulin vials that she had to administer herself to treat her diabetes. Seeing the tiny needle prick her plump finger fascinated me and made my grandfather cringe and look away.

A gust of cold air came in through the sliding glass door as my mom stepped inside. Grandmom June looked at her briefly, narrowing her eyes, and continued talking to me. "Do you really want to spend all your time playing with those little black kids?"

"I dunno." I didn't know what she was trying to say. I didn't see much of a difference—kids were kids, black or white. They all seemed pretty annoying to me.

"June! What are you trying to tell her?" Mom took my ice cream bowl away before I could finish it, whisking it under Grandmom's nose.

"I'm just telling her that if she doesn't like the boat she can live here," Grandmom said. "And let her finish her ice cream, for goodness' sake."

"She doesn't need ice cream. She'll get fat."

"And she'll starve to death on that godforsaken boat! Where is she going to go to the doctor? What if she gets some kind of tropical disease?" Grandmom June, who was normally gentle and soft-spoken, was becoming hysterical. She paced the house's big kitchen, circling faster with each round. Years later, when she was admitted to the hospital to have a mass removed from her brain, we would all look back and wonder how much her personality at times had been affected by the disease that was growing underneath her perfectly-styled curls. I wanted to tell her that it would be okay if I got sick, because there were doctors over there on boats, like Dr. Dog, with whom you could trade and barter for their service.

"June, relax. Tom and I have thought about all of that. We have tons of medical supplies on the boat, and lots of medical books."

When Mom took Carolyn and me by the hand and led us out the door, I thought about staying. The Neale grandparents always had good food around the house, and they let me spend the whole day in front of the TV eating ice cream. For the next two days, I agonized over whether to leave on the boat or stay in West Point. It would be like running away—kind of glamorous.

Granddad and my dad celebrated our pending adventure with a bottle of Wild Turkey. They drank it on the rocks and paced together in the backyard, my dad waving his arms and my grandfather's jowls flashing from stern to set to smiling and back to stern. They discussed mysterious things that had to be discussed away from the rest of the family, and my mom and my grandmother and my sister and I watched them through the tall sliding glass doors of the Neale grandparents' house and wondered what the conversation was about.

We left early the next morning, before I could make up my mind about whether I wanted to stay in West Point. I watched the fog rise off the Chesapeake Bay as we ploughed through the brown water on our way south.

Melanie Neale

Higher in the Gulf Stream

The East Coast and Bahamas • Fall and Winter 1984-1985

Age 5

It takes about sixteen hours to drive from Virginia to South Florida on I-95. When you're on a cruising sailboat, traveling at about seven nautical miles per hour, it can take a month. The first year we went south, it snowed in North Carolina and the decks of our sailboat were dusted with white. Carolyn and I made snowballs and threw them into the brown water where they steamed as they melted. We passed through the bridges—bascule bridges, swing bridges, fixed bridges—concrete and metal structures that stretched across uninhabited water and marked the only trace of civilization we'd seen all day. Eventually, when we'd been making the trip back and forth on the Intracoastal Waterway for several years, the bridge tenders started to recognize us. "It's about time y'all passed through here," they said. I wanted to be a bridge tender so I could sit and look at all the boats that passed through.

The Wittigs had gone south ahead of us on their trawler, and they were already over in the Bahamas by the time we left Virginia. "If you leave now, you can travel with us and we can show you where to go," Dr. Dog had told my dad.

But we waited, because everything on the boat had to be perfect, and because my dad's parents were trying to talk us out of going. "We'll do it the safe way the first trip," my dad had told them. "We'll stay inshore, on the Intracoastal, where we'll always be in sight of land and in VHF range of the Coast Guard." The VHF was a short-range radio that people on boats used to communicate with each other—the nautical equivalent to the truckers' CB.

The palm trees started in South Carolina—scraggly silver palmettos that spiked the banks of the Waterway. The weather turned warm around Fort Pierce, FL, where taller palms of different pedigrees lined the shore, and the water turned bluer than I'd ever seen it. We started shedding layers of clothing, exposing white limbs to the tropical sun. It felt like we were awakening and unfurling, our skin prickling with heat and excitement. Fort Lauderdale and Miami were everything I had imagined they would be—colorful cities where speed boats whipped past our lumbering sailboat and skyscrapers reached towards the clouds. Anchored in Biscayne Bay, our last stop before crossing the Gulf Stream, we could see the Miami skyline lit with neon colors spreading out behind us. I thought it was beautiful.

"Look at all that craziness," my dad said. "All those people, stuck in the city. They have no idea what life is really about." He sat in the cockpit and drank bourbon from a Tervis tumbler. "Miami is an awful place," he said, moving his gaze from the skyline to me.

"Why?"

"Too many people crammed into too little space. Bad things. Crime and drugs." He shifted his gaze again, this time to the blackness that spread out in front of us. A few flashing markers and lights from fishing boats sparkled in the darkness of Biscayne Bay, but for the most part it was black. The wind here was warm and I liked the way it ruffled my bangs and the way it smelled like flowers. I would learn later that the oleander it smelled like was highly poisonous. "Out there," my dad said, pointing into the blackness, "is where we're going. You're going to like it much better than Miami."

I sat and sipped a glass of water and stared at the Miami skyline, wondering what it would be like to be in the middle of all those lights.

I woke up the next morning with a stomach flu. My dad tried to figure out where I had gotten it. He decided that I had probably picked it up from the grocery store in Miami where we had done our last minute provisioning. "Dammit. I should have known better than to take them ashore in Miami," he said, pacing back and forth in the *Chez Nous'* small main salon while I perspired in the forward cabin, leaning over the V-berth every now and then to throw up in a large steel mixing bowl that my mom had placed on the floor next to my bed for that reason. The marine weather was being forecast over the VHF radio, and my dad scribbled notes on a legal pad as he listened to it. The voice from the National Weather Center was computerized, and it reminded me of the words that came from the Speak-And-Learn toy that my Neale grandparents had purchased for my sister and me. "Waves inshore 2 to 3 feet and higher in the Gulf Stream," the computer voice said. My dad wrote it down.

We stayed at anchor in Biscayne Bay for another day, waiting for my fever to go down, but we couldn't wait too long because, according to my dad, we had a "weather window." We didn't know how long the window was going to stay open. Other boats left ahead of us, heading for the Bahamas, their crew calling out to each other on the VHF, excited to be heading into the Gulf Stream.

On the day after my temperature returned to normal, I woke up to the sound of the diesel engine and the anchor chain as it clanked into the anchor locker at the foot of my bed. My dad stood on the deck right above me, shouting back to Mom, who was at the helm, to "motor up on it," and "stop." He operated the electric windlass, which pulled the chain across its cogs and dumped it into the locker. I could smell the seawater and bits of seaweed that clung to the chain, a rich and heavy smell. When the anchor was up, it made a loud bumping sound as it nested securely into its spot on the bowsprit, and my dad's feet thumped on the deck above me as he moved to fasten the chain in place. The hatch above my bed was open, and the same wind I smelled before, heavy with flowers, blew in through my room. Carolyn must have been up in the cockpit, because the berth next to mine was empty.

Chez Nous moved smoothly through the water, and I could hear the splashing of our wake as water slipped past the hull, only inches from where my head rested on the pillow. I closed my eyes and listened—the sound of the engine, the vibration of the boat moving through the water, the splashing and the wind, all of it combined made me sleepy and happy, and my stomach, which been nauseous and unsettled, began to feel better. We began a graceful up-and-down motion which meant that we were getting out into the open ocean. I drifted back to sleep.

I was pulled from my sleep when we slammed into a large wave. It must have been several times bigger than the ones we'd been going through. I stared up at the hatch above me and saw blue sky one second and green foam the next as water rolled over our bow and across the deck. In a solid stream, it poured through the hatch and onto my bed. I sat upright and pulled my blankets around me, hoping to keep them from getting wet. We went over another wave and more water poured through the hatch. I wondered if this meant that we were in the Gulf Stream.

My mom came running up to the forward cabin. "Oh no," she said. "Oh shit. I forgot to close the hatch. I am so sorry, Melanie. She pulled herself up onto Carolyn's berth and secured the latches that held down the hatch, then she stepped down and looked at our beds. "Everything is soaked," she said.

"Are we in the Gulf Stream?" I asked.

"We must be." She smiled and went to work stripping the sheets and blankets from our beds and rinsing them sparingly with fresh water in our shower and spreading them out in the cockpit to dry. I suddenly felt better, and wanted to be upstairs with the rest of my family.

In the cockpit, Carolyn huddled down on the deck with a beach towel wrapped around her and a bucket by her side. She had Saltine crackers in one hand and a Coke in the other. She was seasick. She'd gotten seasick a few times before. I hoped that my mom had given her Dramamine. She looked at me, misery in her eyes, her honey-blond hair tangled across her face. Her hair was always tangled. She was wild, even at three. I felt bad for her. I sat up in the cockpit and stared out across the ocean, which was a deeper blue than I'd ever seen before, and then I realized that I couldn't see land anywhere. This was a first.

I looked in front of us and looked behind us. Nothing. Just the flat horizon and rolling blue swells. My dad sat at the helm, his oversized sunglasses resting on his big nose and sunscreen smeared across his face but not rubbed in. He looked ahead, intent on getting his family across safely.

Two days later, we were anchored off Chub Cay in the Bahamas. It was a small island with a marina where people stopped to clear customs or to use as a jumping-off point for deep-sea fishing in the Tongue of the Ocean, which was the deep stretch of water between Andros and New Providence. A small fleet of Bahamian fishing smacks had anchored nearby. From lines that were strung from bow to stern, conch hung unevenly. Mom examined one of the smacks with her binoculars, the group of Bahamian men who stood in its cockpit staring back through the harsh sunlight with their bare and un-shaded eyes. "It looks like they've hung the conch so that the bodies die and fall out of their shells," she said. Even from our distance of a few hundred yards, we could smell the putrid stench of death coming from the small boats. Dr. Dog and Grandmom Margaret had met us in Chub Cay, on their way back from the Exuma Island Chain. They confirmed that this was the purpose behind stringing up the conch. The fishermen would spend days fishing and conching on the Bahama Banks before returning to Nassau to sell their catch to the restaurants and conch shells to tourists.

At Chub, Dad, eager to try out his snorkeling and spearfishing gear in the clear Bahamian water, spent hours freediving around our boat. He stayed nearby, as he had read to do, in case a shark or barracuda showed up and he had to get out of the water quickly. We watched him from the deck of *Chez Nous*, both nervous and thrilled to see him circle our boat and dive and hunt. Once, we heard a splash as loud as a gunshot, and all three of us turned in the direction from which it had come only to hear it again as a black manta ray with a six-foot wingspan smacked down against the flat calm water, sending spray into the air. The spray fell back to the water like cheap glitter. Mom cupped her hands over her mouth and yelled: "Tom! Tom!"

Dad raised his masked face from the water and spit the snorkel from his mouth.

"There's a giant manta ray over there!" Mom pointed in the direction where the ray had jumped.

"Oh," Dad said. "They are harmless." He ducked back underwater and continued his hunting. A few minutes later, he returned with a yellow and purple fish wriggling on the end of his spear. He hoisted himself out of the water and placed the fish in a bucket and we all watched it as Mom flipped through the waterproof fish book that we kept in the cockpit.

"It's a Queen Triggerfish," Mom said.

"It's pretty." I reached into the bucket and ran my finger along its glistening back.

"Can you eat it?" Dad looked from the fish to Mom and back to the fish.

"Edibility is excellent," Mom said, reading from the book. "The skin is tough, so they are hard to clean. It says that the Arawak Indians used to make shoes out of the skin."

Carolyn, following my lead, stuck her finger into the bucket to touch the fish. But she was three and less cautious, and her finger landed near the fish's mouth. It chomped down, causing her to scream and causing my mother to rush into the cabin for a Ziploc bag so that she could freeze the fish, whole, with my sister's blood still smeared on its mouth. They wanted to save the fish so they could show it to a doctor if Carolyn got any kind of weird infection. Later, Dr. Dog looked at my sister's finger and determined that she would be just fine. I had told her that her finger was probably going to fall off, so she was relieved to get the news.

"The Exumas are the best of the Bahamas," Dr. Dog told my dad that night, as they examined charts together. "The water is clearer and it's the least crowded. And there are people there that we know, that you can depend on if anything goes wrong."

We ended up at Rat Cay, in the Exumas. The harbor was tiny and, like many places where we stayed, we had to enter on a full moon high tide. We must have spent the days doing school work and spearfishing and looking for shells and working on the boat, but I don't remember much about the days. What I remember from Rat Cay is the nights.

George and Joanie lived on a small wooden sailboat called *Gypsy*. Dad didn't like the name of their boat, but I never understood why. George had a gray beard and he carved faces and figures out of buttonwood, which was thick and smooth enough to pass as mahogany. He carved mermaids and old men with beards, which curved across the buttonwood in river-like patterns. Joanie claimed to be blind.

"I can see things most people can't," she told Mom on our second night there. "It's hard to explain. I know what's going to happen to people, and I can talk to people who aren't here anymore."

Joanie drank dark rum and George drank vodka. Both drank it straight from the bottle or from tall stainless-steel glasses. They rarely drank anything else. Joanie's skin was leathery and she had a stout body and muddy eyes. "You don't believe me, do you?" she said to my mom.

"I don't know," Mom said. "I don't disbelieve you."

Joanie used a walking stick to feel her way down the dock, but when she reached *Gypsy* she dropped the stick and clambered onto the boat like she could see perfectly. George said she'd been on the boat so long that it was like a part of her body.

There were many other people at Rat Cay, coming and going, but George and Joanie were always there. My parents drank more than they usually did while we were there, and I think that may be one of the reasons we left and never went back. The harbor glassed over at night, smooth and black, and buttonwood smudge fires lit up the area around the dock. Carolyn and I spent most of the time in a hammock near the fires, watching the adults and listening to our parents' cassette deck playing Jimmy Buffett's *One Particular Harbour* album. "Stars on the Water" played over and over again, and the Bahama Banks spread out west of us with millions of stars reflecting against the shallow black water.

Thick smoke floated over the water from the fires. It wasn't familiar to me at the time, but as I grew older and learned to identify the heady smell of marijuana smoke I always went back to Rat Cay in my memory—the humid nights with their heavy smells and the adults coming and going and the constant fires. I don't believe that my parents ever smoked marijuana, and don't know, with absolute certainty, that anybody at Rat Cay did, but a similar smell hung over the island and was a part of the nights at Rat Cay. Mangroves, if you go near them on a still day, have a smell that's startlingly like marijuana—earthy and natural and smooth. There were many times in the Bahamas when I didn't know which smell was which: mangrove or marijuana. It didn't matter. Both were there, and both belonged.

Night after night, we sat by the fires. People showed up with dolphin fish and grouper to grill, and we ate well. I decided that I wanted to marry someone with a gray beard, and that I wanted to live on a boat when I was grown up. I fantasized about it, thinking constantly about what the boat would look like and where I would take it. I fantasized about living in a world just like Rat Cay, where people from different places came and gathered and contributed to the nightly meals with their day's catches and ship's store of rum.

The adults got rowdy at Rat Cay, and danced around the fires. One night, a wizened and gray-haired Bahamian woman who was staying on the island with her husband began to murmur and beat softly on her legs. She sat by a fire and bowed and raised her head, her voice growing louder as words spilled from her mouth. The words weren't the Bahamian pidgin that I'd come to recognize and understand. They were harsher and faster, one syllable crashing into the next in a jumble that you could almost see as it poured from her and spiraled into the night sky. "What is she saying?" I asked my dad, who had moved closer to where his small family sat huddled together.

"She's talking to a family member," he said.

"A family member?" It didn't make sense to me—she wasn't looking at anyone, or addressing anyone directly.

"Someone who just passed away," my mom said. The woman's chanting was palpable and it made me want to stand up and dance and swing my narrow hips in circles.

"Is she speaking in another language?" I asked.

"It's called 'speaking in tongues,'" Dad said. This was something he had seen many times during his rural Virginia childhood, and something to which the mysterious island chanting could easily be related.

"It reminds me of singing," I said, and I felt myself rising. My body had stopped fighting the urge to dance, and I stood in one place and undulated, feeling my small bones and small hips move to a rhythm that needed nothing more than the gentle sounds of the current rippling along the limestone rocks, the hum of mosquitos, the cracking of the fires, and the woman's chanting to be composed. The woman leaned back, her hands on her knees, and her Adam's apple pulsed as she threw her head so far back that it didn't even look like it was connected to her body anymore. She leaned and leaned until she was lying on the hard ground, and her jumbled words continued to climb into the heavens. She writhed and keened, the pain in her voice striking me as divine. Joanie sat at her side and held her hand, her eyes darting from the woman to me and back to the woman. I lifted my head as well, staring up and up and up into the black night and feeling as if I could see the woman's words trailing upwards like the smoke. Thousands of stars quivered.

Joanie watched me, her eyes little and black, and I wondered how someone who was blind could pay such close attention. "You're grown up," she said to me, poking my leg with her walking stick.

"What do you mean?" I rubbed my leg. It was cold where her stick had touched my skin.

"You act like a little adult," she said. "You're too old for your own good."

"Oh." I wasn't sure what she meant, but I had a feeling of momentum, of things moving faster than I could control them, and of me being pulled along through some kind of rushing current that was going to be my life. There were lots of people and lots of places, and none of them felt like home.

We left Rat Cay and never went back, possibly because it didn't mesh with my parents' ordered sense of the world, but the night sounds and smells stayed with me.

Melanie Neale

Normal People

Virginia • Summer and Fall 1985

Age 6

Because our dock at the wooded property next to the Wittigs wasn't finished yet, we spent the summer of 1985 at Narrows Marina. We reconnected with grandparents, took care of doctor's appointments, and fixed anything on the boat that had broken in our travels and that hadn't immediately been fixed. I rode with my dad in a rented truck to his former law office, where we removed boxes and boxes of old files and took them to a storage unit. The storage unit seemed like a place where you would go to die and I wanted to get out of it as quickly as possible.

In the beginning of September, my books for first grade arrived in white boxes from Calvert School, a private school up in Baltimore that offered a structured phonics-based home-schooling program. I made a big show of opening the boxes, snowing the floor of *Chez Nous* with Styrofoam peanuts, pulling out thin books, yellow #2 pencils with Calvert School written in gold on the sides, larger teachers' manuals for our parents to read, crayons, and construction paper. The thin books were color coded according to their reading level. I took the crayons and drew pictures of myself, dressed like a princess with long blond hair (my own was short and broken off because I didn't brush it enough), into all of the schoolbooks.

When we drove into the small town of Mathews to buy groceries or get the mail, people asked Carolyn and me why we weren't in school. "Because we don't go to school," I told the lady in the post office one day.

When we left, Dad said, "Don't tell people that. Tell them you're homeschooled. Do you know what might happen if people think you're not going to school?"

"No," I said. Carolyn, whose imagination was lively, pretended to be a cat and swiped Dad's shoulder with her fingernails.

"Social workers might come and take you away," he said. "They don't know about people who live on boats. They don't understand that we're different from everyone else."

25

I thought it might be kind of fun to have a social worker come out to the boat and try to take us away. Maybe I'd go voluntarily, just to see what Dad would do. This was more of a fantasy about living someone else's life than it was about leaving my own and defying my dad. We lived one way and everyone else lived another, and I was curious what their lives were like. I watched people watching us, and knew that they were wondering who we were. Mathews was the kind of small town where everyone knew everyone else and had for generations, and we stood out due to the fact that we didn't seem to follow the normal constraints of society—my parents didn't work in a conventional sense, Carolyn and I didn't go to school. We didn't go to any of their churches—Baptist or Methodist, as those were the two main choices in rural Virginia. We went into town when we needed to, but never stayed any longer than necessary. We didn't eat at the restaurants where they ate. ("All those cows eating that greasy food," my dad would say. "They'll probably all have heart attacks.")

"People aren't allowed to be different," Dad said. "That's what's wrong with the world." His nostrils flared and turned red, the way they always did when he was mad about something. He gripped the Oldsmobile's wheel and jerked the car around the curve at the marina entrance. "You girls are going to have so many more opportunities than kids who go to regular school," he said. "You'll appreciate it some day."

The most exciting thing that happened that fall was the grain grinder. Mom ordered it from a health food catalogue because wheat berries stored longer than flour, and when it showed up she spread all its parts out over the salon table. It weighed as much as an outboard motor, and the stainless-steel glistened. She attached the bowl and showed us the stone teeth inside the mouth where the grain disappeared. It reminded me of the triggerfish at Chub Cay that had bitten Carolyn's finger—flat teeth made for grinding and chewing. "What's going to keep someone from sticking their fingers down there?" I asked.

"Common sense," Dad said.

Mom plugged it in and poured wheat berries that looked like tiny golden bugs into the bowl. They seemed to scramble over each other in their race to get into the neck of the contraption, where the teeth waited.

"Watch this," Mom said, and she slid a pan beneath a spout at the end of the machine. She flipped a switch and the thing squealed into action. Carolyn and I stared at the inverted tornado of wheat berries as the machine's teeth ground against each other and pulverized them.

Clouds of brownish flour puffed from the spout, and then a steady waterfall of flour flowed into the pan, piling up in tiny mountains of whole wheat. Mom spread the flour out with a spoon to make room for more. It reminded me of a map—a landscape of whole wheat flour.

School and meals made our days structured and gave us a sense of normalcy.

At breakfast, we all sat around the table in the main salon and ate oatmeal and fresh fruit—the sweet ripe cantaloupes that grew locally, or navel oranges shipped up from Florida.

After Mom cleared the table, she would open the plastic boxes where we kept our school supplies and spread the books and pencils out on the same table. It was perfect for seating four people. A brass trawler lamp hung over the center of the table, casting a warm glow around the cabin even in the daytime when the lamp wasn't lit.

Carolyn's supplies were much more basic than mine: the accoutrements of pre-school. She drew green dinosaurs on thick construction paper and chewed on the erasers of my Calvert School pencils while I learned the basic structure of a sentence. Nouns and verbs and adjectives and adverbs all made perfect sense when diagramed out in my composition books, and I liked figuring out how the pieces fit together. The books I read had simple names like "Mr. Fig." I learned how to write in cursive, practicing each of the letters over and over again. Mom was a patient and attentive teacher.

(Years later, when I turned thirteen, I abandoned the salon table and moved to the forward cabin, the bedroom I shared with my sister, to do my schoolwork. The table where we did everything was becoming too small for me. When I was seventeen, I got tired of the faded varnish on the table, and I unscrewed it from its mount and took it on deck to refinish the surface. When I was nineteen, the fresh varnish on the table was one of the strong selling points of *Chez Nous*.)

At lunch time, we pushed our schoolwork aside and sat around the table as a family, eating sandwiches with homemade wheat bread and ripe tomatoes. Dad continued whatever discussions he'd begun with us earlier while teaching us our history or geography lessons, and we talked about what we were going to do for the rest of the day. Afterwards, he retired to the aft cabin for a nap, and Carolyn, Mom and I finished our daily school assignments, which Calvert School had clearly laid out in its lesson plans.

In Virginia, the exciting days were the ones when we piled into the Oldsmobile and drove to Gloucester, which was bigger than Mathews and had a Wal-Mart. There, we got the same stares we'd get from the lady in the post office in Mathews—stares that said, *Why aren't you in school? How come you're loading up on canned vegetables and dried beans? Why do you need to buy twenty bottles of shampoo at one time?* We'd provision at Walmart and the local Best Value grocery store, filling up carts and carts of nonperishables, which we'd then shove into every bit of storage space that *Chez Nous* had to offer. Storage was something that Gulfstar had taken into consideration when designing that particular model (and all of their motorsailors). There was storage under the settee, under the berths, under the cabin sole. There was so much storage that people in the seventies and eighties dubbed the boats "marijuana barges," seeing as how they'd be ideal for smuggling.

Dinners were spent around the same salon table. Dad sipped his bourbon and mom her rum. She'd taken to rum our first year in the Bahamas, and she mixed coconut rum with Bacardi Gold and iced it down. I loved the smell of the coconut rum.

Some evenings, Dad sat in the cockpit and played folk songs on his guitar while Mom cooked dinner. The deep vibration of his voice as he sang "Old Man River" and "Summertime" rolled across me. On those evenings, the sun was red sinking into the marsh and mosquitoes hummed along with Dad. We slapped them away as we thought of all the poor fools living on land, watching their televisions and living the normal life. What we had was so much more real, my dad liked to say. We lived in the real world and they lived in the rat race. I imagined small rodents rushing through a maze and trying to find their way out. Dad told us made-up stories after dinner, or read to us from *Jonathan Livingston Seagull*, one of his favorite books. It was a fable by Richard Bach and was about a seagull that flew for pleasure rather than for survival. The seagull was different because he cared about flying and was therefore rejected from the flock only to reach a place of higher acceptance and meaning.

In November, we dug up a cedar tree from Granddad Neale's land, an expansive tract of woods and creeks on which he operated a sand and gravel plant. We planted it in a five-gallon bucket and placed it on the stern of *Chez Nous* and tied it to the stanchions so it wouldn't slide around the deck. "I bet we'll be the only people in the Bahamas with a real Christmas tree," Dad said, standing to look at it and smiling. This became tradition—the cedar tree on the back of the boat, so consistent each year that the bridge tenders up and down the Intracoastal recognized us by the tree alone. We covered it in garbage bags for Gulf Stream crossings, to keep the salt from drying it out, and we moved it down into the main salon a week before Christmas and decorated it with shells and ornaments.

The Neale Grandparents didn't try as hard to stop us when we left to follow the Wittig Grandparents south on our second year's migration. They still fed me ice cream and told me I was welcomed to stay, but I didn't consider it as I had before.

Smugglers

Norman's Cay, Bahamas • Winter 1986

Age 6

It was in the early winter of our second year in the Bahamas, and waterspouts spiraled down from heavy cumulous clouds. A cold front was coming, and everything in the Exuma Chain stood impossibly still, waiting for the lead-black line of clouds that hung over the banks in the northwest. Their bellies, which should have been silver, were lined with turquoise from the light that bounced off the shallow Bahama Banks.

We anchored near the wreck of a DC-3 plane that had been deliberately crashed a few years before we came. We were waiting for high tide so we could take the boat over the shoal and into the protected inner harbor called Norman's Pond. We didn't know which would come first: high tide or the wind from the squall line.

"I didn't want to have to come here," Dad said, pacing the cabin. He wouldn't tell Carolyn and me why. Our parents seemed to know something about the place that we didn't. Flies swarmed around the boat, and buzzed through the open hatches and into the cabin. Carolyn and I sat at opposite ends of the salon table, schoolbooks spread in a mess across the table. Lessons for the day seemed to be forgotten, like something more important than school was about to happen.

Mom paced too, the fly swatter in hand. "Those flies know we're in for bad weather," she said. "See, that's one way you can tell." She spoke to Carolyn and me, but her eyes were on the heavy squall line. "Watch the animals. See if they're trying to take shelter."

I rushed into the forward head to check on our hamster, Scruffy.

When I returned to the main salon, Dad had gone upstairs to the cockpit. "You girls should come up here," he said, his voice rattling down the companionway hatch. "You need to know what a waterspout looks like."

The four of us huddled in the cockpit. Dad handed us each life jackets. "You don't need to put them on," he said. "Just keep them by you."

The line of clouds was closer now, and more defined. Mom didn't say anything. Carolyn and I stared out at the clouds, swatting flies and no-see-'ums in the sticky heat. The twister clouds reached down to the water and then pulled back up into the lead-colored mass. I thought of "The Wizard of Oz," and wondered if a tornado could pick up our boat and set it down somewhere else. I wondered what a Bahamian Oz would look like.

"The tide should be high at four," Mom said.

"And the light's going be terrible getting into the Pond. Jesus Christ." Dad was worried. The vein in his neck stood out and pumped blood to his face in rapid jerking motions. "We're not going to be able to see the bottom."

"Look at that one. It's reached the water," Mom said. She stooped between Carolyn and me so close that I could see the beads of sweat that ran down the strands of her short sun-streaked hair. She pointed to a twister on the horizon. It was thinner than the others, and it snaked down to the water and ended in a cloud of steam. "That's where it's picking the water up," Mom said. We watched it withdraw as fast as it had formed, only to be replaced by another one further down the squall line.

"It all starts with areas of different air pressure. That's why the barometer drops when we get a cold front," Dad said. The air felt different now. It pressed against my eardrums and made me think of being underwater.

"Behind those clouds," he said, "the wind is going to swing around and come out of the northwest, maybe as strong as thirty or forty knots. That's why we need to get into a safe anchorage."

It promised to be a bad month weather-wise. There were several other fronts behind this one, all forecast to come through the central Bahamas. My parents had hoped to make it to Pipe Creek before the first one.

By three, the squalls had moved on. Dad raised the anchor and we headed into Norman's Pond. There were people at Norman's that we'd been told to look up, some friends of the Wittig Grandparents, and Mom hailed them on the VHF after we dropped the anchor in the thick grass of what seemed like a stagnant body of water. Maybe it was because there was little circulation back in the pond— water moved slowly through mangrove roots that massed together on the flats all around the island. We'd come close to scraping the bottom on the way in; Dad had slowed *Chez Nous* to a crawl and clouds of silt had billowed up in the water behind us as the prop stirred the bottom. Now we were stuck inside, brought in on the full moon high tide. We'd have to wait until the next full moon to leave.

A man's friendly voice on the VHF said, "Come ashore when you're settled in, Mel, and we'll show you around the island." Mom said we'd be there in about an hour, and she turned the radio back to 16, the hailing channel.

"So who, exactly, are these people? More drinking buddies of your parents'?" Dad spoke from inside the engine room, where he was checking fluids and looking for leaks and listening to the Perkins. He did that every time we shut the engine off—he called it "putting her to bed."

"Tom, my parents don't spend all their time drinking."

"Maybe not all, but a lot." He hoisted himself out of the engine room hatch, which took up most of the space in the floor of the main cabin. When Dad was in the engine room, there was no moving around the boat. Everything we were doing had to be put on hold until he was finished. This was fine if all he was doing was checking the oil, but sometimes he had the floor torn up for days.

About an hour later, we all piled into the dinghy and motored towards the shore where the man had told us to meet him. From the middle of the anchorage, Norman's was a pristine and beautiful island. The hills crouched low, as if they were the bunched muscles of some prehistoric lizard, covered with small mounds of green dry palmetto scrub. We headed towards a dock that was barely visible against the shoreline. When we got closer, Dad slowed the dinghy and wavered his course like he was about to turn around.

The dock was in shambles. It looked like a large vessel had rammed into it and torn down several of the pilings. The pilings that remained were slashed across with red spray paint: "Go Away," and words I didn't understand: crude references to Colombian cocaine that had been trafficked through here a few years before.

A man my grandparents' age strode down the dock waving us over. "Tie up and come on ashore," he said. "Don't mind all that stuff." He motioned towards the jumbled dock, which Dad was being careful to circle around. He took our bow line and fastened it around one of the pilings that was broken in half.

Mom called him The Doctor. I can't remember his real name, or his wife's name, but they drove us around Norman's Cay in a Jeep and showed us Volcano House, where Carlos "Joe" Lehder had lived in luxury and watched his planes fly in and out at night, loaded with cocaine. This was as much as I could understand at six. All I knew was that someone famous had lived here and that the walls had been shot up with machine guns only a few years before. The view from Volcano House was beautiful: the endless shallow banks stretching out west from the Exuma chain, aquamarine and turquoise. I didn't like being inside the house—it felt stuffy and dark, like it didn't belong next to that beautiful stretch of water.

The Doctor and his wife drove us to their house, which was much smaller than Lehder's, and showed us the machine gun holes in their own walls. "They didn't like us being around," the Doctor said. "If you weren't on Lehder's side, you might as well have been dead. We finally left for about a year and let it all settle."

Nothing looked very settled at Normans. I felt like someone was watching us from the shadows. But Lehder was serving a life sentence in federal prison in Illinois, and the only people on Norman's were a few American expatriates and cruising boaters like us.

The bullet holes and the Doctor's calm manners made me nervous and I wanted to get off that island. We were stuck for a month, waiting for the next full-moon tide that would be high enough for us to make it out of Norman's

Pond. Hammerhead sharks haunted the mangroves around the Pond, so I didn't even want to go swimming.

It was a strange time—almost as strange as Rat Cay, but less pleasant. The cruisers who passed through Norman's Cay had potlucks at Volcano House, drinking rum in the tiled rooms and gazing out at the moonswept Bahama Banks where the water stretched shallow for miles. I remember noise and fighting. When the next cold front came through, a large motorsailor dragged down on us in the middle of the night and Dad ran outside in his underwear, screaming at the man on the motorsailor. "I've got kids sleeping inside, and you're threatening our home and our lives." He aimed his high powered spotlight at the man's vessel, which was bearing down on us fast. The man covered his eyes. Of course, Carolyn and I weren't sleeping anymore. We had climbed into the cockpit to see what was going on.

"Tom, it's not his fault that his anchor dragged," Mom said.

"Like hell it's not." Dad walked up to the bow, where the motorsailor's bow sprit was linked underneath ours. He took a boat hook and stepped on the other vessel, pushing its bow sprit down so that it slid out from under ours. Then he used the boat hook to push the other boat away from ours. It slid by in the night while the wind screamed in from the Northwest and chilled my arms so much that my hairs prickled up. The man on the other boat stood on the bow like he couldn't believe what had just happened. He kept dragging anchor toward shore.

Dad ushered us below and back to bed, and then he got in the dinghy to go help the motorsailor. Now that it was past us, it wasn't a threat anymore and he could help without being worried about his own boat and family. That's the way he was. If anything he owned or anyone in his family was being threatened, nothing else mattered and whoever was doing the threatening could go to hell.

Dad didn't have much sympathy for people who dragged anchor. "It's almost always their fault," he said. Whenever we anchored, he made Mom back down hard at the helm until he was sure the anchor was set. He studied the mud on the anchor when it came back up, and remembered the places that had the best holding. And we never dragged.

The space shuttle Challenger exploded off the coast of Florida while we were in Normans Pond, killing all seven people aboard. It was Jan 28, 1986. As with all major news, this information was passed along from boater to boater over the VHF radio, being transmitted through abstract circles of radio reception.

On our last night in Norman's Pond, phosphorescence lit up the water, caused by millions of tiny jellyfish floating out from the mangroves on the full moon tide. The black water looked like a meteor shower was running though it. We stood on the deck of *Chez Nous* and watched, and I felt the boat swinging on the current and knew she was ready to move on.

We never went back to Norman's Cay either.

Tadpoles and Tritons

Little Pipe Cay, Bahamas • Winter 1986

Age 6

Dr. Dog told us about a cistern on Little Pipe. "There's nobody living on the island right now," he said. "So all you have to do is open up the top and dip a bucket." They were always giving us tips on where we should go and who we should meet. We didn't see them much, since their cruising schedule was different from ours (they headed south earlier and were usually on their way back by the time we made it to the Exmuas), but their influence followed us. They'd sat with my parents at our salon table and looked at the charts, marking off in pencil every cruiser-accessible cistern on every island in the Exumas. Most of the fresh water in the Bahamas came from cisterns, built underneath the houses with pipes running from the roofs and channeling rain water.

We docked our dinghy at the crumbling cement pier that jutted out beside the island's east-facing beach. A trail ran up the hill to a clearing, where a deserted cottage sat next to the flat concrete top of the cistern. Since it hadn't rained in weeks, bird shit had caked up on the roof and the pipes, and my mom groaned. "It's a good thing we're not drinking this," she said.

We drank rainwater back then, but we caught it on the clean decks of *Chez Nous*. Every time it rained, we scurried around the decks naked, plugging the scuppers up with clay and opening the fill-pipe to the water tanks. This caused the fresh water that we collected on our decks to run into the tanks rather than out through the scuppers and into the sea.

We had brought our laundry ashore, and we carried it up the hill in mesh bags. Carolyn and I struggled under the weight of a month's worth of dirty clothes.

We set two Rubbermaid buckets side by side next to the cistern: one for washing, one for rinsing. We'd brought a smaller bucket with a piece of rope attached to the handle for dipping water out of the cistern, whose wooden cover slid off easily.

"Oooh, wow." I felt my breath whoosh out of my lungs into the cavernous interior, almost like the cistern was sucking it away from me. The inside looked the same as most Bahamian cisterns' did: the walls were lined with green algae, the bottom glistened brown and gold like the skin of a flounder under several feet of fresh rainwater. Tadpoles wiggled sideways and up and down, and gathered in the shady corners to get away from the sunlight that we were letting in through the opening. "Let's catch a tadpole," I said, elbowing Carolyn.

Carolyn and I dipped the bucket, trying to direct it into the tadpole-filled corners, while our parents admired the view from the top of Little Pipe Cay's low hill. Our sailboat rested at anchor to the east, between Thomas Cay and Little Pipe, in a stretch of aquamarine water lined on either side by shallow brown reef. To the north, the two hills of Compass Cay, Pipe Creek's highest island, rose above the rocks and crags of Joe Cay. White sand flats stretched between Joe and Big Pipe, and smaller islands filled in the spaces between flats and deeper blue channels. "I think this is the prettiest place in the world," Mom said. "I wonder what the view would be like from Compass."

Carolyn squealed and our parents whirled around. "Tadpole! Tadpole!" she said. She thrust her hand in the bucket and clenched it around a shiny brown creature. The tadpole slipped between her fingers and flopped onto the cement. I tried to catch it, but, almost as if it were being magnetically drawn to the water, it rolled over the edge of the opening and into the cistern.

"Don't worry. We'll get another one."

Mom dumped the rest of the bucket into one of the Rubbermaids so she could start the laundry. She poured Tide detergent in with the cistern water. I checked to make sure there weren't any tadpoles swimming around in our laundry.

Dad filled the other Rubbermaid from the cistern, and Carolyn watched the bucket dip in and out of the dark hole, waiting for tadpoles. As soon as he turned his back, she grabbed the bucket and leaned as far into the cistern as she could. She bent in half at the waist. I sat next to my mom, who was looking the other way, hunched over the Rubbermaid and rubbing our clothes hard against a washboard.

"You don't need me to stick around for anything, do you?" Dad's walkabout instinct was kicking in: he wanted to explore the island. It was a new place, a place he'd never seen before. When he was a boy growing up in the marsh surrounding West Point, Virginia, he'd taken his skiff through tiny inlets and creeks in the marsh until he found an island. The islands were small raised patches of dry mud that just escaped the tidal range and were therefore void of marsh. There was almost nothing on them—maybe a pine seedling or two, maybe dozens of little fiddler crabs or a great blue heron. But to my dad, the islands were his. They were unexplored. He could claim them like a colonist. He fantasized, sitting on these muddy islands, about tropical islands that he could explore and conquer. Unlike him, I just wanted to explore and learn. There was no inner colonist in me.

"No. You should put some clothes on before you go anywhere though," Mom said.

"I won't go far. Besides, all the clothes are wet." He nudged a flip-flop against the Rubbermaid laundry tub. Carolyn and I were used to being naked—it made more sense to play on the beaches without worrying about scratchy bathing suits or shorts that would be uncomfortable when they got wet. But our parents didn't go naked as often. Dad usually wore at least a ratty pair of underpants, and mom a bathing suit. Today we were all stark naked, except for flip-flops.

"I guess we should have set some clothes aside," Mom said.

"Just hurry up. We don't want anyone to sneak up on us like this." Dad turned and disappeared in the opposite direction of the old road, making his own path through the scant palmetto scrub, his skinny brown back glistening with sweat and his machete swaying from side to side, hacking at anything in his way.

I watched Carolyn lean further and further into the cistern. The bucket made slopping noises as she swung it back and forth so that it skimmed the surface of the dark water and bounced off, sending the tadpoles darting away in schools. A brown lizard appeared from out of the brush and ran across the sole of her foot.

Carolyn gasped, jerked her foot back, and toppled head first into the cistern.

Her body smacked the water and she screamed. Mom screamed next. "Tom! Help!" She dropped the washboard and ran to the edge of the cistern, where I was leaning down reaching for Carolyn's hand. Carolyn didn't panic. She simply stared up at us, her eyes as big as a frog's, treading water, her arms splayed out to the sides and her legs bent. I saw the terror on her face as she looked around the inside of the cistern, taking in the slimy walls, watching for snakes and spiders. The whites of her eyes glowed.

My dad hadn't wandered far, because he showed up immediately. He and my mom leaned into the cistern together, and grabbed Carolyn by the wrists. They pulled her out with one heave. She didn't say anything, but she stared back into the cistern like she'd seen a ghost. One tear ran down her cheek. She wiped if off and sat down on the cement.

"Oh hell," Dad said. "The bucket's still down there."

"Just leave it. We have more buckets." Mom didn't want anybody else venturing into the cistern. It was only a few feet deep, but the cool dark blackness made it look like an endless cavern.

"Buckets cost too much," Dad said. He went in feet first, lowering his body through the dark hole. "There'd better not be any snakes in here," he said.

"Don't worry, Dad. There aren't any poisonous snakes in the Bahamas," I said. I had been reading field guides with religious fervor.

"Snakes, no. Spiders, yes," Mom said. "Black widows especially."

My dad glared at her and ducked out of sight. He returned a few seconds later, bucket in hand, and hoisted himself out. "No spiders," he said. He slid the cover over the cistern's opening.

Mom rinsed the laundry, and spread our sheets across a bougainvillea bush so they could dry at least partially. We planned to hang the rest of the laundry from the boat's rigging and lifelines with clothespins. My dad dumped the dirty water off into the bushes.

Carolyn lay flat on the ground, trying to dry off. I sat beside her and twirled a hibiscus between my fingers, wondering what I'd look like with the flower stuck behind my ear. The Wittigs had a photo on their boat of my grandmother with a flower behind her ear, holding some sort of tropical drink. I thought she looked exotic and beautiful, the flower a bright red against her brown sun spots and creased skin.

"Hey," I said to Carolyn. "What was down there?"

"Nothing."

"Nothing at all? No snakes or frogs or anything? Lizards?" I wanted to hear something more exciting, perhaps that she'd seen a human skeleton or a chest of pirate treasure. Or a few kilos of cocaine or some other contraband.

"No snakes. No lizards. It smelled funny," she said.

I didn't believe her. "Are you sure?" I said.

"Shut up," Carolyn said.

In the excitement of Carolyn's fall, we hadn't heard the sound of the outboard motor approaching the island. Now all was quiet, except for a few mockingbirds calling to each other through the palmetto scrub. My dad jumped at the sound of voices. They belonged to a man and a woman, and they sounded older, perhaps around my grandparents' age. They floated closer to us, up the hill. My dad reached for the machete.

"Christ, Tom. Forget the machete. Put on some clothes!" My mom scurried around, grabbing damp clothes from the bougainvillea branches. She threw my dad a T-shirt and some swim trunks, slid a bathing suit cover-up over her head, and tossed long T-shirts to Carolyn and me. Our shirts were pink and blue, and said "Hey, Mon," in big block letters on the front. We'd gotten them a few months ago at the tacky straw market in Nassau.

We all covered up with the damp clothing as quickly as we could. My dad, trunks inside out, made sure his machete was within reach.

A man and a woman, both older and friendly-looking, and both just as naked as we had been, rounded the bend at the top of the hill. They stopped short when they saw us, and simultaneously wrapped the white towels that they carried around themselves.

"Hi," my mom said, stepping closer to them. "We were just doing laundry. We're on the *Chez Nous*, anchored out there." She pointed to our sailboat. In the Bahamas in the mid eighties, it was important to identify yourself to other people as soon as you met them. We needed to let people know that we were just a normal family living on a boat. We weren't drug smugglers. We didn't care about anybody else's business.

Strange things happened in the seventies and eighties to boaters who happened to be in the wrong place at the wrong time. In 1980, a sailboat was found drifting on the Bahama Banks just west of Big Pipe Cay, with bloodstains and a corpse in the cockpit. The boat had belonged to a retired couple from the West Coast of Florida. The closest island to where the boat was found was just a small rock with no vegetation or life of any kind. People started calling it Dead Man's Cay, although the name never made it onto the official maps and charts. I learned years later that the couple had left Fort Myers, FL, on their dream cruise, a few months before they had been murdered. The newspaper article I found didn't say much else, except that Carlos Lehder's people at Norman's were suspected of committing the murders.

The strangers on Little Pipe relaxed when my mom told them she was the Wittigs' daughter. "Oh," the woman said. "We saw them a few weeks ago. I guess they're headed back to the Chesapeake now."

"They told us to come here," Mom said. "They said nobody used the cistern, so we could do our laundry here."

"Just don't tell anybody else about it," the woman said. "Sometimes boaters take advantage of this kind of thing. But I'm sure you all know that."

We did. We knew about the bad reputation many liveaboards carried with them from port to port. They dumped their garbage on pristine beaches in the middle of the night, stole water from docks and cisterns, and went naked in populated areas. My dad always got mad at people who, he said, "give the rest of us a bad name."

Sam and Layla were good friends of my grandparents. They were also nudists. I'm not sure what their relationship to Little Pipe Cay was, whether they owned it or simply looked after it for the owners. Not many Americans were allowed to own land in the Bahamas then. Most people leased islands from the Bahaman government for periods of fifty or a hundred years.

They invited us to dock *Chez Nous* at Little Pipe. They docked their trawler, *Dreamer*, on one side of the crumbling concrete pier, and we docked on the other. Layla gave my sister and me chocolate, and she fed breadcrumbs to the rainbow of fishes that gathered under the trawler's stern every evening. A beautiful coral reef lined the shore of Little Pipe, but Layla wouldn't let anybody go near it. "Those are my fish," she said. "They trust me because I feed them. I can't let anyone just come here and catch them." Dad contented himself spearfishing elsewhere.

Little Pipe was a nice place, and was protected from cold fronts. Sam and Layla sat inside their boat with the curtains drawn, doing whatever it was that they did. We were careful never to disturb them. They kept their towels on a hook by the sliding door of their cabin, ready to cover up in case we knocked.

Mom collected shells on the pristine sand bars that stretched across Pipe Creek. Her mother's shell collection spanned years and included majestic tritons, flirty butterfly shells, virginal sand dollars, promiscuous cowries and flamboyant flamingo tongues. The shells told the story of their years in the Bahamas. Mom's own collection was small, but she added to it with a determination. Carolyn and I followed her, our small footprints next to hers on the sand bars, which, when we arrived, were void of any footprints at all. We rarely saw other people on these expeditions—sometimes George and Joannie from our previous winter at Rat Cay drifted by in *Gypsy's* tiny tender, trailing a fishing line and drinking vodka from a thermos. We waved at them and exchanged friendly but distant nods, and went on with our shelling. Dad made fun of us for collecting shells. There was nothing useful about a shell, he liked to tell us. We should be doing something more productive, like joining him on his diving trips and spearing fresh fish that could be eaten for dinner. A shell was just a decoration.

Yet he still picked up the occasional shell for Mom when he was diving. Once he returned to the dinghy with a smooth white milk conch, smaller than the queen conch which we collected and ate regularly. The animal had died and left its shell, immaculate, next to a coral head that Dad checked frequently for spiny lobsters.

Mom wanted a triton. The triton, a majestic sea creature that in the Pacific can grow to over twenty inches long, is really a giant predatory snail. The shells are flecked with brown and gold, with large openings that can be used as vessels for flowers or for other decorative purposes. The Wittigs had several, both aboard their boat and in their home. Mom asked Dad to keep an eye out for one while he was diving, and she searched the shoals day after day for the brown tip of one sticking out of the white sand. We did schoolwork in the mornings, and in the afternoons we searched for Mom's triton.

The crumbling pier on Little Pipe flanked a small beach. It wasn't a good swimming beach, since it was rocky and the bottom was covered with turtle grass and sharp objects like baby conch and sea urchins. Carolyn and I spent very little time on it, even though our boat was docked right there next to it. But one day, while I was waiting for Mom and Dad and Carolyn to finish putting on their sunscreen so that we could go out in the dinghy, I ventured down across the limestone rocks to the small beach and waded out into the water. I wore my flip-flops so I wouldn't step on anything.

Turtle grass freaked me out a little. I didn't like the way it obscured your view of the crystal clear water—a patch of it, shaped the right way, could fool me into believing I was looking at a shark or a stingray, both fascinating creatures that repelled and attracted me. As I stepped through the grass, my feet searching for clear spots of sand that would be free of sea urchins, I kept my gaze out ahead of me and swiveled my neck back and forth, looking for danger. A brown spot about five feet in front of me caught my attention. It was too small to be anything threatening, but the golden color didn't match that of the grass. I took another few cautious steps towards it and leaned forward, the water now up to my waist.

I couldn't tell what it was, so I took a breath and dove, opening my eyes underwater. Without a mask, my view was hazy and blurred, and the salt burned in the same way that chorine in a swimming pool burns your eyes. A small jack moved out of my way as I reached for the object. Could it really be?

The triton was heavy, and as I lifted it out of the water it reached towards me with its thick operculum, stabbing at my hand. The water slid off its surface creating a glistening sheen that made the gold and brown on its shell appear to be melting off. I raised it over my head and yelled. "Mom! Mom! Come see what I found!"

It was over a foot long, and weighed so much that I struggled as I waded back to the shore, this time not paying as much attention to where my feet fell. I squeezed my toes together to grip my flip-flops, which would have been sucked off my feet by the water and mud had I not.

I reached the beach and turned to see Mom striding down the pier at a clip. "Is something wrong?" She squinted through the hot sunlight. Her sunglasses hung around her neck. She'd forgotten to put them on. "What do you have?"

"I found one!" I breathed fast and my heart pounded as I rushed towards her with the creature. It had extended itself from the shell and its thick and glistening muscle writhed. I wondered for a second whether it would fall out, but then remembered what my dad had told me while cleaning conch. Its body was connected to its shell by a strong sinewy muscle, and the only way to remove the body was to cut the muscle, freeze the creature, or hang it up to dry and decompose. With conch, unless you wanted to keep the shell, you pounded small holes through the spiraled top, right above where the muscle would be, and then stabbed though the hole with a knife, reaching around until you felt the muscle give. In a few years, I would become just as good at cleaning conch as my dad was, but not quite as good as the Bahamians.

My arms ached as I raised the triton and presented it to my mom. She stared. "You found one," she said. She took it from me and turned it in her hands, running her fingers across its curves and tracing the spirals. "It's perfect," she said.

"What's going on?" Dad strode down the pier towards us, Carolyn in tow.

"Melanie found a triton," Mom said.

"Oh." Dad cocked his head and gave it a once-over. "Where?"

"Right here!" I jumped a little bit as I pointed to the grassy shallows by the beach. "It must have been here all along!"

"Does this count as one of Layla's fish?" Dad asked, referring to the creatures she fed and which we weren't supposed to kill and eat.

"Well, it sure isn't a fish," Mom said, cradling the triton. The creature had retreated back into its shell, possibly realizing that it may be out of the water for an extended period of time and needing to conserve moisture.

"Do you want to keep it?" Dad took it from her and flipped it over, staring into the opening.

"Yes."

"We can freeze it to get it out of there," Dad said.

But the triton wouldn't fit in our freezer. Dad hung it, using spare line we kept in one of our lockers, from a buttonwood tree at the opposite end of the beach. He hung it with the opening facing down, and after a day flies had found the triton and buzzed and hummed around it as they feasted on the body, which had ejected from the shell and hung limp. A few more days, and the meat had withered and shrunk to half its original size. On the fifth day, the muscle tore from the shell and the body fell onto the ground, where the flies and ants blanketed it. The smell of death coming from the far end of the beach was enough to keep any sane person away, but I checked on the triton daily during this process to see what was happening.

Mom took the shell, which still smelled, and soaked it in a bucket of Clorox and water on the back of *Chez Nous* until the smell was gone and any small pieces of the creature's flesh had washed away.

The triton was the only creature that we ever killed and didn't eat.

Dead Man's Cay

The Bahamas • Winter 1986

Age 6

One morning, Dad was in the middle of shaving when Layla banged on the hull at seven. I always thought it was strange that my dad worked so hard to stay clean-cut. Most men on boats grew beards as soon as they left the States. Most women let their legs go, because shaving your legs with a limited supply of cold water (some people even bathed in the sea) was a bitch.

Layla banged on our hull so hard the boat shook.

"I think Sam's had a stroke," she said.

Dad followed Layla across the dock. Mom made sure Carolyn and I stayed below deck, eating whole wheat pancakes for breakfast. The pancakes were a distraction from what was happening outside.

A few minutes later, he was back in our main cabin, calling the U.S. Coast Guard on the long-range SSB radio. Reception was good that morning from the high-pressure system that sat over the Bahamas, keeping the wind low and the sky clear. The Coast Guard agreed to send a helicopter out from Miami. People all over the Caribbean tuned in their radios to the real life drama. Soon the VHF radio was humming with calls as the news spread locally from island to island. People called out for a doctor, but there seemed to be none in the area. Mom answered some of the calls and ignored some, assuming that people who didn't find out from us would find out from someone else.

The Coast Guard chopper sent the mirror-smooth water into a tornado of ripples and waves that circled out from the cement pier. There was just enough space for the pilot to land. Carolyn and I sat in the cockpit and watched. Small boats and dinghies drifted just off the pier, their occupants waiting to lend whatever hand they could. The noise and action didn't fit Little Pipe, where there was usually no movement save for the clueless fish that Layla fed gliding under the hull of our boats. People had come all the way from Staniel Cay, the small settlement about four miles south.

A twenty-two-foot Mako center console driven by a small man with a gray beard cut through the turbulence, and a silver-haired woman stood in the bow and caught the pier as they pulled up alongside. Nobody tried to stop them, even though it still wasn't safe to come near the helicopter. "Tie her off, Helen," the man said, talking through his nose.

He clambered up onto the pier and rushed over to where my dad and the orange-jacketed Coasties were lifting Sam off the *Dreamer* on a stretcher. My mom told Carolyn and me not to look. She was afraid Sam was already dead.

We couldn't see through the men as they carried Sam down the dock, Layla following, her hand covering half of her face. They lifted him into the chopper. One of my mom's bathing suits flew off the lifeline where it had been hung to dry, clothespins and all, as the chopper took off, sending its whirlwind out to whip at our faces and at the scrubby palmetto trees that lined the beach. For a second, I wanted to be on the helicopter, just because it was going somewhere. I couldn't imagine being back in the States in just a few hours. I was used to slow travel.

The boats and dinghies swarmed in to the dock as soon as the helicopter disappeared. Carolyn and I were allowed off the boat, and we rushed over to the group of people surrounding our dad.

"Sam's about the toughest guy I ever saw," Dad said. "All muscle. Felt like a ton of bricks when I picked him up."

Carolyn and I didn't know the names of any of the people gathered on the dock. They were from Staniel, from Sampson, from Rat and Overyonder and all the other small islands and the boats anchored around them. Any occasion that brought people together in Pipe Creek was rare, and the air steamed with excitement. We shouldered our way through the crowd of legs, reaching our dad. The people shut up.

I didn't want them to leave, because leaving would mean the usual routine: schoolwork until noon, a break for lunch, which would probably be some sort of garbanzo bean salad, school until around three, then a few hours of sitting in the dinghy while our dad went spearfishing. But the sputtering and choking of outboard motors began as the crowd of people headed off to their own secluded lives.

The couple that I had noticed earlier in the Mako waved us over to the edge of the pier. Up close, the woman smelled like jasmine, and the man had a tobacco streak down the front of his beard. His Hawaiian shirt was open, and a brown Buddha belly protruded over his denim shorts. Everything about him was disproportionate: skinny arms and legs, eyes that squinted up through the morning sunlight. "No school for you all today," he said. Carolyn and I liked him immediately.

"Herm, that's up to their mom, not you," his wife said. She stood in the bow and raised her hand to us, shaking as if we were adults. Her arm was tanned and firm, despite the wrinkles on her knuckles and around her elbow.

Herman and Helen Wenzel owned the lease to Compass Cay. They talked Mom into giving us a half-day off of school so we could come see their island.

We ate an early lunch, because Dad hadn't gotten a chance to eat breakfast. Mom set a heavy stainless-steel bowl of garbanzo beans in the middle of the table. "Don't complain," she said to me, before I even opened my mouth. I understood her reasoning: canned garbanzo beans had lots of protein and they kept for a long time. I wondered how many more cans of garbanzo beans my mom had stored in *Chez Nous'* bilge. She set a plate of Wheatsworth crackers and a jar of Jiff peanut butter next to the beans. Thank God. I could pretend to eat a few garbanzo beans and then fill up on Jiff.

Carolyn piled her plate with garbanzos, and went for seconds after she'd wolfed down the first pile. I hated her for actually liking the beans.

"They look like little butts," I said. Carolyn stabbed one with her fork and held it up to the dusty beam of light that filtered in through the galley porthole.

"Actually, she's right," Dad said. He wasn't thrilled about eating garbanzo beans for the fourth day in a row either.

"If you don't like it, then we need to make a trip to Staniel so I can get some fresh vegetables," Mom said.

"Like what? Cabbage?" I didn't think cabbage counted as a vegetable. Fresh tomatoes and lettuce were a novelty in the Exumas, where most of the supplies were shipped in by mailboat. Cabbage lasted almost as long as garbanzo beans.

"Just eat the beans," my mom said. "Maybe we can get some conch and make conch fritters tonight. If we don't find any conch, we can make pizza."

We took the dinghy ride to Compass slowly, my dad navigating between sand bars and rocky crags that jutted into the deeper water running in blue ribbons beside the limestone cays. The shallow water entrance to the harbor at Compass was at the south end, and ran between two adjoining cays called His and Hers. Our outboard motor's prop churned up sand as we crossed the shoal. We hugged the western shore of Compass, where thick-smelling mangrove roots reached into the water.

The current picked up as we approached the deep entrance on the north side of His and Hers, and it welled into the harbor before spilling out onto the Bahama Banks west of Pipe Creek. A small shed with a thatched roof sat at the end of the rickety wooden dock. Herman Wenzel waved to us from the end, where he stood barely taller than the pilings that suspended the dock above the current.

We docked at the small fish cleaning station, and Carolyn and I scrambled out of the dinghy. Herman tried to help, but I took one look at his scaly hands and decided I would rather risk getting a splinter or falling into the water than grabbing his hand. I didn't know yet about the twelve-foot hammerhead shark that grazed the bottom out in the deeper water, or the lemon sharks that used the mangrove swamp as a nursery. And I didn't know yet about the unabashed love and enthusiasm that Herman had for life and would grow to have for my family, or how he would come to be like another grandparent to me.

"They let you out of school early after all," Herman said. He led us up the hill to his house. The path was similar to the one at Pipe Cay: crumbled cement surrounded by palmetto scrub. It crossed a dirt road that ran north to south, from one end of the island to the other. At the intersection, tall gumbo limbo trees crossed over the path, blocking the sun, and the heady smell of cliff orchids mixed with diesel fumes from the island's power shed. "That's our generator," Herman said, motioning off to the left, where the fifteen-kilowatt monster roared in a wooden shed beyond the bushes.

The path turned into stone stairs that ran up the hill, and my breath caught in my throat as my legs struggled to keep up with everyone else's. As we neared the house, the smell of spice cookies funneled down through the bougainvillea and cotton branches that lined the path at the top of the stairs. Helen greeted us with a plate of cookies that looked like pressed flowers. Carolyn and I sat in bucket chairs and ate them until we were stuffed, washing them down with sugar-loaded pineapple soda called Goombay Punch.

"Herm's diabetic," Helen told us. "So don't give him any cookies." She told us to call her Tutu, which meant Grandmother in Hawaiian, and to call him Grandpa.

They sat on their front porch with our parents, swinging in bamboo chairs that hung from the beams on rusty chains. They sipped cold water and talked about the island and about Pipe Creek. The Wenzels had made their money selling tents, retired early on a sailing yacht, and traveled the world, fishing, sailing, and searching for a place to call home until they found Compass Cay. "It had the prettiest beach we'd ever seen," Helen said.

They'd settled in the house and watched everything change on and around their island. "You see that little rock out there?" Herman pointed a crooked finger to a cluster of islands off Pipe Cay. They rested on the banks almost at the horizon, where the water shimmered like mercury. "Dead Man's Cay," he said. He stuffed his pipe with the tobacco he kept in a green pouch, and didn't say anything until he had smoked for a few minutes. Carolyn and I waited, leaving the cookies to soak up the humidity.

A fat tiger-striped cat jumped out of the scrub onto the porch, a bird in its mouth. "Compass!" Helen jumped from her chair and ran to the cat. "Put that poor bird down!" The cat dropped the brown mockingbird at her feet and sulked into the house. "I don't know what he was thinking," she said, scooping the bird up. "He gets plenty of food." She opened her hands and the bird tried to fly but crumpled to the ground instead.

"I'll take care of it," Dad said. He pulled a rag from his pocket and picked the bird up by the tip of its wing, and disappeared down the path. He was back in three minutes. Nobody asked what he'd done with the mockingbird.

I was tired of waiting. "What were you going to say about Dead Man's Cay?"

Herman looked at me over his pipe, but spoke to my parents. "I was the first one to see that sailboat drifting out there a few years ago. I thought it was anchored at first, but nobody anchors there. The holding's no good. The bottom is all scoured rock. So I waited awhile and went out in our old Boston Whaler. When I got up to the boat, there was blood all over the deck. I thought at first maybe they'd caught a big fish and cleaned it on deck, but it wasn't fish blood. I didn't want to mess with anything, so I came back and got on the radio."

"You probably shouldn't talk about this in front of the girls," Helen said.

"Melanie, Carolyn, why don't you all go for a walk?" Mom stood and motioned us over to the side of the house. "Helen, where should they go?"

"There's an old helicopter landing pad on top of the next hill," she said. She showed us where the path started. The bleached jawbone of a whale was propped against the side of the house at the foot of the trail.

"Is that a dinosaur bone?" Carolyn asked.

"No, honey, that's from a humpback whale that washed up on the northern end of the island about five years ago. Now just walk until you get to the landing pad and then come straight back. I'll have another Goombay Punch ready for you." Helen and Mom stood side by side, watching us until we rounded the first bend in the trail.

When I thought we were out of earshot, I said, "Carolyn, why don't we sneak back and try to listen?"

"No. Too scary," she said.

The landing pad was disappointing, which could have just been a reflection of my mood at being torn away from what I thought was a fantastic story about dead bodies and drugs. The top of the hill had been hacked away until it was a flat slab of limestone, with loose rocks and the occasional cactus or aloe plant sprouting through.

"I wonder why they needed a landing pad here in the first place?" I said. Carolyn was busy trying to catch a brown lizard that had been sunning itself on a rock.

The hill where we stood was slightly taller than the adjoining one where the house sat. I had a better view of Dead Man's Cay, and I could see *Chez Nous* docked at Little Pipe. Our boat looked like a white and blue bathtub toy from up here. Compass was crossed by two sections of mangrove flats, so that it was actually three smaller islands connected by sand. A tidal river ran from the north end of the island to the harbor, and lush mangroves lined the edges, with strips of dark turquoise marking the deeper water.

Dad placed a call on the SSB radio to the States the next day to inquire about Sam. He had suffered a massive stroke, and had passed away on the helicopter after leaving Little Pipe Cay. Without Sam and Layla there as our hosts, it was time to move on. Laya made arrangements for someone to come and get their boat, which we had been looking after, and we made arrangements to leave.

A few days later, we were docked at Compass. We went diving off Dead Man's Cay, where the bottom of the sea was scoured in an odd way, almost unnaturally devoid of grass and conch. A Nassau Grouper lived in a small coral head right by the island, but Dad could never manage to spear it. The fish was too smart.

We spent days collecting "rollers," the juvenile conch that had sharp, spiky points on their shells, and transplanting them to the mangrove creek at Compass. My parents said that we were saving the rollers from being illegally harvested by the Bahamians and careless Americans who would take them and use them for bait. We loaded our dinghy down with them, piling so many into the small craft that its stability was compromised and we clung to the sides as we motored slowly, my dad driving, through the shoals of Pipe Creek and up into the mangrove swamp. "This is going to be our special place," Dad said. "If we plant enough conch here, they will grow up and we can come up here every year and find them once they are big enough to eat." He made us promise never to tell anyone about the conch farm at Compass. It was our family secret and it was mystical to me.

There was one spot where the water was about four feet deep and stretched on for the length of several football fields at this depth. The bottom was covered in turtle grass and the small rollers hid well. We snorkeled and squinted into the grass trying to spot the telltale pinkish spikes of baby conch. I collected dozens at a time, cradling them under one arm and swimming them over to the dinghy where I handed them to Carolyn or Mom, whichever one was taking a break from the water. The water was murky here, because of the fine mud and sand constantly being fanned by our flippers, and once a small reef shark darted out in front of me as I cruised over the grass. I didn't see it until I was about eight feet away, and its yellow eyes met mine before it turned its graceful head and swam away. The reef shark was too small to do any damage, as were the barracuda that darted through the shadowy water, but always in the back of my mind there was a twelve-foot bull shark located just outside the range of my visibility. I knew bull sharks liked this kind of bottom, and while I snorkeled I turned in full circles every minute or so to scan the underwater horizon.

Compass Cay and Pipe Creek became one of our homes and we returned to it for years. I was beginning to keep track, in my mind, of places that felt like home.

We stayed there until the end of February, when it was time to go south to George Town, at the far end of the Exuma Chain. The annual Cruising Regatta took place every March in George Town, and since it was the only time of year when we really socialized with other boat kids on a regular basis, it was important for us to be there.

When we left Compass and our conch farm, *Chez Nous* was happy to be underway. I sat beside the mast and wrapped my arms around it, feeling the wind vibrate though the cold aluminum. *You're like my other sister*, I whispered to the boat. *But you're more like me.* I looked at my reflection in the Plexiglas window, and startled myself because my skin was so much browner than it used to be. My eyebrows were bleached white. *Have I changed that much?* I wondered if the boat could understand me.

Seashell

George Town, Bahamas • Winter 1986

Age 6

There were three main beaches in George Town: Volleyball Beach, on the west side of Stocking Island, Hamburger Beach, named for a little burger shack run by the Peace and Plenty Hotel, and the Ocean Beach on the Exuma Sound side of Stocking Island, facing east. The Ocean Beach was about a mile and a half long, with patches of reef where the ocean broke in foamy waves.

The cruising mothers took their dinghies to one beach or another with their kids almost every afternoon so they could body surf or swim or build sand forts and bomb each other with sand balls. I guess we were making up for the lack of social company that we experienced in other places. The mothers, for the most part, were just happy to escape their husbands and the tight confines of life aboard a boat for a few hours. We'd visited George Town the year before, and it, either by chance or by our parents' choice, became our place to socialize. For a month or so out of every year, George Town meant social structure—planned activities such as the Annual Cruising Regatta, weekly potlucks on the beach, afternoon volleyball. For that, my dad resented it. Social structure was what he had taken his family cruising to avoid. And the social structure that was there, he said, wasn't the healthy kind. It was the kind where people did whatever they wanted, partying all day and drinking at noon rather than waiting until a respectable hour like six o'clock. It was the kind of social structure, he said, where adults acted like kids, forgetting responsibilities such as taking care of their boats and finding ways to make money.

The other kids were fun to be around, but I didn't like any of them that much. They were all more athletic than I was, and they wanted to play games that involved running. I was happier sitting alone and thinking, making up elaborate stories about characters I'd created.

The day I met Michelle, I was wandering Ocean Beach, lost in my own head, singing one of the only songs I knew from my parents' collection of cassette tapes. It was Jimmy Buffett's "Son of a Son of a Sailor." I couldn't remember all the words, so I made them up as I went.

A flurry of motion coming from the sand dunes interrupted my singing. I couldn't tell what it was at first, because the sea oats were thick and tangled at the edge of the beach, and the movement was just behind them. Then a wall of sand sprayed out like a boat wake, and a girl about my age tumbled down the dune, rolling over and then somehow landing on her feet right next to me. Her skin was the same color as the sea oats, and she had a sunburned nose and bright green eyes and a mess of black hair.

"I know that song!" she said. Her voice was squeaky, and didn't seem to quite fit her body. She pushed the mop of hair away from her eyes and blinked at me, like it was amazing that we both knew the same song. Lots of parents listened to Jimmy Buffett, especially parents who lived on boats, but somehow this was different.

We sang it together, pulling the words out of our new collective memory, and became inseparable.

Michelle was grown-up at six. She and her father, Gary, lived aboard a 30-foot O'Day sloop called *Indian Summer*. It was close to being the smallest boat in George Town. Her mother had cruised with them for awhile, but at that point she had moved off the boat and was spending all her time back in Michigan. (I don't know when their divorce was actually finalized.) Gary ran an auto repair shop back on the Upper Peninsula of Michigan. During the summers he bought, fixed and sold junk cars, and a buddy of his ran the shop during the winters so that Gary could sail. I was jealous of the things he let Michelle do.

She had her own rowing dinghy, and there was talk that she might even get an outboard motor for it. She rowed it and sailed it around the anchorages off of Stocking Island all by herself. My parents were more cautious. They wouldn't let me take our rowing dinghy out by myself. They wanted to be sure that I knew how to row, so they tied the dingy off the stern of *Chez Nous* and had me row back and forth behind the boat. "It's how I learned to row," my dad said. "What if you got caught in the current and couldn't get back? You'd wish you were tied to the boat." This was typical, overly-cautious, worst-case-scenario Dad.

Michelle sailed circles around *Chez Nous* in her dinghy. She came over to tease me, telling me how dumb I looked wearing my life jacket, sitting in a tethered rowboat.

One day, I was rowing as hard as I could against the tether, trying to see if I could make the big boat move, pretending to be a tugboat captain. Michelle rowed over to me in her dinghy. "We're going to town," she said. "My dad wants to take you with us."

My parents leaned over the lifelines of *Chez Nous*, worried. "When will you be back?" Dad asked.

"I don't know. Before sunset," Michelle said. "We just need to get some fuel and water and food and stuff. He said he'd buy us burgers at Frida's."

"Oh no," Mom said. My family had a rule against buying burgers anywhere in town, because the burgers were cooked on outdoor grills and were supposedly encrusted with flies. Dad told us they were made of goat meat, and he always made sure to point out that the local goat population was a little smaller each time we made a trip to town.

Dad went over in the big dinghy to talk to Gary, I guess to make sure the boat wasn't about to sink and to give Gary some lunch money for me. Dad probably interrogated Gary, threatened him, or at least shook him up a little, but Gary never let on. Michelle and I climbed aboard *Chez Nous* so I could change clothes and grab an extra life jacket. Carolyn threw a tantrum because she wasn't allowed to go. She screamed and tried to bite me, but I managed to push her off. Her teeth were sharp like a puppy's, and they scraped my arm. She took a fistful of her sun-streaked brown hair and pulled it out, still screaming. "I hate you," she said, throwing the hair at us. I'm not sure whether it was directed at Michelle or me. "Why can't I go?"

Mom held her by the elbow and said, "You can do things with your friends too, and Melanie doesn't have to go with you." She guided Carolyn off to draw pictures at the salon table.

Indian Summer was much smaller than *Chez Nous*, and the small engine under the cockpit rattled the whole boat. I knew Gary would rather have sailed the mile across Elizabeth Harbor to Georgetown, but there was no wind. He made sure the companionway hatch was open so Michelle and I had plenty of fresh air while the engine sputtered exhaust into the cabin. We sat on the floor, where Michelle crafted a friendship bracelet out of blue and purple embroidery floss. I wanted some pink in it too, but she insisted that pink wasn't my color.

When she tied the bracelet around my ankle, I thought it was the prettiest piece of jewelry I'd ever seen. I swore I'd never take it off.

"Dad," Michelle called up the companionway, "can we listen to Jimmy Buffett?"

"You know how to work the tape player," Gary said. He was intent on navigating the boat safely across the harbor, and he only took his eyes off the water long enough to look down at us and smile, a smile I learned he only reserved for his daughter. I learned a lot of things about Michelle's family over the next fifteen years.

When Gary worked in the auto shop during the summers, he took Michelle in with him and let her crawl around among the mechanics and tools and grease. The mechanics called her "Bondo Baby," because she always got herself covered with the thick putty used in auto body repair. Michelle's mom, Kathy, was beautiful and wispy, and, while I believe that she and Gary never fell out of love with each other, their divorce was ugly. It was never clear to me whether Gary or Kathy had legal custody of Michelle.

We listened to Buffett's *Songs You Know by Heart,* and it was the first time I heard "Why Don't We Get Drunk and Screw," a song that my parents had dubbed over on our own copy of the tape. I thought it was odd that our tape was missing the track, but didn't think the song was that great. It didn't make a whole of sense.

Michelle and I screamed along with "Son of a Son of a Sailor," and, even though Gary laughed at us, I think he was secretly thrilled. Over in George Town, Gary docked the boat at Exuma Services, the town's only marina. Michelle and I spilled off the boat and ran down the dock without our shoes, Gary yelling something to us about not getting splinters.

Michelle found a group of Bahamian kids who were out of school on their lunch break, running around in their starched uniforms. They chased the scrawny chickens that darted under our feet. My parents never gave Carolyn and me a chance to play with the Bahamian kids. Trips into George Town with my parents were usually all business.

Gary was the opposite of my dad. Dad was careful and conscientious. He dressed up to go to town, made sure to shake hands with the right people, and carried a soft briefcase whenever he went to Batelco, the Bahamian phone company. The Batelco office was the only place on the island where you could make and receive phone calls to and from the States. Gary wore cut-off jeans and didn't mind showing off his beer gut. He laughed a lot more than my dad did, and he knew different types of people.

Gary ordered for us at Frida's. We sat at a long picnic table and watched as the burgers sizzled over the open grill. I tried to find the goats, and Gary pointed to where they were tied next to a small pink house. I'd have to tell my dad that the goats were alive and well.

"The burgers here are so good because they come from Venezuela," Gary told us. "And, you have to get everything on them." He left the table and went over to the grill, pulled some wet five-dollar bills from his pocket, and turned his back to us so we couldn't see what he was putting on the burgers. The smell of beef and charcoal and burnt drippings wrapped around Gary's big body and drifted across the dry grass and sand burrs to our table. Michelle swatted a fly with her hand and wiped it off on the bench, leaving a black smear.

"You just wait," she said. "This will be the best burger you've ever had." My stomach rolled over a couple of times.

When Gary turned around, we saw three paper plates stacked with burgers that might as well have reached the clouds. The top of each bun was sliding off because there was so much stuff piled underneath. "Mayo on the bottom, then the burger, then cheese, ketchup, pickles, onions, lettuce, tomato, and mayo and mustard on the top. And here's more ketchup," Gary said. He set the plates down in front of us.

I could barely get my hands around my burger. Michelle's hands were the same size as mine, but she ate hers like a pro, ketchup dribbling down her chin, lettuce falling all over her lap and the table. Gary finished his in about two bites. When I finally managed to get mine into my mouth, I knew what hamburgers were supposed to taste like. It was well done, because all of us knew better than to eat rare burgers in the Bahamian Out Islands, but it wasn't the cardboard patty that you usually associate with well-done burgers. It was perfect.

Michelle and I followed Gary around town, the three of us singing. I loved the fact that Michelle and her dad didn't think there was anything strange about singing in public. As we climbed back aboard *Indian Summer* for the trip back across the harbor, still full from the burgers, Gary said, "Jimmy Buffett, eat your heart out! This is the life."

Land Kids

Narrows Marina, Virginia • Summer 1987

Age 8

The dock at the land next to the Wittigs was finished, but we'd fallen into a schedule of only spending the beginning of the summer and a month or two in the fall there. The months of July, August and September were spent at Narrows Marina, the marina near Mathews, VA, that we'd discovered while waiting for the dock to be built. My parents may have felt that "The Lot," as we'd come to call our piece of property, was too isolated. Carolyn and I had friends at Narrows—kids that came to the marina from Richmond or Williamsburg on the weekends with their parents.

The parents owned powerboats and partied heartily while they were there, and the kids ran wild through the playground and on the beach. There was a small pool with a sliding board and a diving board and a lifeguard who was only there on weekends. Our parents didn't socialize much with the other parents, but they did have friends on boats at Narrows. They grilled chicken and steamed blue crabs and sat around the marina's picnic tables with their friends.

Narrows Marina was the center of our world in the north and George Town was the center to the south. My land friends talked about what they were doing in school and what they did at camp, and I talked about what happened in George Town.

I sat in the cockpit on Friday evenings and watched the bridge that crossed over to Gwynn's Island, the small island where the marina was situated. The land kids' parents usually got off work around five, which meant they would arrive at the marina between six and seven. I watched the bridge until Jennifer and Julie's parents' minivan or Elizabeth's mom's white SUV crossed it, and then I ran and jumped off the boat and headed to the parking lot where they would pull in momentarily. I hovered while the parents unloaded their bags and carried them into the boat shed, waiting for the kids to be dismissed so we could run to the playground and push each other on the rusty merry-go-round.

There was a family who had two boys, my sister's and my ages. They didn't come to the marina every weekend, but there was always a different dynamic on the weekends that they did. Jennifer and Elizabeth, my two Virginia "best friends," were normally happy to play my elaborate imagining games with me or were content to sit with me in the sandbox and help dig hamster mazes, but they became distracted whenever the boys were there and wandered off to watch television on the boys' boat. Sometimes I followed them, but most of the time I didn't. Dad didn't like me watching television during the day.

"Don't you think it's weird that you don't go to school?" Trey, the older of the two boys, asked me once when I had gone to his boat. We all sat around the main salon of his parents' cabin cruiser, eating store-bought chocolate chip cookies from a bag and watching music videos on MTV.

"I don't know," I said, reaching for another cookie. The cookies weren't nearly as good as the ones Mom made from scratch, but they were sweet and chocolaty and were better than no cookies at all.

"I mean, you don't even know any of these songs," Trey said, motioning to the television where Bon Jovi sang "Livin' on a Prayer."

"Yes I do," I said. My Granddad Neale had given me a small FM radio that summer, and every night before I fell asleep I hid it under my pillow, the volume low so as not to wake up Carolyn. I listened to country music most of the time, but sometimes I switched to rock.

"How can you know about music when you're in the Bahamas all winter without any radio stations?" Trey wouldn't let it go. All the other kids had stopped paying attention to the TV and now stared at me.

I thought about it. My dad always said that it wasn't important to know what music was in the top ten or what clothes people were wearing. "Think of all the other things you know how to do, like clean a conch or open a coconut," he'd say, when I lamented not knowing as much about pop culture as other kids.

"I listen to the radio when we're not in the Bahamas," I said. The bag of cookies was just out of my reach now, so I leaned across the floor to get it. My blond hair fanned out over my arm as I stretched, and I noticed for a second the stark contrast of blond hair on tanned skin. The first time my Grandmom June had seen me that summer, she'd remarked that I looked like a little black kid with blond hair.

"Is it true that your mom grinds her own wheat to make flour?" Elizabeth piped up.

This wasn't a badge of self-sufficiency to these kids—it was something else that was weird about me. "Yes," I said, feeling my cheeks start to burn. "And we catch our own fish for dinner. You don't do that, do you?" I glared around the room.

The other kids simply looked at me, not knowing what to say.

"I heard that your parents don't ever wear clothes when they're in the Bahamas," Trey said.

"Don't know where you heard that. We all wear clothes. We just take them off sometimes when we're washing them or catching rain water or something." I stuffed a cookie into my mouth and stared at the television.

That evening, after the other kids had headed off to their houses in Richmond and Williamsburg, I climbed back aboard *Chez Nous* and trudged across the deck to the cockpit where I kicked off my flip-flops and swung myself down the companionway. "Look," Mom said, standing up from the salon table where she'd been drawing all day in a large sketchbook. Artist's pencils and erasers were scattered around her. She held a piece of paper with a stylized design drawn on it.

"What's that?"

"It's the design for the 'Kids Aboard' flag," she said.

I just looked at her.

"There's a design contest in *Cruising World*," she said, pointing to an open magazine that sat on the table beside her. Next to it, the S.S.C.A. Bulletin, a blue and white newsletter, was also spread open to an article about how boats with kids aboard might locate other boats with kids aboard. The Seven Seas Cruising Association was a network of liveaboard cruisers spread all over the globe. Her parents had been members, and had encouraged her to join for the sake of the cruising tips and advice that could be found in their bulletin. Cruisers mailed letters containing advice and anecdotes to the association's headquarters, which was just a non-specific mailing address in Fort Lauderdale, FL, and the letters were published and distributed to subscribers. The association held annual gatherings and elected commodores, who proudly flew their burgees from the rigging of their oceangoing vessels. "The idea," my mom said, "is that every boat that has kids aboard will be flying a flag with this design on it. That way we can all connect with each other and let the kids meet and play with each other."

"Don't use that word," I said.

"What? Play?" She dropped the drawing back to the table and looked down at it, studying. "What's wrong with it?"

"Little kids play," I said. "Carolyn and her friends play. I'm bigger than that."

"Okay, well, we can fly the flag and find other kids for you to hang out with," she said.

I looked at her design on my way to the forward cabin. I liked it. It was simple and could be easily spotted from a distance. But I didn't tell her that I liked it. It just confirmed what I already knew—we were different. The Land Kids didn't need to fly flags to make their presence known.

Boarding

The Bahamas • Spring 1988

Age 8

We left Gun Cay at two in the morning, in the spring of 1988, planning to cross the Gulf Stream while it was still dark so we could reach Port Everglades, the inlet at Fort Lauderdale, FL, in the morning. It was a nearly non-existent weather window, with a low pressure system forming overtop of us and threatening to develop into something tropical and disastrous, so we had to make sure we were in a safe harbor as soon as possible. Normally we wouldn't have left the Bahamas at night.

We passed through the narrow cut between Cat and Gun Cay, and headed into the open ocean. Mom and Dad told me to stay in bed, but the sound of the diesel engine, the clanking of the anchor chain on the bow, and the luff and slap of the mainsail sliding up the mast drew me up to the cockpit. The shallow banks glowed purple behind us. Even at night, we could see the change in water color as we neared the drop-off. It went from lavender to purple to black under our bow.

Off to our right, a few lights sparkled on Bimini, an island we avoided because of the shallow water, expensive marinas, and tourist crowd. "What's that?" Mom pointed to the dark stretch of water between Bimini and Gun Cay. Dad and I followed her gaze. An unnatural glow swept the water, flickered off, then came on again, lighting up a round patch of the banks.

"It looks like a searchlight," Dad said. He turned off the autopilot and altered our course away from the light.

We couldn't see the boat that the light was coming from. Whatever it was, it had no running lights. The light moved slowly back and forth, like whoever was on the boat was determined to cover every inch of seabed between Bimini and Cat. I was eight then, but I didn't need to be told that something was going on that we didn't want to know about. I had heard stories of midnight drug drops, where planes would fly low over the water, dump cocaine and marijuana onto the Bahama Banks, and speedboats would sweep in from the unlit islands nearby to pick up the packages. This was part of the landscape, and boaters who weren't involved knew to stay away.

"Let's turn off the running lights," Dad said. "I don't want them seeing us."

Mom ran down below and switched off the running lights, and we watched the searchlight's glow as it faded behind us on the banks. After awhile, I went back to bed.

Carolyn and I were still too young to take watch on our own, so we usually slept through these night passages. She had been knocked out with Dramamine, because nobody wanted to be stuck cleaning up puke on a rocking boat in the middle of the night.

The smell of coffee brewing in the galley, the sideways pull of a tidal rip once we crossed the drop off, then the steady movement of ocean swells made it hard for me to sleep. Mom had closed the forward hatch, the main source of ventilation into the V-berth, so we wouldn't be drenched with sea water when *Chez Nous* buried her bow. The shape of her hull helped her take waves more gracefully than most boats, but salt spray still found its way over the bow with each wave.

I lay in bed, letting the up-and-down motion pull my body. When the boat fell off a wave, I pushed off the bed with my hands and let my body become suspended until we hit the trough, then I crashed back into the mattress. I drifted in and out of sleep this way for what seemed like hours. At one point, I stood and opened the hatch, wanting to smell the ocean. The dirt-rich smell of the Bahamas came in with the salt, so I knew we hadn't gotten far.

It was sometime around the new moon, so there wasn't any light other than our navigation lights, which Mom had turned back on. Through the hatch, I could see the red and green reflection of the bow lights against the full jib. We were sailing nicely, and the swells had evened out so I figured we must be close to the Gulf Stream.

I drifted into sleep again, but jerked out of it when I heard footsteps pounding on the companionway stairs. Mom took them two-at-a-time and rushed to turn off the lights at the chart table and in the galley. I leaned out of bed to see what she was doing. The whites of her eyes glowed against the black cabin. She had her life vest on, but she covered it with a black sweat shirt. "Mom," I said, swinging my feet around and onto the cabin sole.

"Shhhh." She moved faster than I'd ever seen her move before. She held the key to the gun locker in one hand, and she put the other on my shoulder. "Go back to bed," she said. "Just pretend to sleep." She looked over at Carolyn, who had her head turned to face the hull. Carolyn's ribcage rose and fell in steady, sleeping rhythm.

"What's going on?" I pulled myself back into the V-berth.

"Don't come out on deck," she said. "Just stay here." She shut the door, then changed her mind and opened it, latching it into place. She looked at me and clenched her jaw, grinding her teeth like she did when she was stressed.

Dad's silhouette filled the companionway hatch, and he hissed down at her. "Mel," he said. "Hurry up." He held a heavy flashlight, the kind police officers use to knock people out. He had turned the lights in the cockpit off as well, so the space behind him was gray, the only light a green glow from the engine gauges on the instrument panel.

Mom disappeared into the aft cabin, and I turned so that I was on my stomach. I leaned as far out as I could without falling out of bed. I heard the teak door of Dad's gun locker slamming open.

She held a small handgun up to where Dad's arm hung suspended in the darkness above her head. I didn't know anything about guns, but I knew that Dad had never taken this one out of the locker before. She stood like that, arm stretched, gun offered, for what seemed like five long minutes. Dad kept his hand unnaturally still then dropped it to his side without reaching for the gun. "No," he said. "If they're smugglers and they see us with a gun, we're dead. Put it back, but leave the cabinet unlocked." Mom retreated to the aft cabin.

I wanted to get out of bed, and at least go to the main cabin where I could look out the window, but something in Dad's voice made me stay where I was. I couldn't move. I felt like my arms and legs were pinned in place. Night terrors, later in life, would give me the same sensation. I couldn't see Mom and Dad out the hatch anymore.

The sound of the wind and the water was overpowered by a wild roar of engines, and the beam of a strong searchlight swept over *Chez Nous*. I heard Dad on the megaphone, asking someone to please identify themselves. The roar got closer and then it was right alongside, and our boat rocked violently and something thudded on deck. I wanted to move now more than ever, but I still couldn't.

Dad's voice boomed through the megaphone again. "This is a private vessel. We have two small children aboard. Please identify yourself."

I wondered how Carolyn could sleep. She sighed and rolled over, but her eyes stayed shut. Outside, voices echoed and bounced, distorted by the night. I couldn't understand a word they were saying. I heard Dad's voice and realized that he wasn't speaking into the megaphone anymore. The hull of another boat squeaked against ours.

"Just don't wake the girls up." I could hear Dad now, but couldn't tell what the other people were saying. Footsteps heavier than my parents' pounded over my head. A silhouette filled the companionway: an unfamiliar man, dressed in a jeans and a T-shirt that didn't conceal his holster and gun. Two more stood behind him. Could they be pirates? I felt bile rise in my stomach and a strange twinge of excitement too—what were these unfamiliar and young and somewhat glamorous-looking men doing on our boat in the middle of the night? The one in the companionway jumped downstairs, and I faked sleep.

I pulled the cover around my ears and closed my eyes halfway so I could watch the man. He walked the length of the boat, sweeping the beam of a flashlight into corners and opening cabinets and peering inside. He made his way into the bedroom.

The man was less than two feet away from me now, and I stared at him through squinted eyes. He opened my clothes locker and pushed aside my Barbie dolls. I must have moved, because he turned to look at me. He was young, almost a teenager, and he smiled. His teeth were bright white, and I thought he was handsome, like a Disney prince, but didn't like him there in my bedroom in the middle of the night. "Go back to sleep, sweetheart" he said. "Everything's okay."

The two other men searched the rest of the boat, and Mom made them coffee. Dad stayed on deck. They took extra time in the aft cabin, and I heard them banging around in the gun locker and talking in clipped sentences. Dad showed them a stack of papers, and their voices relaxed a little bit.

The next morning, once we had reached the shallow U.S. waters on the west side of the Gulf Stream, Dad told me that they were U.S. Drug Enforcement officers. They had gotten a tip about a drop off of Bimini, and they had seen us leaving the area and chased us down.

"They came up with no lights," Dad said. He hadn't looked right all day, like he hadn't slept in a week. The veins on his neck were swollen, and his nostrils flared. "I almost shot at them," he said. "They could have been anybody."

When we reached Port Everglades and the hustle of Fort Lauderdale, Dad made Carolyn and me sit out on deck and wave at the Coast Guard, Customs, and Marine Police boats that patrolled the inlet. "They aren't going to pull us over if they see that we're a family boat," he said.

We cruised by them just fine, Carolyn and I waving and looking like innocent boat kids.

We found out later that the D.E.A. made one of the biggest cocaine busts of the year a few nights later off of Bimini. Even though the eighties were almost over, drug traffic between Miami and the Bahamas was still relatively heavy.

Kids Aboard

Fort Lauderdale, Florida • Fall 1989

Age 10

We were docked in Fort Lauderdale in the fall of 1989 when we met Rod. He came aboard *Chez Nous* without being invited, in the usual manner of liveaboard kids. I was nine and Carolyn was seven. We'd been flying the "Kids Aboard" flag. Mom had sewn a flag with the winning design (someone else had won, although her design had been a close runner-up and had been featured in a magazine article), and we'd started seeing the flags on more and more boats up and down the coast and in the Bahamas.

Rod made all kinds of noise out on deck, and Dad popped out from underneath the flipped-up galley steps. "What the hell was that?" He was busy installing our first watermaker, a contraption that would pump salt water up from the sea and turn it into fresh so that we would no longer have to depend on finding abandoned cisterns or collecting rainwater on the deck. Dad was beginning to make a little bit of supplemental money writing articles, and he added equipment to our boat as necessity arose and finances allowed. He had a three-quarter inch hose in one hand and a screwdriver in the other.

"It sounds like some kind of animal," Mom said. She pushed the companionway hatch open and Carolyn and I climbed up the stairs behind her. Rod stood in the cockpit holding a plastic machine gun.

"Hi," he said. Then, "Oh, you just have girls."

"Excuse me, but what's wrong with girls?" I was ready for battle.

Rod just stood there in our cockpit, looking down the barrel of his toy gun. He was shorter than me, had round cheeks and a buzz cut, and something about him reminded me of Bart Simpson. Maybe it was the skateboard he'd propped on a banyan tree next to our boat. "Well," he finally said, "Nothing's wrong with girls, but I wanted to play war." He set the gun down on the cockpit cushion. "I guess we don't have to," he said.

"You can shoot Melanie's Barbies," Carolyn said. Mom and I both turned to look at her, surprised to hear her talk. She was usually shy around new kids. I stepped on her foot.

63

"Where are your parents?" Mom looked around the dock, which was really just a stretch of seawall along the New River where the City of Fort Lauderdale made a few extra bucks tying up sailboats.

"On the boat smoking dope," Rod said. He puffed his chest out and looked at all of our faces to see what kind of reaction he'd gotten from us, then he pointed the gun over to a Taiwanese canoe-stern sloop that was docked three boats up the river from us. I covered my mouth and sucked back a giggle. This guy was ballsy to say something like that. And about his own parents? It struck me as hilarious. This, after all, was a world where one false accusation or one stray joint could land a cruiser in jail for supposed smuggling of drugs. To hear him speak so callously about something that my parents handled with such righteousness and delicacy made me feel like I would burst with excitement.

Mom glared at him for a moment before saying, "Do they know you're over here?" She didn't address the dope comment, but I was sure she would question his mother about it in private.

"Sure," he said. A woman with long blond hair popped out of the companionway of the sloop, which was named *Wind*, and waved over at us. A black cat shot out the hatch next to her, and jumped onto the seawall. "That's Geraldine," Rod said. "She's nineteen years old and she's blind. She'll claw your eyes out too, if you're not careful."

Rod's parents were Lynn and Joe. Joe was a Vietnam vet with a bad back, who received enough money from the government to pay for the boat and to keep Lynn and Rod happy. Rod announced to Carolyn and me later that Joe wasn't his dad so he was technically a bastard. Lynn was almost a foot taller than Joe, and she wore Western shirts and jeans. If she hadn't been living on a sailboat, I think she would have worn cowboy boots too. I liked her clothes, and I followed her around so I could pay close attention to everything she did and said.

Once Mom had talked to Lynn and determined that it was okay for us to play with Rod, we poured off the boat and into a large banyan tree. We weren't allowed to go any further than the tree, because Fort Lauderdale was a dangerous place, full of child molesters and bad people and God knows what else.

We strung a hammock up under the banyan, and the three of us climbed in and rocked it back and forth until it flipped over and dumped us onto the hard-packed Florida dirt. It was quiet in the banyan tree, and nobody bothered us. The New River, with its boat traffic and horns and current and mish-mash of wakes, flowed past us, and we pretended to be Greek gods. Rod, of course, was Zeus, and Carolyn cried when he threw a lightning bolt at her. I was Aphrodite, which pissed Rod off because he said I was too fat to be Aphrodite.

Rod's parents and ours decided to give us two days off school, because we were all ahead on our coursework. None of us knew when we would be around other kids again. Rod was a Calvert school kid too, a grade behind me, so we'd all read the same books and learned the same things. We went from playing Greek gods to pretending to be Hobbits to creating our own mythology in which Rod was the captain of a ship named Argo (represented by the hammock), I was the beautiful, but fat, cook, and Carolyn was the ship's cat.

Dad finished installing the watermaker in those two days, and the engine room of *Chez Nous* was now lined with heavy duty reverse-osmosis filters and hoses running from thru-hulls to the filters then to our water tank. Our time with Rod was over.

We steamed out of the New River in tears the day we crossed to the Bahamas, but Rod was on the way to George Town. We knew we'd see him again in a couple of months after we had spent our alone-time in Pipe Creek and at Compass Cay. Dad liked to have his own time of peace before we made our way to the social madness George Town, so there would be days and days of school in the morning, diving and shelling in the afternoon, and quiet dinners around the table on *Chez Nous* before we would be around kids again.

Girly Dive

George Town, Bahamas • Winter 1991
Age 11

The Monument on Stocking Island was always the first thing we saw of George Town. It rose out of the Exuma Sound off our bow, a green hill with a flat face, topped with a crumbling concrete beacon. Nobody knew what the Monument stood for, but it marked the graves of many well-loved boat pets, including our first hamster, Scruffy. It was probably built as a navigational beacon for island hopping schooners and sloops back in the days before loran and GPS made navigation something you did by pushing buttons.

I got giddy when I saw it.

To me, the Monument meant other kids. It meant Volleyball Beach, bonfires, the end of long days on the boat with nobody but my family for company. George Town was called Chicken Harbor by other boaters, because people always stopped there on their way to the Caribbean with the intention of provisioning in the small town on Great Exuma or making a few repairs. Most of them chickened out and ended up staying for months. It was that kind of place.

When Dad saw the Monument, his ears turned red and the vein in his neck started pumping the way it did when his temper was starting to flare. To him, George Town represented everything that he and Mom had moved onto the boat to escape—social structures, crowds, bad influences on their kids.

The winter I was eleven and Carolyn was nine was the first time I remember caring much about my looks. When we caught the first glimpse of the Monument looming off our bow, I ran below to put on a pair of shorts that wasn't ripped and a pink tank top. It was the kind I'd seen on the cover of *Seventeen Magazine* in the aisle at Publix back in the States: a skinny blond model with tanned shoulders and a giraffe neck had sported the turtleneck tank top as she lounged on a beach chair. I took my hair out of its ponytail and brushed it over my shoulders, wetting my hairbrush to calm the flyaway strands. I squeezed some strawberry flavored lip gloss out of the tube I kept by my bunk and rushed out on deck to see if the Monument had gotten any closer.

Carolyn sat on the bow pouting. I joined her. "Look at all the masts," I said. A forest of sailboat masts was beginning to appear underneath the Monument. Dad changed course slightly as we entered the harbor. The channel was narrow, and required his concentration. One or two boats went up on the reef each year, usually because they came in at night or during bad weather, relying too heavily on poorly-surveyed U.S. government charts or the boat's electronics.

Mom chattered on the VHF radio, calling all her friends to let them know we were here. She'd changed clothes too, preparing for the inevitable onslaught of dinghies we would face as soon as we anchored.

"I don't like George Town," Carolyn said.

"Why?" I thought she must have been crazy.

"Too many people," she said.

"You're going to have to start liking people one of these days," I said.

"Did you dress up for Rod or something?" She wrinkled her nose the way she did when she was pretending to be a rabbit. I didn't think her question warranted an answer.

The harbor opened up turquoise and violet in front of us, and Dad steered through the deep channel toward the Monument. We dropped anchor off of Hamburger Beach, almost directly below the Monument.

Dad stood on the bow and yelled back to mom, who had replaced him at the helm, to put the boat in reverse and jerk the anchor. "Goddammit," he said, when the anchor pulled out of the grassy seabed for the second time. This was one of the reasons why he hated George Town. The holding was terrible. It took three tries to get the plow anchor to bite. After we were anchored, he hid in the engine room for slightly longer than necessary, checking the fluid levels on the Perkins.

By the time the sun went down over Great Exuma, we'd received at least a dozen invitations to cocktail parties on people's boats, potlucks on the beach, and other kids' birthday parties. The social onslaught of George Town had begun. "We're only going to stay here a week," Dad said at dinner, but that's what he always said and we knew not to take him seriously.

The next morning, I woke up around 6:30 to hear Dad talking on the VHF. Mom was already up, and the tea kettle whistled in the galley where she was heating water for instant coffee. I dragged myself out of my bunk and up to the main cabin.

"Can you be ready in twenty minutes?" I didn't recognize the other man's voice on the VHF.

"Make it thirty," Dad said. "I need to eat breakfast. The light won't be good for another half hour."

"Okay. Back to 16," the other voice said.

"Hey Tom," a woman's voice broke into the VHF conversation.

"Morning," he said.

"Sorry to be eavesdropping, but you know how it is. Can Rod come along with you guys? He hasn't been diving in awhile." It was Lynn. I didn't know why she would apologize for listening. Everybody knew that the VHF wasn't private, and listening to other people's conversations was part of everyday life out here.

"Sure," he said.

"I'll run him over there in the dink so you all don't have to come get him," Lynn said. "I'm going to let him have the day off school so he can go with you."

Dad turned the radio back to 16, the stand-by and calling channel, and disappeared into the aft cabin mumbling something underneath his breath about babysitting other peoples' kids.

"Where are they going?" I sat on the galley steps and watched Mom stir raisins into a pot of oatmeal. The smell nauseated me.

"Diving," she said.

"I didn't know there was anyplace to dive around here."

"They're going offshore," she said.

"Can I go?"

"Better ask your dad." She spooned some of the oatmeal into a bowl and handed it to me so I could put it on the table. "If you're going, you'd better eat some of this."

My stomach rolled over and I turned away from the oatmeal so I couldn't smell it. The raisins looked like black insects in the mush. I decided to go without breakfast. I also decided not to ask Dad about diving. I changed into a bathing suit and a long T-shirt, put my hair in a ponytail and hoped nobody would notice that I hadn't brushed it, and spread some sunscreen on my nose. I hopped up the stairs to the cockpit and got my diving stuff together—mask, snorkel, fins, weight belt, spear, Hawaiian sling. We didn't scuba dive, because it was illegal to spearfish with tanks. Dad had a tank, but he only used it when he had to repair something underwater.

Lynn zipped up in the dinghy and barely slowed down to let Rod jump off. Rod waved at his mom and stood there on the deck with his mesh gear bag slung over his shoulder. "You're not going, are you?" he said.

"Yup."

"This isn't a girly dive," he said.

"What's a girly dive?"

"You know, shallow water, to look at pretty fish," he said. "We're going to go kill stuff."

I picked up my Hawaiian sling and stretched out the cord, pretending that the spear was cocked into place, and let it go in Rod's direction. "I'll shoot you if you don't shut up," I said.

When Dad came upstairs, he looked at me funny and asked, "Are you going with us?"

"Yes." I glared at him and then at Rod, and picked up my dive bag and spear.

"Okay," Dad said.

We skimmed across the harbor toward the inlet in a hard-bottomed inflatable dinghy that belonged to a guy named Sean—the man Dad had been talking to on the VHF. Sean was a professional captain, hired to run and take care of someone else's sailboat. Dad had met him back in Pipe Creek the week before. I thought his graying beard and deep tan made him look the part of a professional captain. His dive gear was all new, and the Yamaha outboard on the dink was the latest model.

I sat in the narrow V of the bow and leaned out over the water, looking at the coral heads as they flew underneath us. It was flat calm, and I could make out the details on each fish: black spots running down the side of a barracuda, the purple stripes on a triggerfish's mouth.

Sean cut the engine off just outside the inlet. Large swells lifted and dropped the dinghy, but their surfaces were glass-smooth. "There are a couple of good reefs down there," he said, pulling on his fins. "Let's throw a line in and drift."

I spit into my mask and rubbed my saliva around inside to keep it from fogging. By the time I had finished, everybody else was in the water. Sean and Rod swam ahead of the dink, and Dad held onto the line that was tied to the bow. I sat on the edge and let my fins trail in the water. I tried to guess the depth, but the sun was behind the clouds and I figured it probably wasn't as deep as is looked. I hoped Dad had taken a thorough look around for sharks and barracudas.

As I slipped into the water, I thought about my mom and sister and Lynn. I wondered why none of them wanted to be out here. They all seemed to be content back on the boats, reading, studying, doing boat work. Maybe Mom was working on one of her paintings. She'd been commissioned to do a large yacht portrait for some yacht club yuppie back in Virginia. I wondered if something was wrong with me for preferring the company of a bunch of fish-killing guys to the more civilized company of my mom and sister.

I spun in a complete circle to let my eyes adjust to the filtered light underneath the water. I was looking for sharks, even though I didn't want to admit it. The circle of visibility spread out about seventy feet on all sides, then faded into gray-blue shadow where coral heads and schools of amberjacks loomed against the muted rays of sunlight.

Rod and Dad took turns pulling the dink, swimming slowly underneath it holding a line tied to the bow, and Sean did most of the diving. I watched him dive and come up with a twenty pound grouper thrashing at the end of his spear, a cloud of fish blood trailing behind him. Two barracudas followed him up, circling underneath, but they slunk back into the shadows as soon as the grouper was in the dinghy.

I wanted to get out of the water, but didn't. I tried not to think about the guy I'd seen on Volleyball Beach last year. He'd been diving off Andros a few months before, and a reef shark had taken a chunk out of his leg. His whole calf was concave, and he half-ran half-limped around the sand volleyball court. He'd been spearfishing, and the shark had come up out of nowhere. He'd never even seen it, just felt something hit him hard and then he looked back and a chunk of his leg was gone. Shark attacks were like that. I was an expert on them.

I'd read every book about sharks that I could convince Mom to buy me. Somehow, it made me feel better to know what I was up against. The bloodier the pictures in the books, the more I liked them. I wanted to study shark behavior someday, and I fantasized about going down in one of those steel cages while a great white gnashed its teeth against the bars. I'd read that shark attacks didn't even hurt until afterwards. When they happened, you just felt numb.

Something nudged against my shoulder and I jumped. It was Dad. He pointed down at the bottom with his spear, waving it towards a sandy patch between clumps of dead elkhorn coral. There were forests of dead coral all over the Bahamas, where Bahamian fishermen had bleached the reefs in order to chase grouper and lobster out from under ledges and into waiting nets.

I had to let my eyes adjust all over again to see what he was pointing at. There were dozens of conch spread out across the sand. They looked tiny from the surface, but their shells had the flared lips of full grown queens. Dad stuck his head above the surface and motioned with his thumb for me to do the same.

"I don't think I can go that deep," he said. "My ears can't handle it. Why don't you try it?" (He'd injured his eardrums as a child and always wore earplugs when diving.)

"How deep is it?" I tried not to swallow water.

"I don't know, forty-five at least."

We ducked back under, and I took a couple of deep breaths through my snorkel. I didn't know at that point that you're supposed to hyperventilate before you dive. I didn't know any of the technicalities or rules or fancy terms. I just knew to clear my ears when they started to hurt, which was a matter of instinct.

The conch were huge, some over fifteen inches from spiral to tip, and their shells were thick from living with that much water pressed down on top of them. They were crusted with coral and tufts of seaweed, and my hand looked small and white, like it didn't belong, when I reached out for the closest one. I scooped up two, one under each arm, and kicked towards the surface. The dinghy and the other divers were small black spots against the round sphere of sunlight above me.

Rod dove with me on the next trip down, but he only made it halfway to the bottom. I came up with two more conch.

Dad tapped me on the shoulder after my fourth trip.

"What?" I said.

"You didn't see them?"

"See what?"

"The reef sharks," he said

He didn't need to say anything else before I was climbing into the dinghy. "Where were they?" I pulled my mask off and wrapped my arms around my chest, suddenly cold.

"They followed you down that last time," he said. He pulled himself into the dink, and Rod and Sean followed. The whites of Rod's eyes seemed twice their normal size through his mask.

"How many?" I said. I was glad I'd skipped breakfast, because I knew that had I eaten it the oatmeal would have come back up.

"Two," Dad said. "They circled right over you a couple of times."

"He tried to chase them away," Rod said, pointing at my dad, who was peering into the glass bottomed bucket we always took with us on diving trips.

"They're still down there," Dad said. I leaned over the bucket, pushing him aside. Through the scratched glass, I could see the two sharks, small gray silhouettes against the sandy bottom. They swam in unison, their bodies moving as naturally as the water around them.

Sean laughed. "I don't think they were hungry. They were just looking." He smiled, white teeth against tanned skin, and started the outboard, and Dad set the look-bucket down in the dinghy's bilge.

Rod pulled a towel around his shoulders and spit into the water. "My sinuses were hurting," he said. "That's why I couldn't dive as deep as you."

Dad rolled his eyes at me, checking first to make sure Rod wasn't looking.

"How deep was it anyway?" I said.

"I can tell you." Sean flipped on a handheld depth sounder and dropped the transducer in the water. "Fifty-three feet," he said.

"Why didn't you tell us you had a depth sounder?" Dad said.

"Because none of you would have gotten into that water if you'd known how deep it was." Sean covered the grouper and the conch with a wet towel and turned the throttle until the dink was planning back towards the harbor. When we neared *Chez Nous*, the smell of just-baked whole wheat bread trailed downwind from the open hatches. I was hungry now.

Cold Front

George Town, Bahamas • Winter 1992

Age 12

Michelle was in George Town the year I was twelve. We'd bumped into each other yearly, although not at any consistent time or place. Her dad's cruising schedule was much less regular than ours. Sometimes he spent months at Norman's Cay, and sometimes he sailed straight to George Town. Once we saw each other in Nassau for a couple of hours, and that was the only chance we had that year to catch up. We spent the time gabbing incessantly over boys and music. Gary had just remarried and bought a Morgan Out Island 41 named *Summer Wind*, a tub of a boat, but one with a hell of a lot of room, which was good because his new wife had plans for lots of kids. My parents were friendly with Gary, and always went out of their way to make sure Michelle and I could see each other, but yet there was this subtle difference between our families that at that age I sensed but couldn't define.

By 1992, Michelle was one of those strong girls who could arm-wrestle any of the guys on Volleyball Beach until she made them cry. She had spark-green eyes and lots of dark hair that she didn't really like to brush so it always hung in her face. Terry, her step-mom, gave her a layered haircut that made her look like an upright mop.

Michelle wore a baggy New Kids on the Block T-shirt over her bathing suit every day, trying to cover up her changing body. When I saw her for the first time that year on Volleyball beach, I told her that her legs would look thinner if she shaved them. That's what Trey and the kids at Narrows Marina in Virginia had told me the summer before. They'd also told me that my hips were too big. They stood behind me while I walked, my thighs rubbing against each other, and called out, "Thunder thighs! Buffalo Butt!"

"Really?" She raised her black eyebrows and leaned forward so she could look at her legs. "Do you think they look fat?"

"Um, no," I said. Michelle's legs were a lot thinner than mine.

Michelle and I sat on an old splintery picnic bench under the biggest Australian Pine on Volleyball Beach. It was on the west side of the beach, opposite the volleyball courts, and we could look across the harbor, though the mess of anchored boats, to town, which was just a sprinkling of pink and white buildings against the low green scrub of Great Exuma. We were old enough to be on the beach by ourselves now—my parents usually dropped me off after school.

Michelle turned a paperback book over in her hands. Its cover was green from the mildew that grew on every bookshelf on every boat. "Hey, you should read this," she said.

"Oh yeah?" I'd gone through every Nancy Drew book in the George Town library, and had read *The Hobbit* and *The Lord of the Rings* stories multiple times, so I was eager for new recommendations. I could always reread *The Island of the Blue Dolphins*, but after seven times it was getting predictable.

"It's a ro-mance novel," she said, overstressing the first syllable.

"Is it good?"

"Listen to this," she said. She read something about a throbbing erection and we both burst out laughing.

"That's sick," I said. "Does your dad know you're reading stuff like that?"

"Hey, it's Terry's book," she said.

A burst of giggling erupted from behind the Australian Pine, and Carolyn and one of her ten-year-old friends started pelting us with the tiny hard pine cones that covered the beach. They whooshed through the air and stung when they hit our sunburned shoulders and chests.

"Hey, don't do that!" I stood on the bench and tried to swat the pine cones as they came, missing most of them. Then one flew at me extra hard and from another direction and hit me on the chest. Rod had joined the younger kids in the attack, and now he jumped up and down and screamed.

"Whoo hoo! Right in the boob!" He grabbed another handful from my sister, who was scurrying around the brush and gathering them as fast as she could.

"Rod, you're a jerk," Michelle said.

"You can do better than that." Rod hurled a cone at Michelle, but missed. "Why don't you call me an asshole? What, you're not allowed to say bad words or something?"

"Just ignore him." I sat back down next to Michelle.

"That never works," she said. She covered the back of her head with the romance novel.

Rod jumped up on the bench behind us. "Hey, you all should come see the fort we built," he said.

"Where is it?" I turned just in time for another pine cone to graze my cheek.

"Back in the bushes," he said. He pointed to the middle of the beach, which was actually a peninsula jutting out into Elizabeth Harbor. The center of the peninsula was overgrown with palmetto scrub and buttonwood and sea grapes, and people were always losing dogs and children in there.

"I bet it's a crappy fort," Michelle said, but she left her book on the picnic table and we followed Rod into the bushes.

Carolyn and her friend were already way ahead of us. "They're building their own fort," Rod said. He stopped at a clearing somewhere in the middle of the peninsula.

"This is it?" Michelle looked around, her hands resting on her hips. "This isn't a fort."

"It kind of is," Rod said. "See, these are the walls." He pointed to some vines and palmetto thatch that he'd laced between the branches of a sea grape tree. "It's got a nice floor," he said, thumping the sand with his foot.

"Yeah, but that didn't take any effort," Michelle said.

I stared up at the twisted branches overhead. I kind of liked it back here—at least it was shady. The slanted beams of sunlight that made it through the scrub danced on the ground in orange patches. It was getting late.

"I'm leaving," Michelle said.

"Don't go!" I didn't want to go back out to the beach, but I was suddenly a bit nervous at the prospect of being left alone with Rod.

"It's time for me to go home and fix dinner," she said. Michelle had more responsibilities than any other twelve-year-old I knew.

"What are you making?" Rod took his sunglasses off and hung them on a branch.

"Mac and cheese." She stormed off, not bothering to say goodbye. That's the way she was—always on some kind of mission, always in a hurry to get to the next thing. I admired the way she moved.

Rod and I were stuck in the fort, standing at opposite sides, awkward as hell.

"Um, maybe I should go too," I said.

"Maybe not," Rod said. He crossed the fort and put his arms over my shoulders and stuck his tongue in my mouth. Somehow he managed to be a smooth talker at twelve. I guess some people are just born with it.

I hoped it would be over soon, even though I knew I was supposed to be enjoying this. I wondered if my sister and her friend were hiding somewhere, watching us. I figured they probably were.

This was a kissing marathon, like we were trying to see how long we could go without choking on each other's spit. It wasn't my first kiss—that had been a few weeks ago, under the Monument, with Rod. It had been a lot quicker and softer and a lot more pleasant. This just felt like something we were supposed to do, even though neither of us enjoyed it that much. We'd decided, in some childish way, that we were boyfriend and girlfriend, which really just meant that we snuck off every now and then to kiss.

The light was turning orange, and I knew Dad would be coming ashore soon to pick Carolyn and me up, so I pulled away from Rod. On the way back to the beach, I spit several times, trying to get Rod's saliva out of my mouth. I hoped he wouldn't notice.

Dad stood by the Australian pine, staring straight at us. "It's time to go," he said. He didn't acknowledge Rod. He set a book he'd been holding back onto the picnic table, and turned to where our aluminum dinghy was pulled up on the beach. Carolyn was already in the dink.

When I passed the table, I saw the book was Michelle's romance novel, sitting open, the pages fluttering like signal flags. I grabbed it and tucked it under my shirt. I wondered which part Dad had read.

That night, a cold front rolled over the Exumas, and the wind funneled through the hatch over my bed and brought rain and earthy smells in with it. I thought about the rain pouring down the face of the Monument, dislodging sand and rocks and the small coral fossils that we found there all the time. The only way to describe the smell of rain in the Bahamas is to say it's green, like when you crumple leaves together and their juices leak onto your hands and you smell them still living even though you've just broken them.

The air was clean and dry in the morning, and I sat in the V-berth with a heavy math book over my knees, trying to work out some pre-algebra equations that seemed impossibly hard. I didn't know when I'd be able to get off the boat again, because the wind was blowing twenty knots and cold air was pouring down the forward hatch from the front that had passed through overnight. *Chez Nous* pulled at her anchor chain, her bow riding over the waves that rolled down Elizabeth Harbor. Getting into the dinghy to go ashore would be uncomfortable, if not downright treacherous, for a day or so.

The lead on my #2 pencil kept breaking, and I kept getting up to sharpen it over the trash can in the galley. Carolyn sat at the table in the main cabin, building something out of modeling clay.

"Melanie, can you come back here for a minute?" Dad stood in the doorway to the aft cabin, one foot at the top of the steps. Carolyn rolled her eyes at me as I walked past. I wondered what he'd do if I said no.

The aft cabin was always darker than the rest of the boat. Dad had his computer set up on a big slab of a desk that he'd hired a carpenter in Virginia to fit into the space between the foot of the queen-sized bed and the door to the aft head. The little bit of light that came into the room filtered through the two portholes in the stern. It was always dusty back there, because Dad didn't like any of us to come in and clean while he was writing his articles. He had papers scattered all over the floor and the desk. I sat down on the bottom step, not fully inside the cabin.

"What do you want?" I asked.

He leaned back in the folding chair at his desk and saved his work on the computer. His hair stuck up straight on top of his head, and I thought about how Mom had said once: "He's afraid it'll fall out if he brushes it." He just left it looking like a rat's nest until it was time to make a trip into town. Then, he'd comb the top layer so that it was smooth over the tangles.

"I saw you and Rod come out of the bushes yesterday," he said.

"Uh huh," I said, trying to sound like it was no big deal.

"What happened back there?" he asked.

What did he want me to say? I felt uncomfortable as hell, like Mom should be asking me this stuff and not Dad. After all, Mom was the one who, three years before, had given me the sex talk. I think I must have been the only kid alive who, at nine, had no idea how babies were made. Sex-ed wasn't part of the home school curriculum. I'd asked her something about the Virgin Mary and she'd asked me if I knew what a virgin was, and we'd spent the next three hours sitting in the forward cabin talking about the logistics of reproduction. That night, I told Carolyn, horrified at the idea that she would have to live in the dark as long as I had.

"Um, he kissed me," I said.

Dad's knuckles turned white on the arms of his folding chair. "Is that all?"

"Um, yeah, that's all."

"Well, I just want you to know what people will think of you if they see you coming out of the bushes with a boy," he said.

"Huh?"

"Just don't let it happen again."

"What are you talking about?"

"People see you come out of the bushes with Rod and they'll laugh at you," he said. "They'll call you a slut and it'll make our whole family look bad. That's not the way we're raising you."

I had no idea what he was talking about. I wasn't doing anything on Volleyball Beach that the other kids weren't doing. I just got caught. "I don't think anybody's going to call me a slut, Dad," I said.

He just frowned and stared at his computer screen. "You don't think that people will, but they will. That's just the way the world works, and I don't want people to think bad things about you," he said.

"What will people think of Rod?" I knew the answer, but I had to ask. I had to hear what my dad would say.

"It's different with boys. Boys brag about kissing girls and people encourage them to act that way," Dad said.

"Then nobody is going to call Rod a slut."

"No." Dad and I were both silent as we both pondered this. We both knew how wrong it was, but we both knew that it was undeniably *true*. "The world isn't fair, Melanie."

"I don't like that." And somehow, somewhere in the deep, deep recesses of my mind and the flesh and bones of my being, I knew that I would fight that unfairness.

I decided that afternoon that I simply wouldn't get caught next time. And I decided that I would not change my behavior simply because I was afraid of what people would say. I knew that part of my dad's lecture had to do with the way he wanted the world to perceive our family. We were wholesome and harmonious. We lived on a boat and baked our own bread and caught our own fish for dinner. We were smart and pure. We were not slutty. But I also knew that my dad didn't want me to be blind to the way the rest of the world would perceive a girl who did her own thing and ran off on the beach to make out with boys.

Some cold fronts take their time. They stall out on top of you and kick the waves into a frenzy, and when they finally pass you're stuck with air that's unnaturally cold for February in the Bahamas.

The one that came through the night after Dad caught me making out on Volleyball Beach lasted three days. On Day One, the wind came up out of the Southeast—masses of air being sucked across pressure gradients before the front. In the middle of the next night, *Chez Nous* swung 180 degrees on her anchor chain as the wind moved around to the northwest. Since Elizabeth Harbor ran diagonally across the compass from northwest to southeast, the wind funneled straight down the harbor in both directions.

I woke up the next day with the feeling that something was terribly wrong. Carolyn was already up in the main salon, and I smelled oatmeal. I realized I had slept much later than the rest of my family. It was already eight thirty, and we had a rule about starting school exactly at nine, but I didn't want to get up. The bow moved up and down over the waves that were rolling through Elizabeth Harbor, and big raindrops pounded on the deck. Someone had closed the forward hatch, and it was hot and stuffy inside the V-berth. Even though I never got seasick, the stuffy air and the oatmeal smell made me feel queasy. Dixie, the yellow parakeet we'd begged our parents for last summer, whistled and banged her beak against the metal bars of her cage, which was almost directly over my bed.

I tried to remember what was wrong. I heard Dad talking on the VHF radio to some other boater about the weather. "It might blow like this for three more days," he said. I didn't hear the response. Dad's voice sunk into my stomach and I remembered: I was a slut. I felt like it was written across my forehead in big black letters. It was there, but underneath it was written something else. I was a fighter. I was a Fighter Slut. I would fight the unfairness of being labeled. I waited until he had gone into the aft cabin to write before I got out of bed and made my way up to the table. Mom had left a bowl out for me, and the stainless-steel pot of oatmeal was still on the table.

Carolyn was already doing her schoolwork, sitting at the chart table with the Calvert School fifth grade syllabus spread out across her lap. "You slept too late," Carolyn said. "I'll be finished with school before you."

"I don't really care," I said. "It's not like we're going to be able to do anything this afternoon." I didn't see the point in rushing through my schoolwork when the weather was this bad. I opened the lid to the oatmeal, but before I could spoon some of the sticky goo into my bowl my stomach gave out and I threw up all over the salon table. I managed to get most of it into the pot of oatmeal.

"Eeewww!" Carolyn threw her book onto the floor and jumped up. "You puked in the oatmeal!" She danced around the cabin, waving her hands over her head. "Melanie puked in the oatmeal!"

Dad came out from his office and opened the companionway hatch to let in some fresh air. The sound of rain pelting the bimini top over the cockpit drowned out Carolyn's shrieks. Dad didn't say anything, just looked at the mess and shook his head. Mom put on her yellow foul weather gear and climbed out the hatch with the pot of oatmeal and puke so she could throw it overboard. I tried to clean up the rest of the mess.

Mom took my temperature once we had restored a sense of order to *Chez Nous*. I didn't have a fever, and I felt fine. She made me eat some wheat bread, and I crawled back into the forward cabin to start my schoolwork. I sat where I always did, propped up on my bunk with my feet on Carolyn's side and my books spread over my knees. I kept all of my books and papers in a file box, which stayed at the foot of the V-berth when I wasn't using it. I tried to focus on a page of geometry problems, but I couldn't. I looked in the back of the book for the answers.

I wondered if this was what happened to kids in regular school who had problems concentrating. I'd heard about attention deficit disorder, and about how parents relied on drugs to make their kids concentrate. Maybe I needed drugs. Instead of reading the chapters in my history textbook about the Civil War, I pulled out a blank piece of paper and wrote a poem. Maybe I just needed to write. Maybe I'd send it to some poetry contest when we got back to the States.

I was starved by the time Mom fixed lunch. She fried falafel in vegetable oil, and Dixie, the parakeet, tried to mimic the frying sound. "Stupid bird," I said, and opened the cage. I wondered what would happen if Dixie flew into the frying pan. Instead, Dixie flew up into the main salon and perched on top of Carolyn's head. Carolyn acted like she didn't even notice, and Dixie clicked her beak as she chewed on honey-blond strands of Carolyn's hair. Dad came out of the aft cabin and we all sat around the salon table for lunch.

"It still smells like puke in here," Carolyn said. She held a piece of falafel up to Dixie, whose beak dripped with oil.

"We're trying to eat," Dad said.

"I don't smell anything," Mom said. We finished lunch without talking.

It rained for the rest of the day, and Mom and Dad spent the afternoon arguing in the aft cabin. Carolyn and I sat in the salon and listened to them speak to each other in clipped and harsh tones. Mom had lost the lens to one of her cameras, and Dad ranted about how much it would cost to replace. "We're on a limited budget," he said. "We can't stay out here forever if we keep having to replace expensive equipment. I'm trying to make money for us by writing but I can only make so much." I couldn't hear Mom's response, although I imagined it to be rational and quiet, reminding him that there was still plenty of money saved up and that our lifestyle wasn't threatened by the loss of a camera lens. I decided, as I listened, that it wasn't so bad to be a slut. I'd heard my parents call each other things that were just as bad when they lost their tempers. Dad was most likely to lose his temper during cold fronts. It could have been cabin fever, or the possibility weighing in the back of his mind of another boat dragging into us. These were the days, when we were stuck aboard, at anchor, with no safe way to reach the shore, that I wondered what it would be like to live in a big, comfortable house like the kids back in Virginia.

On the third day of being stuck on the boat, I woke up after nine. I hadn't been able to get to sleep the night before, because I'd stayed up late reading and eating Hershey's kisses from the bag I'd snuck up into the forward cabin. Mom always made sure we had a good supply of chocolate on the boat, and I knew where all the storage spaces were. Mom and Dad slept in too, because they'd stayed up drinking boxed red wine.

It wasn't raining anymore, but the waves were still pitching *Chez Nous* around, and the salt spray outside felt like rain. I didn't want to work on geometry, so I cheated on my math problems again and focused on writing a poem. Carolyn threw a tantrum when Mom tried to get her to diagram sentences. Dad shut the door to the aft stateroom and ignored us all, lost in his writing.

Michelle called on the VHF sometime during the long afternoon. We switched over to channel 72, which was my favorite because it rhymed with *Chez Nous* and I liked saying it.

"How are you all holding up over there? Over," Michelle said. She was well-trained in proper radio etiquette, and, like me, I think she enjoyed knowing that her voice was being transmitted across the entire anchorage. The range on most VHF radios was at least ten miles, depending on the signal strength and the height of your antenna.

"Okay. Everyone's fighting. Over," I said.

"Oh, yeah. We're all fighting here too. Over," she said.

"It must be the weather. Cabin fever. Over."

"It must be. Well, maybe we'll be able to go ashore tomorrow. Over."

Before we could finish talking, Dad was in the main cabin grabbing the microphone from me. "That's nobody's business," he said. "Don't you know everyone in the harbor is listening?"

"Just let me finish talking to Michelle," I said.

"Melanie, are you there? Over." Michelle's voice sounded smaller.

"Yeah. I have to go. *Chez Nous* clear. Over," I said. I switched the radio back to 16.

Carolyn sat back and waited for whatever was coming next, and Mom pretended not to be paying any attention. She was brushing gesso across one of her canvas boards, preparing to start another painting, and the air inside the boat smelled like acrylic paint and thinner. "What's wrong with what I said?" I hung the VHF microphone back up over the chart table.

"I just don't think everyone in George Town needs to know what goes on in our family. It's none of their business," Dad said.

"Do you really think everyone in George Town is listening in to my radio conversation?"

"Yes," he said. He stormed back into the aft cabin, and shut the door again. He was busy writing his own version of our life, one that had begun appearing in all the big boating magazines. He was writing about perfect beaches, serene anchorages, and home-schooled kids who got perfect scores on all the standardized tests. He was writing about how living on a boat brought families together in ways that were impossible on land.

My dad could be good at anything he decided to do, and what he had decided to do was become one of the best and most popular boating writers in the industry. He wrote because he enjoyed it, and because the payout from a structured settlement that he'd won for a client and which had supported our family in our early years of cruising was running its course. He had to find a new way to make money. When he'd started writing, he submitted his articles to the boating magazines with fervor, tossing the rejection letters aside and submitting again until his articles were accepted. The cruising community loved his sense of humor and his practical tips and his how-to guidance on raising a family aboard. But, as anyone with his sense of propriety would do, he only wrote about the things he wanted people to know. His daughters were growing up around him and doing the things that post-pubescent girls do, and this dose of reality weighed heavily on him. He could not, as much as he wanted to, write his way back to the days when he and I sat on the back of *Chez Nous* slurping down raw oysters and dreaming of heading south.

Skinny

Virginia • Summer 1993

Age 13

Rod broke up with me by letter after we left George Town. The problem was that I didn't get the letter until after another boat kid had stopped in Pipe Creek and told me that Rod had been going out with a younger, thinner girl with bigger boobs than mine. "They even go over to the Ocean Beach and mess around," she told me. I cried and nursed my first broken heart as I listened to sad country music on cassette tape and stashed bag after bag of Hershey's Kisses in the cabinet above my bunk. I ate them while I was doing schoolwork and while I was reading or just hanging out in my room and hiding from the world. The chocolate gave me a high that made everything else fade out and seem unimportant. Even though I was physically active, going diving with my dad almost every afternoon and hunting for conch and grouper and lobster, my weight crept up and my self-esteem crept down.

Halfway back up the Intracoastal, I decided that I would lose a bunch of weight and that Rod would most certainly like me again when I returned to George Town the following winter. I asked my mom about diets and she told me that she'd tried several. There was one where you ate less than 1,200 calories a day and one where you ate less than 20 grams of fat. The low-carb craze was still about ten years in the future. Mom applauded my dieting, but reminded me that I needed to keep eating healthy things like fruits and vegetables.

If one could lose weight on 1,200 calories a day, it made sense to me that one could lose even more on 900. So I started measuring everything I ate, carefully portioning out one-cup servings of Special K cereal and eating light yogurt cups. We were back in Virginia, docked at "The Lot," so convenience food was an option whereas it wouldn't have been in the Bahamas. I went grocery shopping with Mom every week, selecting diet-friendly foods: fat free Fig Newtons, SnackWells, lean lunch meats and low-calorie bread. On these same shopping trips, Carolyn haphazardly tossed bags of Oreo cookies into the shopping cart, and anger boiled in my stomach as I looked at her skinny legs and narrow hips and the way her hair cascaded across her shoulders and down her back to her waist. It was so easy for her to stay thin. She was always eating, scarfing down candy and cookies while I ate my 70-calorie artificially-sweetened yogurt cups one tiny bite at a time, hoping that the next bite would satisfy my hunger. I told myself that hunger was a virtue and that it made you feel more. I was convinced that, when hungry, I could write better poetry and be a more creative person.

"The Lot" was lonely. There were no other kids around, and we spent most days performing maintenance on the boat and finishing the season's schoolwork. Carolyn and I stripped down and repainted an old sailing dinghy that my parents had owned for years, work that Carolyn hated but that I relished. My arms felt strong as I sanded, and I loved seeing the fresh paint glisten as it dried in the hot Virginia sun. I loved the way it smelled clean and metallic, the copper in the antifouling paint that we put on the bottom to keep seaweed from growing seeming to jump into the air in tiny sparks. When we finished, it was to become our own sailing dinghy. To us, this was just like having a car. That summer was particularly hot, and the jellyfish blossomed in the Chesapeake Bay earlier than usual. Dad cursed them as he dove on *Chez Nous* to scrub barnacles from the prop.

Soon I was eating fewer than 700 calories a day. Breakfast was a cup of Special K, lunch was half a piece of bread with some lettuce and some lunch meat, and dinner was whatever meat Mom had cooked and a small portion of vegetables. I ate as little as I could eat without being called out by my family. I weighed myself every day, happy to see my weight falling and falling. My clothes were baggy and my thighs no longer rubbed together. I started running in place up in the forward cabin every morning, blasting music. I ran for an hour before I let myself eat breakfast, and I ran so hard that my feet wore a hole in the carpet that covered the teak-and-holly cabin sole.

The hair on my arms and my face began to grow thicker, although the strands were fine and brittle. My nails broke easily and sometimes I felt dizzy. Sometimes I felt so angry that I wanted to be violent. Carolyn, eating her Oreos and drinking calorie-laden orange juice, infuriated me. Once, as I walked behind her on the wooded path leading from where we kept our car parked to the dock, I watched her brown back glistening in a scoop-necked bathing suit. Her hair flowed down her shoulders and the sun coming through the trees set it on fire. How was she so beautiful and thin without even trying? I carried a bucket that I'd been asked to fetch from our Oldsmobile. Without thinking, I drew my arm back and hurled the bucket at the small of Carolyn's back. It hit her with a thwack and bounced off, landing in the dry leaves and rustling to a stop. Carolyn turned to look at me, her eyes wide and her mouth open.

"Um, I'm sorry," I said, panicking inside. Why had I done that? What kind of evil lived in me that would make me want to hurt someone without even thinking about it? My dad's temper was dark, but never physical. Was whatever was inside me even darker?

Carolyn scampered down the hill, putting distance between herself and me. She never told Mom and Dad about it. Or if she did, nobody said anything to me.

Occasionally, the Neale grandparents drove to "The Lot" and took us out to dinner in Kilmarnock, the small town located nearby. We went to a family restaurant that served giant burgers and steak fries. I would order a burger and eat the entire thing, returning later to *Chez Nous* to hurl into the toilet in the forward head. I learned to do this quietly, shoving my fingers into the back of my throat until the vomit came out in a stream, any sound stifled by my hands, now cupped over my mouth. Our boat was small and it would be easy for someone to hear me, but I don't think anyone ever did. As I looked in the mirror I stared at my jaw line which now seemed so well-defined and strong and so much more beautiful than the soft one I'd had a few months ago. *Rod will have to like me now*, I thought.

My parents finally noticed that I had a problem. Only a couple of months had gone by since I started my diet, but at this point I was constipated and eating about 500 calories a day. They pulled me into the aft cabin to talk to me about how I'd gotten "too skinny" and how they were afraid I was anorexic. My mom fed me oatmeal and whole wheat bread until my system started working properly again, and by August I had regained some of my weight. I was still thin, and when we left "The Lot" to spend some time at Narrows Marina, the Land Kids were much more accepting. They still teased me for being different, saying things like, "Do your parents still run around naked?" but it was more good natured and more out of habit than anything else. I was no longer Thunder Thighs or Buffalo Butt. I wondered if the simple act of getting skinny had suddenly made me more socially acceptable. I knew it had but I questioned why this was so important to people…weren't we all taught that what mattered the most was on the inside? It felt good to be accepted, but part of me hunkered down at that point and prepared to battle. I would not be normal and I would not fall into the trap of judging people for their outside appearances or their ages or their gender or status.

We spent time in the playground more as a place to hang out. "Playing" was what kids did. There really wasn't much to do at Narrows besides hang out on people's boats and watch TV and movies. Since we didn't have a TV in our main salon and my parents didn't believe in watching TV during the daytime, I spent all my time on the weekends on one of the powerboats inside the rickety boat shed. Trey's boat was the biggest.

One Saturday morning in August, I climbed onto Trey's boat to join the usual kids, who were sprawled out on the floor watching some action movie and passing around a bag of potato chips. A blond boy in the corner caught my eye. I had never seen him before. He had eyes that reminded me of an owl's, except they were blue and spaced far apart, and his lanky body was draped across the couch. Unlike Trey and Rod and the other boys I was used to hanging out with, he had thick blond hair on his arms and when he spoke to me his voice was deep. On autopilot, I took a seat next to him. "I'm Will," he said, and shook my hand like one adult would shake another adult's. And that's how I felt—like we were the only two adults in the room. His legs were long and his skin was tanned, and it unnerved me when he looked at me.

The other kids watched the movie and Will and I chatted. He lived on a farm west of Richmond, which he hated. He and Trey had known each other since fourth grade, and coming out to Narrows Marina with Trey was a way to escape the monotony of the farm for a weekend. He listened to country music and he was fascinated by Edgar Allan Poe. Later, when the group of us moved to the V-berth to hang out, Will pulled me over and kissed me. I was surprised but went along with it. This was different from kissing Rod. I didn't feel like I needed to spit afterwards.

We exchanged addresses on Sunday, and he wrote me a letter the next day. When my dad handed me the envelope after his daily run into down to the post office, he squinted at the return address as if he wasn't sure whether or not he should give it to me. I took it from him without speaking and settled into my bunk to read. The letter was written on lined composition paper, and Will's handwriting was neat and small. He apologized for not giving me a proper good-bye. Trey's family had left so hastily that he hadn't had time to find me. But he thought he was in love with me and hoped that he would see me again. I wrote back, telling him that we would be at the marina for another month or so if he could come down again with Trey, and that I would like to see him.

He came down on Labor Day weekend, but Trey did his best to keep us away from each other. We walked on the beach on Saturday, holding hands, and talked about life on the farm and life on the boat, and later sat pressed together on Trey's boat watching movies. But by Sunday Trey had convinced his parents that they needed to go out for a cruise on the Piankitank River. Out on the boat, away from me, he'd have his best friend to himself. The weekend ended abruptly and, just like the time before, Will and I didn't get a chance to say goodbye.

The Tuesday after Labor Day, Carolyn unpacked her Calvert School boxes for seventh grade and I started high school. Calvert only went through eighth grade, so my parents had researched high school home school programs thoroughly and chosen to use the curriculum provided by Brigham Young University. One of my mom's four sisters was Mormon, but other than that we had no ties to the religion. It was just a good, medium-priced program that met the accreditation requirements of the Commonwealth of Virginia and would provide me with a real, honest-to-goodness, high school diploma from Mountain View High School in Orem, Utah. The classes came packaged separately, each with their own teacher's manual and textbooks and materials. Unlike Calvert, the teacher's manuals were written for the student and not the parent.

I had been teaching myself for a few years now, confining myself to the space in the V-berth for my lessons while Mom worked with Carolyn in the main salon. I still consulted with her for the more difficult math problems, and Dad liked to teach history lessons, seating me on the floor in the aft cabin while he preached his interpretation of historical events (the Civil War was really "The War Between the States," and had less to do with slavery than it did with states' rights and the embargo against European industrial goods that made it difficult for Southern states to sell cotton) and retold the great stories that he said made up our society and culture. "You need to learn history so that you can learn how to avoid the mistakes people have made in the past," he said. He spent the hours when he wasn't writing or working on the boat preparing history lessons and reading the textbooks that came with our programs. He underlined the passages that he wanted us to remember and thought of ways to make the material interesting.

Now, with the new program from BYU, I was officially my own teacher. The independence was refreshing. I listened to music while I focused on the less-demanding subjects like literature and English, and learned how to get the more difficult subjects over with first thing in the morning so that I had more time to do the things I enjoyed.

Will wrote me a letter a few weeks after Labor Day, saying that he had gotten back together with his "old girlfriend," who had helped him through a difficult time when his grandmother died. It seemed like an oddly mature thing for a thirteen-year-old to say. I wrote him back telling him that I was sorry to hear about his grandmother, and that we were getting ready to leave Virginia and head south. I secretly wondered what Trey had told him about me. Maybe he'd told Will that a year ago I'd been nicknamed Thunder Thighs.

I told myself that Will and I would never have been able to date each other anyway, since he lived miles away on a farm. He would need the company of local girls who listened to country music and could do things with him like go to the State Fair and kiss on the school bus. Long-distance relationships would surely be a part of my life, but to someone who didn't live on a boat this was a hard concept to grasp. Will was everything that was normal to me and everything that I was sure I was destined not to have—the school dances, the movie dates, the making out in a parked car out on a dirt road where nobody could find you. I grieved through the fall and told myself there would be lots of boat boys in George Town that year.

The Dream

Fort Lauderdale, Florida • Spring 1994

Age 14

The winter flew by with the usual patterns—we spent a couple months in the Pipe Creek area, and a couple months in George Town. Will continued to write me letters, mainly between break-ups with his hometown girlfriends, and I wrote him back as a friend, because I'd found an audience in him that loved to hear about my life and the things we did that, to me, seemed mundane because we did them all the time. But he was fascinated by the fact that we speared all of our fresh fish and received our mail by boat. Michelle and I were inseparable that winter. We talked about the George Town boys in the V-berth of *Chez Nous*, Carolyn laying in her bed and hiding beneath her comforter, pretending not to listen but hearing every word we said. Michelle dated a boy who was four years older than her, and we tried to keep it a secret from her dad. Her dad would never have approved of him, both because of his age and because he wasn't a Jehovah's Witness, a religion that Gary had adopted as part of his marriage to Michelle's stepmother.

Coming back to Fort Lauderdale in 1994 was like coming back almost every year. *Chez Nous* rolled across the Gulf Stream on a near-perfect day, I spent most of it on the bow looking into the deep blue water and trying to come up with words other than blue to describe it. When I tired of writing, I tuned into my small FM radio to see if I could pick up the stations out of Miami. I learned that Kurt Cobain had just shot himself, and when I had tried to reach my friends in George Town over the long-range SSB radio to tell them, Dad grabbed the microphone out of my hands. "This is an emergency radio," he said. "Someone might think that somebody important died." I didn't bother trying to explain that Cobain was important. I kept quiet and watched the ocean.

We caught a dolphin-fish on the fishing line Mom had trailed out behind the boat, and it slapped its green and yellow tail against the deck and speckled everyone with metallic smelling blood before Mom poured rum down its gills and it went quiet. I cleaned it. I was pretty good with a fillet knife at fourteen. I'd spent a lot of time watching my dad and other men clean fish, and I was starting to read Hemingway, so fish blood seemed natural.

89

Fort Lauderdale looked like a massive freighter on the horizon, loaded with cargo, then it turned into a spiky forest of skyscrapers as we got closer. This didn't seem like a bad thing to me then. It meant cheap payphones, ice cream, FM radio stations, *YM* and *Seventeen Magazines*, the Galleria Shopping Mall on Sunrise Blvd., Borders and Barnes & Noble, clean laundry, Miami Subs, and wacky evening news stories on Channel 7. South Florida was a different kind of homecoming than arriving in the Bahamas or the Chesapeake, but it felt just as good.

I was starting to attach myself to South Florida in a way I didn't understand: the same way I'll never understand home, or know where it is. But the dark underbelly of it drew me in: the freak show at the local grocery store, the secretive hookers on U.S. 1, the murders in the mystery novels I read by John D. MacDonald. The novels featured a guy who lived on a houseboat at Bahia Mar marina and who got caught up in all these great adventures that involved boozing, sleeping with various women, and solving mysteries. But he lived on a boat. In Fort Lauderdale. So he must have been a good guy.

We docked at the city docks at Las Olas, two blocks west of the beach, and checked in with customs and rented a car. Dad and I ran out to Publix, where we bought Haagen Daz ice cream for dessert that night and fresh bagels and smoked salmon for breakfast the next day. We went to the Miami Subs on 17th Street and ordered onion rings and Italian subs. The dolphin we'd caught earlier would have to go in the freezer. We'd been eating fresh fish and beans and rice for six months, and getting back to the States called for a junk food celebration.

Mom was out on deck when we got home, hosing the salt and fish blood off the cabin windows. The sun sank down into the Everglades, leaving a trail of orange across the Intracoastal Waterway, and the Las Olas Bridge let off five short horn blasts to indicate that the 7:30 opening was over. South Florida was hot even at sunset, from the sticky asphalt and concrete and glass reflections off the condos.

"Melanie," Mom said as soon as Dad and I stepped onto *Chez Nous*. "You need to call Michelle."

"Why?"

"The people on that boat just came here from Indiantown." She pointed over to a thirty-six foot trawler, a boat I recognized from the Bahamas even though I didn't know the people. Indiantown was the small town in central Florida where Michelle's dad had bought property and set up a car lot, and where Michelle now lived during the summers. It was right on the Okeechobee Waterway, and the Indiantown marina was well-known for being one of the cheapest marinas and boatyards in Florida.

Mom coiled the hose on the dock. "They said Michelle's boat caught fire."

"Very bad?" I set the grocery bags aboard *Chez Nous*, and held onto the teak railing, feeling like I suddenly knew why South Florida was so unnaturally hot.

"The whole family had to move off, I think," Mom said.

I had to call Indiantown Marina and leave a message, since the phone line on *Summer Wind* was dead. I left the number for our slip in Fort Lauderdale, since we had temporarily set up a phone line at the marina. I didn't hear back from Michelle for a couple of days. When I did, she said, "Terry thinks it was my fault." Michelle had been babysitting the kids while Gary and Terry were at the car lot, and something had shorted out in the engine room. She smelled fire and got the kids off the boat before running back in to grab the fire extinguisher and start flipping off circuit breakers.

Fiberglass has to reach extreme temperatures before it burns, but when it does it goes fast and it smells almost like human hair or fingernails burning. Michelle grabbed a few things off the boat—photos and letters—and stood on the dock with the kids, keeping them as far away as she could, until the fire trucks showed up. The marina owner cut *Summer Wind* loose from the docks, so it wouldn't catch any of the other boats on fire, and Michelle said she tried to jump back aboard to see what else she could save, but they wouldn't let her.

"You've never smelled anything like it, Melanie," she said. "And it still smells. They put the fire out and the boat's still in one piece, but that smell is never going to go away."

I was seeing it all, playing it out for her in my mind while she told me about it. I saw flames licking through the portholes and reaching up around the mast. *Summer Wind* was a Morgan Out Island 41, one of the toughest fiberglass boats ever built, and I couldn't imagine it burning that easily.

"Did you lose much of your stuff?" I asked.

"No. Terry did, though. You know how their cabin is right by the engine room."

"Is she pissed?"

"She's always pissed."

"What are you all going to do?"

"My dad has a trailer sitting in the car lot. We're going to bring it down to the marina and live in it while they get their house built," she said.

"They're building a house?"

"Yeah. I'm not moving in though. I'm going to stay on *Summer Wind* and get her back into shape."

That was how Michelle moved onto *Summer Wind*, completely on her own, at fourteen. Her dad and Terry and the kids were moving ashore, and she couldn't do it. She said the boat was like a person, that she felt like it needed her, especially after the fire.

She drove out to the coast with her dad a few days later, for the Dania Marine Flea Market. Gary hauled all of the things they didn't need from the boat to Dania and set up a booth, and he and Michelle sat in it for three days trying to sell old outboard motors, Michelle's sailing dinghy, her windsurfer, old sails and anything else from the boat that hadn't been too badly damaged in the fire.

My dad and I met up with them on the first day of the flea market. We drove down U.S. 1 past the Fort Lauderdale airport, into the seedier and more comforting parts of South Florida, past the Dania Jai Ali, where the flea market was set up in the huge parking lot, with aisles and aisles of broken down boat stuff. We found Michelle and Gary sitting on their gray inflatable Zodiac dink, planted solid on the asphalt. Neither of them looked like they wanted to be there.

Michelle and I ran into each other's arms, squealing, and Gary hoisted himself off the dink, a button popping off his shirt, which hung mostly open around his belly. Sweat dripped off the corners of his moustache. "Don't know what to think about all this, Tom," he said, slapping my dad on the shoulder.

Dad jumped a little, then relaxed, but I could see the vein pumping in his neck and I secretly hoped Gary had managed to smudge a little bit of outboard motor oil on his slick Polo shirt so he'd fit in with the Flea market crowd a bit better. Dad always wore Polo shirts that had the *Cruising World Magazine* logo stitched on, partly to let people know he was a writer and to remind them that whatever they did or said could possibly end up in a magazine article and partly to promote the magazine.

"Must be a sad time," Dad said. He scanned all the junk set up in Gary's booth. Michelle's windsurfer was propped up against the U-Haul trailer, and the Janet Jackson lyrics Michelle and I had painted across the board looked sloppy and crooked.

"Yeah, well, you know how it is," Gary said. He yawned and put his hand on Michelle's shoulder. "Gotta move on. The wife doesn't want anything to do with the boat anymore. Guess the fire was some kind of sign, not that I believe in signs, but everything happens for a reason, ya know?" His Michigan accent kicked in.

"You guys are building a house?" Dad was shifting from one foot to the other, and looking over Gary's shoulder the whole time. He was supposed to be meeting his buddy from the Marine Industries Association.

"Yeah. Opening a car lot. The plan is to sell a few El Caminos to the Guatemalans," Gary said. "Nobody else will finance them out there, ya know?" Indiantown was smack in the middle of orange country.

"Oh. Hey, I'm sorry Gary, I've gotta talk to someone," Dad said. He waved to a man in an equally snazzy Polo shirt. "Gary, this is Hank," he said.

They all shook hands, Hank spelled out his Marine Industries Association credentials, and Gary just said, "Nice to meetcha, Hank. Boy, that's a good handshake. Your arm must get tired." Hank opened his mouth then closed it, at a loss for words.

Michelle and I had been sitting on the dink. "Oh God," she said. "My dad is embarrassing your dad's friends. Hey, let's walk around a little bit and let them bond."

"Sure." I was eager to get away. We stepped out of the shade and into the glorious April heat wave to explore the other booths. We saw a few people we knew from George Town, sailboaters carrying huge canvas bags, people with dark tans and home-styled hair cuts, cut-off jeans and faded T-shirts that smelled like old sunscreen and pot smoke. I filled my lungs and my soul with it. Young kids that might have belonged to the other boaters or to the flea market gypsies ran around, hiding behind engine blocks and stands that sold cheap tie-dye shirts.

Michelle stopped in front of a bulletin board that had local ads for boats and marine services tacked up, overlapping each other in a sloppy mess. "Look at that," she said. "A Morgan 41, and they want $120,000 for it. Ha! Someone could get a good deal on *Summer Wind* now if my dad decides to sell her."

"You really think he's gonna sell her?"

"Why else would we be here getting rid of all our stuff?" She looked around like she was trying to find a place to sit, but settled for leaning up against the bulletin board. "I love that boat," she said. "Maybe not as much as I loved *Indian Summer*, but a lot. You know what I mean. It's like it's human or something."

And I did know what she meant, because I'd always felt the same way about *Chez Nous*, even though I never talked about it. Sometimes I thought I shared a soul with the boat, because *Chez Nous* and I were born and built on the same year. "You'll be able to fix her," I said.

A tear came out from under Michelle's sunglasses, but she pushed it away with the back of her hand and smiled. "Yeah. But you know how I feel, right? I don't think anybody else does. Except my dad. You know, I wish it was still just him and me on *Indian Summer*. Before Terry and the kids and everything." She turned back to the board and ran her finger over the ad for the Morgan 41. "Wait a second," she said, and I could hear her breath catching in the back of her throat.

I looked at the board. Her finger had fallen on another ad, one for a smaller sailboat. It was an O'day 30, 1978, almost identical to *Indian Summer*. The ad said: "Atomic 4 gas engine, good condition, new sails, shoal draft…$7,900." It was a nice, practical boat, but right below it was an ad for a Tartan 27, smaller, with cleaner lines, almost the same price. I think it hit both of us then—one of those earth-shattering moments that feels kind of like a déjà vu. Our similarities and our differences were summed up in those two boats—Michelle's choice more practical, mine based on the Tartan's pretty lines. But the dream was the same.

"Let's buy a boat together," Michelle said.

"Now?"

"No, silly. When we're 17 or 18. We'll save up for a few years, then we'll live on it and sail around, go different places and work."

It made perfect sense at the time. I wanted to yell and scream and tell Michelle how much I loved her.

BOOK 2

My Tribe

At Work

Newport, Rhode Island • Summer 1995

Age 15

The summer of 1995, we sailed up the coast to Newport, Rhode Island, so Dad could go to work in the *Cruising World Magazine* office. He had just started writing a monthly column for them, his Chesapeake Bay cruising guide had just come out, and International Marine (McGraw Hill) was about to publish his second book, *All in the Same Boat*, which was about how other families could do what we were doing.

We picked up a mooring off of Jamestown, on the southern side of Narragansett Bay, and three days after we arrived Dad invited the entire staff of *Cruising World* out to the boat for a cocktail party. That's how I met Tim.

Tim said he'd been to George Town when he was a teenager. He was twenty-eight and one of *Cruising World's* editors. He spoke French and German, and had a master's degree in journalism. He and Carolyn and I sat on the boom, straddling it and holding the lazy jacks (a rope system that helped to catch the mainsail when it was dropped) for balance. When he laughed, the mast shook. I felt drawn to him the way I have to only a few people in my life—that feeling that tells me that this is someone with whom I will share a great deal. That feeling has never been wrong.

Jamestown was cold at night, even though it was July and the days were perfect. Fog rolled in from Block Island Sound and covered Narragansett Bay, and I had woken up early that morning to hear the sound of foghorns tumbling through the forward hatch of *Chez Nous* like ghosts. When I had gotten out of bed and gone out on deck, the fog was so thick I couldn't see the end of our mooring line. It simply disappeared into a cloud.

I shivered and watched Tim, who was playing my sister's guitar. "I want to know how you felt about growing up aboard," I said. "I mean, how do you feel about it now that it's over and you're living ashore?"

What I really wanted to ask was something I couldn't comprehend, not to mention express. Did he feel like he had a home or was he rootless, the way I felt sometimes?

97

"I wanted to keep doing it," he said. "I didn't want to go to college or move ashore."

"Then why did you?" I watched the lights of a commercial fishing boat flash over Tim's shoulder, as it came into the dock behind us.

"I don't know. Circumstances. I changed. That happens, you know." Tim handed the guitar down to Carolyn, who had jumped from the boom and was watching all the people on our boat like she was waiting for them to leave us alone.

"I don't know if I'll change," I said. "I mean, sometimes I think I can't change." I wasn't sure whether what I was saying made any sense, but Tim seemed to understand. "I want to keep living on a boat. Actually, my best friend and I have a plan," I said.

"What is it?" His already-large and brilliant eyes widened and he looked straight into me.

I told him about Michelle, and about how we were saving our money to buy a boat as soon as we turned eighteen. How we would split the costs down the middle, and live aboard and cruise to the Bahamas, and keep going south until we found a place where we could work for a few years. We were already thinking about what kind of boat to get—maybe a Bayfield or a Seafarer. Something in the $10,000 range, under 30 feet long. Michelle and I wrote long letters to each other, reminding each other that we couldn't spend our lives waiting to do this. We had to do it now, while we were young and had the energy and desire.

"I don't want to wait until I'm thirty or something like that," I said.

"I'm almost thirty," Tim said.

"Well, do you wish you'd done things differently?" I watched him scan the foggy harbor, his eyes settling on one boat and then the next. The boats were just black silhouettes against the New England night—sloops and yawls, slender lines and feminine hulls.

"Sometimes, yeah," he said. "I was actually going to do the same thing with my best friend when we were about nineteen. The thing is, I don't even know what happened. We were looking at boats and we were convinced we were going to do it, and then we just stopped looking."

"Just like that? You stopped?"

"Well, it wasn't just like that," he said. "But it wasn't conscious either. I started crewing on a schooner down in Annapolis, and he went in a different direction. Life happens, and you don't really know how things are going to work out. I got married, then divorced. Now I'm here, editing *Cruising World* and reading about people like you who are actually out there seeing the world by boat. And all I want to do is go sailing."

"What about your friend?" I said. "Did he just give up on it?"

"He runs a boatyard up in Biddeford, Maine. I don't think either of us ever really gave up on it. Things just happened differently. We still look at boats and talk and dream."

Tim didn't seem to have any more of an explanation for why his life had gone differently than what he had planned, and I wondered how a dream as strong as the one Michelle and I had could just fade. "I don't think that's going to happen with Michelle and me," I said. "We want it too bad."

"I hope you get your boat," Tim said. "And don't wait until you're my age."

I had just met him, but I believed in him more than I'd ever believed in anybody else. He understood me. He'd grown up the same way, rootless, homeschooled, sailing with his parents from place to place without ever staying put long enough to call one place home. Now he was here, working for one of the biggest boating magazines in the world, but his job at *Cruising World* seemed dreary to me.

Later that summer, when I started going into the office with Dad and doing random jobs so I could earn a little bit of extra money, I realized just how dreary it really was. Tim sat in a cubicle. So did my dad. The people who worked for the magazine gathered around the water cooler and gossiped, drank too much coffee and ate microwaved lunches. I organized the books in their library, which was really just a dusty bookshelf between the design and layout offices and the editorial offices. I stuffed envelopes and correlated copies. I stared out the window at the grassy yard that sloped down into a foggy pond. I lived for the moments I could spend with Tim, sitting in the lunchroom and talking about boats. I composed poetry as I stared out the office windows and wrote it down later, curled up with a composition book in the V-berth of *Chez Nous*.

Every week or so, Michelle and I talked on the phone. I would call her from one of the payphones in downtown Newport, and talk to her while I watched the tourists line up outside of the fudge shops and lobster restaurants. "I put another hundred dollars in the bank today," I'd say. I had a bank account in Lancaster, Virginia, which was technically our home town. All of our mail came to a post office box there, and it was where my parents' property was.

"That's getting closer to our boat," Michelle would say, and I felt like my heart was about to jump out of my chest.

Tim started coming out to the boat for dinner every week, and he and Carolyn played the guitar. He taught her new chords and brought new music with him every time he came. One song was by Dar Williams. It was called "The Ocean," and every time I listened to it I thought about the boat that Michelle and I would get in a few years. *Chez Nous* glowed inside with Tim's music and the kerosene trawler lamp that Mom kept lit over the salon table. The nights were warm and comfortable and Tim became like a member of our family.

We left Newport as soon as it turned cold. I started the school year the day we left, hauling my books up to the forward cabin and spreading them across my knees. BYU's curriculum allowed me to take college-level creative writing and literature classes as substitution for the required high school ones, and I buried my nose in a poetry anthology as *Chez Nous* pounded through the waves.

The Boat Show

Annapolis, Maryland • Fall 1995

Age 16

We made Annapolis by October, and moored off the Naval Academy with dozens of other cruising boats, all on their way south. Dinghies crisscrossed the mouth of Spa Creek as the town and harbor filled up with brand new boats, fresh from the factory, for the Annapolis Sailboat Show.

Carolyn and I stood in the *Cruising World* booth, helping to sign people up for yearly subscriptions and signing copies of our dad's book while he rushed around meeting people and giving seminars in the big Marriott conference room. His seminars were packed, and people flocked to the booth after each one, asking Carolyn and me whether we liked being home schooled, and whether we were ever afraid of storms. They brought their kids to talk to us, hoping we'd tell them how great it was to live on a boat. Most of the kids were reluctant.

The booth faced a dock lined with shiny new sailboats, and I watched the people climb on and off, stars in their eyes. There weren't many boats in the show that appealed to me. Most of them were too new and flashy. In the booth next door, a thin boy who looked a little older than me hoisted and dropped a small sail over and over again. The display was for a sail flaking system made of small lines that were threaded through the sail at various points and helped to guide it into place when dropped. The zip of the sail rising and the whoosh of it dropping, zip, whoosh, zip, whoosh, was like the frantic heartbeat of the Annapolis Boat Show.

"Why is that guy looking at you?" Carolyn jutted her elbow towards the sail. "Doesn't he know that staring is rude?"

"Guess not," I said. I could feel his eyes burning into the back of my neck as we turned around to talk to another dreamy-eyed future cruising family. Two girls, both a couple years younger than Carolyn and me, slunk behind their parents, one clutching a walkman and the other holding an ice cream cone.

"Can you two tell them that we're not going to get hit by any big storms?" the dad said. "They're afraid to go out on the boat with me because they think we're going to sink."

"I saw on the Discovery Channel how typhoons can come up out of nowhere," the girl with the ice cream said.

"Well, there are storms out there," I said, watching the mother's face turn dark. "But you just have to pay attention to the weather and make sure you're in a safe place when they hit." The mother looked a little more relaxed.

"But your family has never been caught in anything bad," the dad said.

"Once the boat actually got picked up by a waterspout." Carolyn, who had been quiet up to this point, waved her arms as she spoke. "We were anchored in the marsh in Georgia," she said, "and it formed right on top of us. Mom looked up and there it was. So we all put on our life jackets and stayed in the main cabin until it was over. The boat lifted a couple feet out of the water. You could feel it thud back down."

The girl with the ice cream looked like she was going to cry, and the mother's face darkened again. In the booth next to us, the sail went up and down.

"It was scary," I said, "but no scarier than walking around in a shopping mall." Something had clicked inside of me. These people had a story that they wanted to hear, and selling it wasn't hard. You just had to anticipate their objections and overcome them, or anticipate a problem and offer a solution.

"How's that?" The dad held onto the ice cream girl's hand.

"Well, in a mall you never know whether you're going to get ripped off or kidnapped or murdered," I said. "The ocean is a lot nicer than lots of people." I realized that I sounded like my dad when I said this, but brushed the thought aside.

The mother didn't look any more relaxed, but she made a good effort at smiling. "What about school? The girls are afraid they'll miss their friends too much if we move onto a boat," she said.

"They probably will, but just make sure you take them to a place like George Town where there are lots of other kids on boats," I said. Carolyn nodded.

They bought a copy of *All in the Same Boat*, thanked us for signing it, and rushed off to catch our dad's next seminar at the Marriott. "He's still looking," Carolyn said, glaring over at the sail. Zip, whoosh, zip, whoosh.

"He'll get tired of it after awhile." I said. Another family came to talk to us, kids in tow, asking the same questions about storms and school and other kids. Just like the kids before, these stood back and let their parents do all the talking.

"Excuse me." A guy's voice broke the momentary silence between families. I turned around to find the thin boy from the sail flaking company standing just outside the *Cruising World* booth's blue carpeting. "I'm Ben," he said, reaching out his hand. "I just wanted to come over and meet you."

"It's about time," Carolyn said. "You've been staring at us all day."

"Hey, it's not like I have the most exciting job in the show," he said. "You guys are famous. You get to talk to people all day. All I do is raise and drop that damn sail."

He was eighteen and he was from Connecticut. He worked on the company's design team, creating CAD drawings of boom-vang preventers and sail flaking systems. And he lived on a boat. A Soverel 28. His own.

Ben came to visit me in Virginia a few weeks later, driving his truck through the night and arriving at Narrows Marina along with a cold front. We were ready to head south, and the cold air that pushed its way across the Chesapeake was another reminder that the Bahamas were a little over a month away. Ben stayed in a room at the marina's dilapidated motel that looked like a giant chicken coop. He stayed for two nights, during which I didn't venture near his room. I wasn't afraid of him. I was afraid of what my dad would say.

He gave me an antique compass and a piece of his boat—a round cut-out that he'd removed while installing a new depth sounder. We sat on the dock overlooking the channel between Gwynn's island and the mainland and examined the layers of fiberglass. Geese flew over us and a gunshot went off somewhere in the woods across the channel—deer season had opened a few days before.

"What do you think—is the hull thick enough?" Ben held the fiberglass cutout up to the afternoon sun.

"For what?" I asked. "I mean, are you planning on sailing her around the world or just around Long Island Sound?"

"I dunno. I'd like to have something a little bigger for going around the world. But maybe I'll bring her down to Florida. That's what I want to do. Would you help me make the trip?"

"I don't know. It would be nice."

"You should," he said, throwing his arm around my shoulders and leaning over to kiss me. "We would both be so happy."

Kissing him was different from kissing Rod or the other two boys I'd kissed: Will and a crazy British boy I'd met in George Town. Ben was older, and I could feel how much he needed me. Something moved in the pit of my stomach, and for a brief moment I considered sneaking into his hotel room to see what sex was all about. But I didn't. I wasn't ready yet.

It seemed so easy at that point: to just leave my parents' boat and move in with this boy I barely knew. Guilt was the only thing that kept me from doing it.

Ten years later, Ben emailed me right before his wedding and told me that he'd named his boat's autopilot after me. Twenty-five and sitting in my first big-girl office at my first job with health insurance, I'd pondered this for a few minutes before emailing him back. I was flattered, I told him, wondering how it was possible for me to make such an impression on someone who I'd barely known.

Melanie Neale

Not My Type

East Coast and Bahamas • Winter to Summer 1996

Age 16

The winter of 1996 was a series of cold fronts that came through fast, stirring the Bahama Banks into waves that made it uncomfortable to get off the boat. Michelle wasn't in George Town that winter, and I spent most of my time working on school, and writing poetry and bad short stories. In my stories, someone always died in a boating accident.

I did my schoolwork up in the forward cabin, where I could focus on it without listening to Carolyn's lessons or Dad cussing in the engine room. Now that it was sixteen years old, the big Perkins was a constant headache for him. I had started doing most of the basic maintenance on it: changing the oil with a cranky drill pump, draping my body over the heated block to unscrew the filter. The engine made sense to me. Everything was interconnected and ordered. To my Dad, a sixteen-year-old engine must have made more sense than a sixteen-year-old girl.

Right before Christmas, I had finished a correspondence class on rebuilding gas engines. We had been docked at the Las Olas City Marina in Fort Lauderdale, with the stern facing out to the Intracoastal Waterway. Dad and I took apart a small Honda generator and put it back together on the stern, watching boats go by and talking about them as we worked. We got along best when we were putting our minds together on something mechanical. I loved riding around Fort Lauderdale with him in the rental car, going to machine shops on State Road 84. We could find everything we needed for the boat, engine and generator behind Lester's Diner on 84. The grease-covered men in the shops always gave me funny looks until they realized I was there with my dad and then they smiled and wanted to know how they could help us. By then I was long past puberty. With my dad's crazy hair and both of us in grungy clothes and grease stains, we must have looked like a kidnapper and his teenage victim. In the machine shops and marine supply stores, I was comfortable being looked at as one of the boys. Part of it was a feminist streak and the other part of it was the ultimate in anti-feminism: a deeply rooted need in me to be accepted by my dad and by other men. If I could do the same things as them, I would be accepted into their world.

In George Town I didn't have anything to work on other than school. I wrote long letters to Michelle about our boat. We wanted to call her *Mother Ocean*, after a Jimmy Buffett song. We were narrowing the search down to what we thought we might be able to afford, maybe a Catalina 27 or an Ericson 27. Maybe a Bayfield, if we could find one that was cheap enough. Ben wrote me a letter every day, so when we got our packages of forwarded mail there were always about thirty letters from him. Some were short, and sometimes he put a week's worth of letters into one envelope, but he managed to write every day. I wrote him back once or twice a month.

Rod was there, but he and his girlfriend, who was twelve, spent all their time together and didn't socialize with the other boat kids. They disappeared to the ocean-side beach for hours, leaving everyone to guess what they were doing. People talked but as far as I knew nobody referred to her as a slut. Rod was fifteen, and the difference in age that, back on land, would have put him in high school and her still in junior high, meant very little out here. Maybe the "slut" tag would have been more appropriate in a place where social structures were more defined. She was cute and dramatic and complimented Rod's alpha-male persona perfectly. The other kids that year were scattered into cliques that were almost like the cliques you would find in a normal high school. I was starting to understand why Dad hated George Town.

Carolyn found her own group of fourteen-year-olds, and they had sleepovers and beach days and gossiped on the VHF. She had two friends named Tara. They were both blonds—one pale and wispy and the other freckled and animated. Both Taras came over for lunch one day. They piled into the main salon with Carolyn, who seemed to balance them out perfectly—she was mellower than the hyper one, and more hyper than the mellow one. Carolyn had recently had her braces removed (she only wore them for six months, because the dentist wouldn't be able to adjust them while we were traveling) and her hair was cut in a sharp bob. It was the first year that she didn't look like a kid. She held court over the Taras, who studied her every move and tried to emulate her even though neither of them were aware of it. To them, Carolyn was the real thing—someone who was completely attuned to life as a boat kid. They were still trying to adjust, both being first-year cruisers.

I sat at the chart table to eat pizza left over from the night before. The Taras and Carolyn were eating grilled cheese sandwiches. We had made the pizza from scratch, and I was trying to be healthy by making mine without cheese—a pile of vegetables on whole wheat crust. I figured that cheese-less pizza was better than starving myself or binging and throwing up. Occasionally, I still did this, but I fought the urge most of the time.

The freckled Tara stood over my plate and stared at it. "Why are you eating pizza without cheese?" She raised one eyebrow at me and wiped her hands on her jean shorts.

"Because I like it," I said.

"Oh. Hmm. Are you a vegetarian?" The freckled Tara wasn't going to go away.

"Sometimes," I said.

"My parents used to be, when we lived in California. But now that we're on the boat they eat pretty much everything," she said. "Hey, how old are you?"

"Sixteen."

"Cool. You should meet my brother. He's seventeen. He refuses to come to the beach, though. Maybe you could talk him into it."

"What does he do?"

"He spends all his time sailing in his dinghy."

"Sounds like a better way to spend your time than going to the beach," I said.

When the Taras left, the freckled one said, "I'm going to know you from now on as the one-who-eats-pizza-with-no-cheese."

I thought she was a strange girl.

Carolyn went over to the freckled Tara's boat for lunch the next day. When she came back, her cheeks were flushed and she bounced down the companionway stairs. "We listened to Jimmy Buffett and her mom made cheeseburgers and we swung from the halyards into the water," she said. "They have a great boat. Melanie, you would like it. It feels homey," she said.

"What kind is it?"

"I dunno. Something Taiwanese. A Spindrift 43, maybe? Oh, and Tara's brother is really cool. His name is Cole. He wants to get his own boat as soon as he can. He really loves sailing." Carolyn pushed past me into the forward cabin. I stood in the galley with Mom. We had been talking about school before Carolyn came home, discussing whether or not I should apply to any colleges. To Mom, applying was the only option. I wasn't so sure.

"That's weird," I said. "How come I haven't met him?" The circle of cruising kids in George Town was usually too small for anybody to go unnoticed, but it looked like Cole had done exactly that.

"I've seen him," Mom said. "And he's not your type, which is probably why you haven't met him."

"I'm not looking for a boyfriend, Mom. Come on," I said.

"Well, I'm just saying that I don't think he's your type," Mom said.

"What's my type?"

"Oh, I don't know. Someone who's going to go to college and become a doctor or a lawyer," she said.

"But not this guy?"

"I just don't think he is as ambitious as you are. That's all." Mom wiped her hands on a dish towel and tabled the subject. She turned away to pull a loaf of bread out of the oven.

I wondered if she was serious. I didn't think I was going to meet any future doctors or lawyers in the Bahamian Out Islands. But one thing was certain: I had to meet Cole.

Cole's family lived aboard a Taiwanese-built ketch named after a line from a Jimmy Buffett song. They had left California and bought the boat on the East Coast, and now they were cruising indefinitely. Cole and Tara did their schoolwork through an informal program that their mom had set up. "All that means is that their parents are too lazy to give them any kind of formal education," Dad said as we sat around the dinner table that night eating black beans and rice.

"They're smart though," Carolyn said between mouthfuls of rice. The kerosene lamp swung in small circles over the salon table as *Chez Nous* rolled through another cold front. Carolyn, like me, was beginning to figure out that not all of Dad's preconceived ideas matched her own.

"I'm sure they are, but if they don't get some kind of formal schooling they're not going to be smart for long," Dad said. "Your mind turns to mush if you don't use it."

"You know, people might say the same thing about us," I said. "I mean, we're not really getting formal schooling either."

"It's different. You're going to get your diplomas, they're not. And no college is going to take them without a diploma," Dad said. "Why are we even talking about it? You know better than that."

And we did, or at least we knew what Dad would say, but it was fun to challenge him. BYU would give us each a real high school diploma from Mountain View High School in Orem, Utah. I had never been to Orem and I had no desire to go. It seemed weird that a piece of paper mailed out from a place we'd never see was that important.

"Tara is a pretty good writer," Carolyn said.

"Oh great, just what the world needs. Another writer." Dad clanked his fork against his plate as he emptied the pan of beans. "People don't know how hard it is to break into writing. They think that you just have to write something and it's automatically going to get published."

"What does she write?" I asked, thinking that maybe she could show it to me and we could critique each other's poems. I didn't have any friends who were interested in writing.

"Poetry, mostly," Carolyn said. "Hey, they want to have a party on their boat on Saturday. You're invited. They're inviting all the kids in George Town."

I wasn't sure about going to a party on Tara's boat. After all, she was Carolyn's friend. But it would give me a chance to meet the mysterious Cole.

Their ketch floated above the dark water like a lighthouse. Even though it was March, the parents had strung Christmas lights up the mast in much the same fashion that trailer-park gypsies would decorate an old Airstream. The boat cast a multicolored trail across the water.

Cole helped us aboard, taking Carolyn's hand and then mine and hauling us out of the dinghy in one pull, his feet braced against the teak rail. The first thing I noticed about him was that he took up a lot of space. It wasn't that he was overweight—he wasn't heavy enough at that point to be really considered fat. His blond hair was too long and fell around his round face in a don't-give-a-damn way. He had blue eyes and spoke with a lisp. But he had the happiest aura I had ever felt. It filled the air around him with a warmth that felt like sunlight even though it was dark and a smell that was part laundry detergent and mostly sweat and salt water. It was part of the reason why he seemed to take up so much space, and it made me immediately comfortable in his presence.

"So, the famous Neale girls are on my boat," he said. "Wow."

He didn't mean to be sarcastic, even though remarks like this usually were. They also usually came from adults—kids didn't seem to care who we were. Almost everyone who was living aboard and cruising read Dad's articles in *Cruising World*, and most sailing families had a copy of *All in the Same Boat* stowed somewhere on the bookshelf. Carolyn and I rolled our eyes in unison, which was our usual response even though we never planned it that way.

Cole laughed. "Ok, I don't want to make you uncomfortable. Come on, let me show you the boat." He motioned back toward the cockpit, and I followed. Carolyn made a beeline for the main salon, where the two Taras were giggling about something in a teen magazine.

Their parents had gone over to another boat for cocktails. They had left heaps of food on the salon table, and Carolyn and the Taras and a few other boat kids sat around eating. "There's plenty of food if you want something," Cole said.

"Um, no thanks." I'd already topped my calorie limit for the day. I chose a seat behind the wheel. I liked the old fashioned teak styling, and I ran my finger along the edge, thinking about how, if this were my boat, I would sand and varnish the wheel until it glistened.

"That's right, I hear you only eat whole wheat pizza without cheese," Cole said. I wondered what else Carolyn and Tara had told him about me.

"I make exceptions sometimes," I said. "So why don't you ever come to the beach?"

"I come to pick Tara up in the dinghy. Doesn't that count?" Cole's eyes were sparkling in the dark, either laughing at me or just laughing.

"I guess. You're not missing much. Just a bunch of kids who wish they were back in high school and a bunch of adults who want to rule the volleyball courts. Did you know that they actually imposed age limits on volleyball a few years ago, to keep the kids from playing?"

"That's harsh," Cole said. "So, you see why I don't hang out on the beach like everyone else?"

"I guess. What do you do, sail all day?"

"Pretty much. Or work on the boat. Or read. Do schoolwork. Whatever. I don't want to be around people who aren't happy to be out here," he said. "This is my dream—to just take off sailing and never have to go back, so why would I waste my time on people who don't appreciate it?"

"Makes sense," I said.

"What about you? You're not the most social person in George Town. You just eat veggie pizza all day?"

How could I explain what I did? Could I tell him that I spent too much time fantasizing about the boat that Michelle and I were going to get? The anchor lights in Elizabeth Harbor hung like low planets in the dark, and there was no way to tell whether we were looking at sky or water. George Town at night was a sea of floating lights, kerosene and 12 volt, shimmering across the water. Rather than navigating by the stars, people navigated by anchor lights: they were thick in the popular anchoring spots, sparse in the deserted areas. A portable generator hummed from another boat, the sound of it and the smell of dirty gasoline drifting across the water to us.

"Well? What do you do all day?" Cole sat back on his heels and laughed at me. "I mean, you asked me first," he said.

"I want to get a boat," I said.

"You already have one. And that's not something that you spend all day doing."

"No, when I'm old enough to move out. And I spend my time on schoolwork and letters and books."

"What, you're sick of living on your parents' boat? I mean, to most of us you've got the life. I remember reading about you guys before we moved aboard and thinking about how great it must be to never have lived ashore. *Chez Nous* is a hell of a boat, but I can see why you'd want to get your own."

We talked about boats for the rest of the night. If Cole could have his ideal boat, it would be a Bristol Channel Cutter or a Nor'Sea 27. He laughed when I said I wanted a Hinkley Bermuda 40. "It's not a very good cruising boat," he said.

"You're right. But it's gorgeous. I mean, realistically, I'd settle for a 28' Bayfield. Or anything that's old enough to have been built when the builders weren't sure how much fiberglass and resin to use. They always ended up using too much, so those old fiberglass boats are bulletproof." I told him about Michelle, about Tim, and Ben—the only other people I knew who didn't think I was crazy. We talked until it was time for the long dinghy ride home, navigating by anchor lights.

When we got back to Fort Lauderdale in May, I had a letter waiting from Cole. *I don't want to make you feel uncomfortable, but I have to tell you this, he wrote. I have never met anyone like you and it means a lot just to be your friend. If you're ever ready for more, I'll be here. Maybe we'll meet in some harbor halfway around the world, on our own boats, years from now.*

I had a dream later that night in which I woke up with my head on Cole's shoulder, and I woke up afraid that if I ever saw him again I would act on it. Michelle came out to see me in Fort Lauderdale for a couple of days, and we took the aluminum dinghy up and down the New River and all through the canals, looking at boats.

Michelle looked like the winter in Indiantown had been hard on her. She already had tiny lines on her face, around her lips and her eyes. She was working for her dad and living on *Summer Wind*. Michelle detailed the cars that came into her dad's lot, to help him out, and detailed boats for extra cash.

"The men around the car lot are awful," she said. We were motoring along in the dinghy, going slow so we could look at the boats and talk to each other. "They grab my butt as soon as my dad's not looking. And the cars are awful too. You wouldn't believe some of the stuff I find in them. Dirty diapers. Cockroaches." The cars that Gary bought were all old—if he had something on the lot that was newer than ten years, it was a rare exception.

"You ought to tell your dad about the guys," I said.

"Why? He's got enough to deal with." Michelle trailed her finger in the dark water of the New River.

"I guess you're right. And he might overreact."

"And Terry would just say it's my fault."

"For what?"

"I dunno. Just for being there. Thank God I'm not living in that house with them." She was happy on the boat. She had her own space. "And she's getting way more into the Jehovah's Witness stuff. I go to meetings with them just to make my dad happy, but it's weird," she said.

When we reached Virginia and collected a month's worth of mail, I had thirty letters from Ben, a few from Will, and a handful of religious pamphlets from Michelle. They were called *Awake* and *The Watchtower*, and she didn't say anything about them in her letters; she just sent them in the same envelopes. I looked at the pictures, tried to read them, and threw them away. Her letters were all about boats—the boats she was detailing, the boats in her marina, boats she'd seen for sale.

Cole and Tara arrived at Narrows Marina in Virginia in the middle of June. They came without warning—no letters, no phone calls. They just showed up one day, docking two slips down from *Chez Nous*. Mom and Carolyn and I saw them from the bridge that connected the island to the mainland as we drove home from Gloucester, where we had just bought a Senegal parrot. The cage sat in the backseat next to me, fastened with a seat belt, and the bird hopped from one side to the other, trying to peck me through the bars. Carolyn swiveled her neck around when she saw the Taiwanese ketch. "I knew they'd be here soon," she said.

Cole and Tara were waiting for us on the deck of *Chez Nous*, our dad standing with his hands in his pockets making small talk with their parents about the weather and their trip up the Waterway.

"Oh my god," Tara said, pointing at the parrot. "He's so cool!"

"Jolly Mon is his name," Carolyn said, after we'd all hugged hello. "From the song." He was a Senegal parrot, green with a gray head and an orange band around his neck. He was supposed to be smarter than a Quaker parrot or a Sun Conure, but it wasn't evident. Once we were inside the cabin where we could take him out of the cage, Jolly Mon jumped off Carolyn's finger as fast as he could and tried to fly towards the open companionway hatch. He fell to the carpet. His wings had been freshly clipped at the pet store.

We spent the evening playing with the bird and not talking about anything important. Cole never mentioned his letter, and I never brought it up, but neither of us had forgotten about it.

Our parents ate dinner aboard the ketch, and when they came home Dad rushed to the shower, grimacing. He waited until Cole and Tara were gone to tell us why.

"Cockroaches," he said. "All over their boat. We sat down to eat and as soon we'd been sitting for a few minutes they started coming out from everywhere."

"He's exaggerating, right?" I looked at Mom.

"Actually, no. They have a cockroach problem. I hope they're planning on taking care of it." Mom stuck her finger in Jolly Mon's cage, and the parrot bit it.

"I'm sure they are," I said. "Cockroaches are kind of a fact of life."

"I know, but we've never had them that bad. And we would never let them get that bad," Dad said. "It's not that hard to clean up after yourself, is it?"

We were careful, never bringing any paper grocery bags or cardboard boxes aboard, always examining produce before buying it. We'd had the occasional rat or palmetto bug, but the only bugs we'd ever had a real problem with were boll weevils. They got into the wheat berries that Mom kept aboard for flour.

From that point on, the only thing Dad talked about when Carolyn or I mentioned Cole and Tara was the roaches.

Newport during the summer was all sailing races and tourist shops and ice cream. The anonymous feeling of melting into the crowd at Bannister's Wharf, a crowd of wealthy travelers shopping for T-shirts and overpriced sailing tours, suited me in a weird way. I liked walking around unrecognized on the weekends, going into the soap shops and the music shop on Thames Street, looking for clothes at Gap or Express. The other side of Newport quietly loomed in the background: the commercial dock where all the lobster and quahog boats unloaded. The pilings were heavy with tar and the air smelled like dead fish and marijuana. A block over it smelled like cinnamon. Something about the commercial docks stopped me whenever I walked by: a familiarity, like it was more the stuff I was made of than the tourist Newport. People who worked hard physically for a living made more sense to me than the office crowd at *Cruising World*. I worked at *Cruising World* again, writing poems during my lunch break about how much I hated working in a cubicle. I mailed each paycheck down to the bank in Virginia.

Cole and I kissed for the first time in a movie theatre in Newport. I dressed in flip flops and peasant blouses the summer I turned sixteen, and I wore bead jewelry that I made in my spare time with silver peace symbols and blue glass beads. This was my hippie phase, and rebellion against anything and everything came naturally. Cole's family didn't give a shit about propriety or college or pieces of paper from obscure high schools in Orem, Utah. They just cared about having fun and about not caring.

Cole stroked my hair in the movie theatre and I thought he was being too careful, like I was going to break if he pressed too hard. Cole and Tara and Carolyn and I were perfect together that summer—Carolyn and Tara became best friends and Cole and I entered into the romance that would define my late teenage years. Michelle knew about it before I even told her. I called her from a payphone near the dinghy dock at Bowen's Wharf in downtown Newport, and she said, "I knew from the way you talked about him that you would get together."

Tim blended back into our family, recapturing the harmony that had been established the previous summer. Tim's house in downtown Newport was haunted. When we had dinner there, he showed us a vase that kept falling to the floor for no reason, sliding to the edge of the table and then crashing in the middle of the night. When he came out to dinner, I picked him up in the dinghy next to a smaller dock where the commercial boats landed. He played the guitar and sang, and Carolyn sang with him. Tim introduced me to most of the music that would define my life—alternative folk and singer-songwriter artists whose words ran through me as Tim played their music in the low light of the kerosene glow. I was getting to know him better, and I loved the time I spent with him. I ached when I dropped him off at the wharf and the evenings were over, and wondered if my life would turn out the way his had.

It was early September, getting to be time for us to head south. After our second season in New England, we knew better than to stay too late.

The Graduate

Staniel Cay, Bahamas • Spring 1997

Age 17

There was no graduation ceremony when I finished high school. I finished my last exam from BYU and didn't tell anyone for two days. We were in the Exumas, anchored off of Big Majors Cay, between Pipe Creek and Staniel Cay. I'd grown to like the central Exumas better than George Town, because there weren't as many people and because the water was clearer.

In the years we'd been going to the Bahamas, Compass Cay had turned into a marina when Herm and Helen left for good and their caretaker took over. Dead Man's Cay became a popular diving spot for cruisers, who all anchored or docked at Compass and acted like they were the first to discover it. Talk of drug smugglers and piracy had dwindled to whispers left over from the eighties. Little Pipe Cay, where Sam and Layla had fed the fish and sat on the stern of their boat naked, was being developed into some rich man's dream. A megayacht was tied to our old spot on the face dock, and statuesque coconut palms had been planted along the beach, where fresh sand from the bottom of Pipe Creek had been piled to make the beach a little whiter and a little more post-card perfect. Sometimes I wondered what the new batch of cruisers who visited Pipe Creek now would have thought ten years before, when the murder stories were fresh.

After I graduated, I wrote hard for two days, finishing a short story about some college girls from Miami who stumbled into a drug-smuggling scheme on their Spring Break. It seemed natural to keep working on something, even if it wasn't school. Then I wrote letters to Michelle and Cole, telling them that I was through and now what? Now Michelle and I could start thinking seriously about our boat. I had almost $10,000 in the bank, from the summers working at *Cruising World* and a summer of crewing on Adirondack, a 78' schooner that sailed out of the Newport Yachting Center.

I stumbled out of the forward cabin for lunch a little after noon on the third day after graduation. "Well, I'm done," I said to Mom, who was poring over a slide display set up on the table in the main cabin. The slides were shots of Dad covered in mud from the anchor. They were bound for Newport, to accompany one of Dad's articles.

"Done? With what?" Mom looked up from her slides, pushing her glasses up on her nose. Her face gleamed with sweat—a thin healthy layer over her tanned cheeks. She still didn't have wrinkles, even though almost fifty years of sun had been harsh on her skin.

"School." I sat down on the settee so I could look at her slides.

"What? With all of it?" She sat up straight and gave me a long look, like she was wondering how I had managed to finish high school behind her back. I had been following my own lesson plan for almost four years, reading the syllabi and teacher's manuals for all of my correspondence classes, doing all the work on my own. And now I had finished early—it was the beginning of March, 1997. I was seventeen.

"Shut up," Carolyn said. She was working on pre-calculus at the chart table, a heavy book on her lap and crumpled sheets of scratch paper on the floor. I had opted out of pre-calc, filling my math requirement by taking an easy geometry class in ninth grade. I had read the diploma requirements carefully, and chosen all the easiest classes that I could take. Instead of biology, I took a college-level poetry class. I got out of some of the standard requirements simply by taking advanced classes in things I knew how to do. "You suck," Carolyn said.

"Well, congratulations," Mom said. "How do you feel?" Before I had time to think of a response, she rose out of her chair to give me an awkward hug, then stuck her head through the door to the aft cabin, where Dad was banging on his keyboard and staring into his computer screen. "Tom, Melanie just finished high school," she said. That sense of momentum, of things moving faster than I could control them, surged up in my stomach and I pictured water rushing through a narrow inlet on a full-moon high tide, just moving along because this was what it was supposed to do.

"What?" Dad knocked he keyboard aside when he jumped up. "Did you know she was close to finishing?"

"No," Mom said. "I mean, I knew she was getting there, but I thought she still had a month or so."

"Well, we have to have a celebration," Dad said. This meant diving for conch and making conch fritters and inviting whoever was in the anchorage over for dinner. We would also have to find someone who was flying back to the states and could take a batch of mail with them. The Bahamian postal system was still unreliable, and I wanted to make sure my final exams and papers reached BYU so that the teachers in Utah could get busy and give me my coveted diploma.

My parents fussed about it for the rest of the day, calling everyone they knew on the VHF radio. I busied myself by going out with Dad later that afternoon and diving for conch, feeling good just to be out in the dinghy, skimming across the flat Bahama Banks. I drove while he snorkeled from coral head to coral head, the tiller for the outboard motor vibrating against my hand. Dad and I had perfected a system in which I always followed him thirty to forty feet behind, keeping the dinghy's bow pointed in his direction so that I could speed over to him if he speared a fish or saw a shark. I never went ahead of him, because the sound of the outboard may have chased the fish away. Some of the barracudas in the Bahamas were trained to follow the sounds of an outboard motor because they knew outboards usually meant there were divers in the water and fish to be cleaned. Sharks were less of a problem because they were rare and usually alone. Barracudas schooled together and would stalk a diver just outside of her circle of vision.

I could drive the dinghy by feel, and didn't have to think about what I was doing. I knew to throw it into neutral when Dad dove, just in case he surfaced near the prop, and to avoid any sudden bursts of the throttle. Now that I was a high school graduate, I felt somehow out of place and disconnected, like I'd suddenly lost my sense of direction. I would need to find a new one as soon as I could. I'd been letting my mind wander on these diving trips for years, thinking and fantasizing about boats and boys and writing and what I would do when I grew up. Now that I was through with high school, I wasn't sure that I was ready to leave the Bahamas.

I thought about what it would be like to be seeing the Bahama Banks for the last time, watching the yellow shallows dip into aquamarine flats, then deepen into purple over beds of turtle grass and deep coral. I had a map of the Banks drawn inside of me, one that I'd been creating since I was five. I could go to college. I could move off *Chez Nous*. I could buy a boat of my own. I could do whatever I wanted. Dad raised his hand from the surface, holding a queen conch, and I eased the dinghy over to him and took the conch. When I set it in the Rubbermaid bucket we kept in the dinghy's bilge, a golden conch fish flopped out gasping. These fish spent their whole lives living inside their host's shell, and when they were shaken into the world they died quickly. I scooped the fish up and dropped it into the water, where it headed straight for the bottom to find another conch.

My parents' friends who came over that night asked me what I would be doing next. "Have you applied to any colleges?"

I had taken my SATs two summers ago, in a trailer that belonged to a high school in Williamsburg, VA, where the kids who were there all knew each other and stared at me like I didn't belong.

"Yes, but I'm not sure if I want to go."

"Yes you do," Dad said. "You might need another year on the boat to decide, but I'm sure you'll decide to go."

"Actually, I want to get my own boat," I said.

"That would be nice," the friend's wife said. "But it would be a lot of work." She had a perfect manicure and she flew back to the States every month or so for a haircut.

"I don't mind working."

"I'm sure you'll do whatever you set your mind to doing," the husband said.

When we got to Fort Lauderdale, Michelle and I wandered around the Dania Flea Market like we did every spring. We bought a *Sailboat Trader* and looked carefully at all the boats under $10,000. Michelle had started her own boat detailing business in Indiantown, and she was making decent money looking after all of the boats that were put into summer storage in the yard at Indiantown Marina. She hadn't finished high school yet, and didn't know whether she would. "I just don't have time for it," she said as we browsed through a table of used nautical books. "I'm either helping my dad at the car lot, watching the kids, or working on boats." College wasn't an option, even though Michelle was smart enough to do anything.

There was a Bayfield 29, in bristol condition, for sale in the yard at Indiantown, and Michelle called the owners to check on the price. They were asking $30,000, which we knew was well above our price range. We shifted our search to boats that had thick growths of oyster shells on their bottoms and mildew stains running down the hulls.

I got my acceptance letter from a state school in Virginia, the only college I had applied to while Michelle was visiting. I opened it, read it, and stashed it behind one of the books above the V-berth on *Chez Nous*. The letter encouraged me to apply for financial aid, and offered a list of all the scholarships and loans I might be able to get. I didn't tell Michelle about it.

I found out about a correspondence program for designing boats—the Westlawn School of Yacht Design, out of Connecticut. It would give me a technical degree, and was supposed to take two or three years to complete. I figured I could start it aboard my parents' boat and finish when Michelle and I moved onto our own.

Runaway

Annapolis, Maryland • Fall 1997

Age 18

The Westlawn program came with all kinds of drafting tools, and I felt good spreading tracing paper out across the salon table and arranging my splines and weights and drawing half-sections of yawls that all looked too much like Hinkley Bermuda 40s.

I didn't study much that summer, because I was working full time in Newport aboard the Adirondack. I made $8.00 and hour, but on a good day I'd take home $200 in tips. I learned to wear short shorts and throw my whole body into the halyards when I raised the sails, bracing against the wooden masts with my topsiders. The tourists loved it. Tim came sailing a couple of times, and came out to dinner aboard *Chez Nous* as much as he could. There were moments when I loved him, and moments when I thought he probably loved me back. But mostly there were long conversations and dinners and guitar music and sailing and an understanding that we were made of the same stuff. *Chez Nous* stayed anchored off of the Ida Lewis Yacht Club in Newport Harbor. It was a crowded anchorage that was always full of weekend boaters and kids in sailing dinghies. Carolyn got a job selling tickets for another tour boat, and started crewing after a few weeks. She and I waved at each other across Narragansett Bay in the evenings, while we ferried groups of drunk tourists past the Kennedy Estate and the Castle Hill Light House.

Cole and Tara had been in Annapolis for two years now. Their parents had decided to settle in one place and try to save a little bit of money before going cruising again, so they docked the boat at one of the liveaboard marinas and the whole family went to work. The dad and Cole worked at a sailing school in Baltimore, Tara worked at a restaurant, and the mom worked at a chandlery. Cole and Tara came up to Newport to visit us a couple of times, and we saw them when we were passing through the Chesapeake on our way north or south. Cole and I talked on payphones and wrote letters, caught up in the only kind of romance I knew how to have: an odd long-distance one whose survival relied on the wind and tide and the whims of my parents.

Right before the Annapolis Sailboat Show that fall, Cole bought an Ericson 35. It had the sleek racing lines of a boat built in the '70s. Cole's parents had owned it along with a partner in Marina Del Rey, California. I never knew what kind of price they gave him, but I'm sure it was good.

The Ericson was shipped from California on a truck. The four of us waited at Jaban's Boatyard on the morning it was supposed to arrive, shuffling our feet through paint chips and oyster shells, the smell of polyester resin crisp in the October air. We watched the road coming into the marina, Tara and Carolyn sitting bored on a picnic bench and Cole and I giddy with anticipation. It seemed larger than its 35 feet when the truck pulled in. The hull was white with a blue Ericson stripe, and the name, *Gypsy Lady*, was painted down each side in blue letters that were bigger than they should have been—an in-your-face statement speaking out against the conservative Right and, I thought, people like my dad.

Cole signed the papers on Tara's back, his hands visibly shaking, and the yard crew slid it into the water. Inside, the cabin smelled like gas from the Atomic 4 engine that sat directly in the center of the boat, under the U-shaped dinette. The mast had to be put back on, the stanchions reattached, and the boat cleaned inside and out to get rid of a country's worth of road dust. I helped Cole put the boat together, spending hours squeezed into the anchor locker or contorted under the cockpit sole, covered in caulking and epoxy.

Gypsy Lady became the party boat for the cruising kids in Annapolis. We drank wine coolers and hung beer over the side in mesh bags so it would cool in the Chesapeake Bay. Drinking was part of our everyday life. I'd started drinking in Newport, snatching beers from the cooler on Adirondack and finishing bottles of champagne after the evening sunset cruise. I rarely got drunk, but the taste seemed to compliment the life we lived—salt water and tequila, sweaty days working on the boat and cold beer, sunsets and champagne. Our parents didn't know, but I didn't think they would really mind. After all, drinking was part of our legacy. Cole and I shut ourselves in the V-berth on these nights and made out, each time more intense, our clothes pushed to the end of the berth. Our friends and our sisters pounded on the hatch overhead and yelled down to us.

I had a temporary job driving *Cruising World*'s photo boat for their Boat of the Year competition during the week after the show, ferrying my dad and the other judges back and forth to the show boats, trying to keep the big inflatable still while the photographer snapped sailing shots of brand new Hunters and Catalinas.

On my third afternoon of driving the photo boat, *Gypsy Lady* came cutting through the new Hunters and Catalinas like a warrior, her blue and white hull a little duller than those of the new fiberglass sailboats, but much sturdier and tougher. She and Cole were headed to Baltimore, where he had a liveaboard slip lined up at the sailing school where he taught. He waved at me from the helm as I pulled alongside. I was in between fares, so I had the inflatable to myself.

"I just wanted to tell you that you're welcome to come to Baltimore with me," Cole said. He leaned over and caught the bow line that I offered him. I cut the inflatable's motor and drifted with *Gypsy Lady*.

"I can't," I said. "I've got this job for the week."

"And then what? Your dad's going to find another silly reason for you to stick around and he's going to convince you that it's the right thing to do," Cole said.

"Not necessarily," I said.

"Look, your dad's a manipulative asshole," Cole said.

"He says the same thing about you."

Cole sighed and let the bow line go before either of us had a chance to say anything else. I had to go back to work, and Cole had to get into his slip before dark.

There was nobody aboard *Chez Nous* when I got home that afternoon. I left a note apologizing for bailing as the driver, took the Water Taxi ashore, and caught a cab to Baltimore. I had no idea what the address was for the marina where Cole was headed, so I asked the cab driver to take me down by the water. I was sure I could find it once I could see the water.

The cabbie and I drove around the industrial section of Baltimore, looking for an out-of-the-way marina that I'd never seen before. I didn't have a phone and Cole didn't either, so there was no way to get directions. The marina wasn't in the glitzy Inner Harbor part of Baltimore, and as we passed industrial buildings covered in graffiti I wondered if I had made a terrible mistake. If the cabbie had wanted to, he could have just run off with me and nobody would have ever known how to find me. Eventually the marina popped up like a small and unexpected blessing. I paid the cabbie and headed down the long floating dock towards *Gypsy Lady*.

The companionway hatch was open, so I climbed aboard and threw my backpack down onto the settee. Cole jumped and looked up, and for a second his face was blank as if he didn't recognize me. I wondered whether I should turn around and leave. "Oh my god," he said. "What are you doing here?" Then, "I had a feeling you would come."

"Well, do you mind?" I said.

"Um, no." He looked around the boat for a place to set my backpack. The boat was a mess. The gasoline smell from the Atomic 4 made me dizzy, and I sat down and closed my eyes, trying to figure out what I was doing here and what was next. I wasn't sure what I had planned on—I had only brought enough clothes for two days, and hadn't expected to stay any longer, but now that I was here I wondered what would happen if I just decided to stay. I could probably get a job at the sailing school, and Cole and I could live together. He sat down next to me and wrapped his arm around my shoulders. "Are you going to stay?" he said.

"I don't know."

"What did you tell your parents?"

"Just that I was going away for a few days."

"What about the boat driving job?" Cole wiped his thick glasses on his T-shirt.

"They'll find someone else. I don't really think they needed me in the first place," I said.

"Well, you're old enough to make your own decisions," he said.

"Yeah, I guess." I didn't feel like it. I was eighteen, and I was finished with high school. I'd have my captain's license in a few months. There was nothing to keep me from leaving home. Except I knew I'd miss the Bahamas and *Chez Nous*. Winter in Baltimore would be gray and cold. Staying with Cole would mean disappointing my parents. Leaving would mean disappointing Cole. This wasn't a compromise that could be easily made.

"I'm not going to stay here all winter," Cole said. "I'm going to follow my parents down the ICW in a few months. You could help me make the trip."

We walked to a Mexican restaurant for dinner, avoiding talk about anything important, and we woke up early the next morning, both still clothed. Sex was the last thing on my mind as I agonized over the decision I would have to make. We spent the morning moving and fueling the sailing school's boats. There were no classes that day, so each of the boats had to be checked over and cleaned. We worked together without talking, and somewhere near the end of the day I realized that I had never really planned on staying. My mom, frantic and broken-hearted, called Cole's parents to find out where I'd gone, and Tara left a message for Cole at the school, telling him that my family was worried. I thought that Dad was probably more concerned about the way it would look to other people for his daughter to be running off to Baltimore, chasing a guy on a sailboat, than he was about me. After all, what was there for him to be worried about? I was an adult. I wasn't in any physical danger. I had left them a note explaining that I would not be around for the next few days. Was Dad worried that I was too sensitive and impressionable to make my way in the world or to make the right decisions?

I went home two days later, on my dad's birthday, like nothing had happened. Nobody said anything, and after a few weeks, nobody seemed to remember that I'd gone away. But I remembered the decision I had made. I had officially learned how to break a heart.

Licensed and Worldly

Florida and the Bahamas • Winter 1998

Age 18

I took the exam for my captain's license in Fort Lauderdale with a bunch of bearded old men who gave me suspicious looks. While I waited for the exam to be graded, sitting in Sea School's waiting room, Phil Collins and Genesis sang music from the *Miami Vice* soundtrack. Cheesy, I thought. But appropriate. South Florida was growing on me. In our world of back-and-forth, it was a constant, and the drug-smuggling days, while long over, felt like part of my history. I waited and waited, eager to find out whether I would receive the ultimate in nautical credibility—the license that would allow me to drive boats for a living. My dad didn't have a license. I wanted to be better than him. The room was dusty and smelled like mold, and when they came out and told me I had passed I let my breath out slowly, exhaling the humidity and sinking back in my seat. Some of the gray-beards with whom I'd studied weren't so lucky. I watched them trudge out of the building, heads down, knowing that they'd have to spend a few more months learning light configurations and whistle signals.

Cole and a friend of his sailed south on *Gypsy Lady*, trailing behind Cole's parents aboard their ketch. They arrived in Fort Lauderdale right after Christmas. Cole got a mooring near the Las Olas bridge, a couple hundred yards from where *Chez Nous* was docked. Our parents gave us curfews each night we went to *Gypsy Lady*, and Carolyn and I always found them waiting up for us when we came home, sliding up to the back of *Chez Nous* in the aluminum dinghy.

For Cole's birthday in January, we crowded onto his boat with a bunch of other kids and smoked cigars and drank beer and watched the multi-million dollar yachts make their way up and down the ICW, sliding through the Las Olas bridge and showing off the helicopters parked on their decks and the sparkling evening attire of their passengers. A cold front had just passed through and we were bundled in jeans and sweatshirts. "We've got a millionaire's view for a few bucks a night," Cole said, pulling me across the cockpit and onto his lap. I felt at home on his boat, watching the rest of the world go by. The mooring field at Las Olas was close enough to the ocean so that the air smelled like

Sargasso weed and salt, and the current rushed under the boat on its way out Port Everglades, sending us sliding and swinging on the mooring line. The lights from cars crossing the bridge shone down on the decks, and they flickered across the cabin and bounced off brass and chrome inside of *Gypsy Lady*. Cole and I ended up in the V-berth, our clothes on the floor and the door to the cabin locked behind us. I'd decided a few weeks ago that I'd lose my virginity to him on his birthday.

When he climbed on top of me, I wondered if our sisters could hear us. I hoped they couldn't. He fumbled with a condom and I stayed as still as I could, holding my breath. I didn't have any illusions that losing my virginity would be an amazing, life-altering experience, and maybe by expecting the worst I somehow denied myself of any enjoyment I could have felt. The sound of cars on the Las Olas bridge drowned out Cole's heavy breathing. The feeling of tenderness that Cole always had when he touched me, the same feeling that made me think he was afraid of breaking me the first time we kissed, was completely gone now. We were partners and co-conspirators, defying convention in our act of having sex on a small sailboat surrounded by mansions and money. We were bound nowhere— not to college, and not to regular jobs. We didn't know where we'd be in a month. I didn't even know if I wanted to be with a man.

When I was sixteen, I met a suntanned blond girl who looked like a competitive swimmer, and one night she slept over on *Chez Nous*. We talked about losing our virginity and what it would be like, and how we thought that seventeen was an appropriate age for one to do so. We talked about Rod and Will and Ben and the boys in our lives, listened to music and held hands in the dark. Sometime during the conversation I felt my cheeks grow warm and her hand got heavy, and I pulled mine away wondering if I could have possibly just been attracted to a woman. I wiped my sweaty palm against my comforter and then held it to my chest and felt the rise and fall of my own breath under my small breasts. She and I had a brief but intense friendship before she escaped the boating life by hopping on a plane in Nassau and heading home to Maine. I noticed people—whether they were men or women—and I loved them and felt for them in different ways. Maybe there were different types of love…the deep and sisterly love I felt for Michelle was nothing like the crush I had on this other girl, and my unrequited love for Tim was not like my rebellious love for Cole. These were the things I thought about the first time I had sex with what, had I been a normal teenager, would have been my high school sweetheart. Around us, the salt and seaweed smell blended with the smell of the boat's gasoline engine. I would forever think of this night when I smelled the gas-drenched interior of a boat with an Atomic 4 marine inboard.

For the next week, I waited for my mom to say something. I was sure she could tell that I was different. I felt different. I must have looked different. Nobody said a word.

My parents put *Chez Nous* up for sale that winter, listing it with a broker they knew in North Carolina, and started looking for another boat. They felt that they needed a bigger boat for many reasons, not the least of which was that my Dad wanted Carolyn and me to stick around forever and wanted us to have separate cabins so we could come home after we had ventured out into the world. We looked at boats over 50 feet long, boats with three staterooms, boats that were so old that the cored decks felt like sponge under your feet.

Cole and Tara got a job crewing on a big trimaran with a devout Christian family. I never knew where the family was from—they just appeared in the Las Olas mooring field one day: two grumpy parents and four good-looking boys. They invited the other cruising kids over to their boat for movies and dinners and games, and took us wakeboarding behind their monster inflatable dinghy. When we left to head for the Bahamas, they followed a few weeks behind us, pulling into George Town and anchoring right next to us.

"It's like that Cole is following you everywhere," Dad said as Carolyn and I climbed into the dinghy. "I don't like it."

"Get used to it," I mumbled, knowing that he couldn't hear me over the outboard motor.

When we visited the family on their boat, we were instructed by the mother to cover up our bathing suits. Once I dove with Cole to replace a corroded sacrificial zinc on the propeller shaft of their boat. Under the greenish murky water in George Town's harbor, I kept an eye out for barracudas as I pulled myself down underneath the boat and felt my way across the whale-like hull to the shaft, allen wrench and zinc in-hand and Cole following behind. The T-shirt that I wore over my conservative blue one-piece bathing suit billowed out around me and got in my way as it crept up my belly and swished in the current.

On one breath, I removed the old, corroded zinc, watching pieces of it tumble down through the water towards the grassy bottom. A small barracuda darted over to see if the pieces were edible, and then disappeared back into the murk. I could hold my breath longer than Cole, but I resurfaced behind him when he had to go up for air. "I can't work with this shirt on," I said. The family stared at me, blank-faced, as I pulled the shirt over my head and draped it across the dinghy.

I dove back under, moving freely in my one-piece and feeling nothing more than my hair swirl around me. Wearing too many clothes underwater seemed not only unnatural, but an unnecessary risk—why would you inhibit your body from moving as freely as possible? Cole and I met back up at the zinc, and laughed through our face-masks at the scene that we'd left above—the mother terrified that her boys would like what they saw: the curving and graceful tanned flesh of the siren who worked diligently underwater to replace a crumbled piece of their vessel.

Another day, we picked Cole and Tara and the Bible Boys up and headed to the small beach inside the first hole (past Volleyball Beach) where we could land and walk across Stocking Island to the ocean-side beach, tearing across the water and cutting and tilting the outboard seconds before hitting the beach. The dinghy slid ashore still on a plane. We laughed as the boys grabbed at anything they could and hung on. "You'll get used to it," Cole said. "You can't trust the Neale girls to take it easy."

Carolyn and Tara and I took off all our clothes and swam on the ocean beach in George Town in front of the Bible Boys, secretly hoping it would get back to their mother. We'd stopped going naked aboard *Chez Nous* when we'd hit puberty, and swimming in the clear warm water on the ocean-side beach made me feel like a little kid.

Cole and Tara flew back to Fort Lauderdale when the Bible Boys and parents decided to continue south to the Caribbean, and we skipped Fort Lauderdale altogether on our way back north. We crossed over to Fort Pierce, where we docked at the City Marina. We were planning on staying there for a week or so and renting a car so we could drive over to St. Petersburg to look at a few boats. Now Mom and Dad were looking into trawlers.

The day we crossed, I realized my period was a week late. I stayed in the V-berth most of the day, wondering what I would do if I turned out to be pregnant. *Chez Nous* rolled underneath me as I sat in the V-berth and read the same passage in my naval architecture textbook over and over again. The shape of the hull—wide and round, made the boat prone to long and smooth rolling motions as she made her way over the waves. Head-on, she would pound terribly, but today, with the swells on the beam, she rolled and the plates in the galley cupboard rattled against each other. Maybe I would just leave for good—go join Cole on *Gypsy Lady* and have the baby. That would be a way to get started on life, wouldn't it?

"Why aren't you up in the cockpit?" My mom stood in the doorway to the forward cabin, her hands braced on each side against the rolling. Her skin was oily with sweat and sunscreen, and she still had on her oversized sunglasses. "We're going to see land any minute." Even though this wasn't exactly our first crossing back to the States, the tradition of watching for the skyscrapers looming over the beaches of South Florida and yelling "Land, ho!" was still fresh to us. Every time, the skyline looked a little bit different but the feeling of returning from the sea was the same.

"I don't really feel like going up there," I said.

"Are you feeling sick?" Worry flashed across her face.

"No." I pushed my face closer to the book.

"Then what's wrong?"

"Nothing. Really." I tried to scowl at her, but it didn't work. The lump of panic and fear in my throat pushed up until I let out a small gasp.

"Tell me what's wrong." She entered the cabin and leaned against Carolyn's bunk.

"I might be pregnant," I said. Just like that.

She stared at me, obviously not ready for the answer I had given her. "Why do you think that?"

"My period is late. It's never late." I stared at my book.

"Have you been having unprotected sex?"

"A few times." Condoms in the Bahamian Out Islands were nearly impossible to get, and buying them meant you had to go into the small grocery store where all the other cruisers that you knew shopped, ask for them behind the counter, and pay while everyone watched. It was like buying dirty magazines or rolling papers.

"With Cole?"

"Geez, Mom, who else do you think I've had sex with?"

"Well, I didn't know. How long has that been going on?"

"A few months."

"Oh." She looked only slightly relieved. "Well, it is probably a false alarm. Give it another day or so. Sometimes your period can come late if you're stressed about something or if you're not eating right. Are you stressed about anything?"

I just stared at her.

"Well, okay, I guess this is a little bit stressful. But it will probably be okay."

"Just don't say anything to Dad." I said.

"I won't." She left the forward cabin then, and made her way back to the cockpit as the boat continued to roll on the Gulf Stream swells.

The Fort Pierce City Marina was dismal. Within walking distance, the town was a jungle of economy food stores, a few antique shops, and some cowboy bars. Mullet jumped in the eddies of brown water around the floating docks, and large amberjacks whooshed into the corners to swallow them. There were a few liveaboards at the marina, but most of the boats were abandoned and slowly falling apart. The boats that nobody cared for made me sick—I couldn't imagine someone buying a boat and then not wanting it, letting mildew grow on the canvas and letting the teak fade and the varnish curl off. I called Michelle from the payphone next to the marina showers.

"I'm ready to leave Indiantown," she said. She was still living on *Summer Wind*, but her dad wanted to sell it. "I'm going to come up to Newport this summer. Do you think you can get me a job on *Adirondack*?"

"We can start looking for our boat," I said.

"I know."

I called Adirondack's owner, who said that if I recommended Michelle he would hire her. Things were falling into place—I was certain we could find a boat in Newport. There were more sailboats up there than anywhere else in the world, except maybe for Annapolis, and if we couldn't find the perfect boat in Newport we could go down to Annapolis in the fall and buy something in the Chesapeake.

That night, Dad asked me to come out onto the dock with him. There was no moon, and the lights of Fort Pierce were dim compared to the dark ICW east of us, lit only by a passing tug and barge. "I wanted you to come out here because I don't want your sister hearing this," he said.

"What?"

"Your mother tells me you've been fucking Cole," he said.

"What difference does it make to you?" I didn't know of any other way to respond—the only thing that made sense was to fight. My feet felt like they were encased in the concrete dock, and I was nauseous.

"It makes a lot of difference," he said. "And now you might be pregnant?"

I wished I hadn't told Mom, but somehow I had thought it was okay to tell your mother things like that. After all, I was eighteen and Cole and I had been together for two years. I didn't see anything wrong with us taking our relationship to the next level.

"It makes a difference because you've just gone and thrown your life away," he went on. "You're a goddamned slut and you've just ruined your life."

"You're not making any sense," I said. I wondered what it would feel like to reach out and slap him or claw him until his cheek bled. The skin around his neck was getting loose and it would be easy to grab and twist, maybe tear. Here was that violent streak again—the darkness inside me that made my desire to fight so much stronger than it should have been. I didn't want to cause physical harm to my dad, but the fire coursing through my body told me that this was the only thing to do. I stood still and pushed it back and stared at my dad.

His nostrils flared and the veins in his neck stood out. "It makes perfect sense—nobody is ever going to respect you now, or respect me or anyone else in our family," he said.

The only thing that made sense to me was to walk away, but I felt like that would be giving in somehow. I wanted to fight but I didn't know how. *Fighter Slut.* The phrase that I'd coined for myself years before, after I'd kissed Rod on the beach in George Town, came back to me. At that time, I'd wanted to fight the double standard that made women who kissed boys sluts but that championed the behavior in the same boys. Now I was an adult and my morals were more defined. They just didn't match my dad's and my dad's words didn't match what I understood of the rest of the world, which seemed, until now, to be a fairly logical place. "Go on," I said. "I don't really understand what you're getting at."

"Cole is a dog, and fucking him makes you the same thing to the rest of the world. You are better than he is. Or at least you used to be. You have options and places to go. Just look at his family—they don't care about their futures. And now you're acting just like them," he said. "If you make the decision to live like that and just do what you want to do when you want to do it then your future is shot." He went on like that for awhile, and I listened to him and waited until my feet didn't feel like they were part of the concrete dock anymore. *Fighter Slut. Fight or flight.* Flight seemed like a better option. Mom's face floated for a second in the open porthole next to us, looking out at us, but she turned away quickly when she caught my eye. I understood then that she hadn't had a choice in whether or not to tell Dad, and that the bond between a husband and wife can be stronger than the bond between a parent and child.

Years later, I would reconsider the telling of this fact, the Melanie-is-having-sex-and-might-be-pregnant news that I had shared with my mother in confidence. Perhaps the use of this fact in conversation with my father had been something in which she had no choice. Perhaps my father, in his idealism and his naivety that sometimes so grossly contradicted his life experience, believed that my sister and I would stay aboard his boat forever. Perhaps he believed that I would become a naval architect and that my courses from the Westlawn School of Yacht Design would provide me with the skills I needed to work from home and continue the lifestyle that we had lived for nearly twenty years, the four of us, on the same boat, self-sufficient and close and strong. Perhaps my mother told him: "Melanie doesn't want to design boats. She likes to draw boats and she loves their lines and thinks they are beautiful, but she doesn't have an engineer's mind. She wants to be a writer or a poet and she's not going to stay here forever."

In Fort Pierce that night, in my bed, I listened to my sister breathe. She slept only three feet away from me in the forward cabin and her breathing bored through my head and distracted me so much that I couldn't even think about sleep. My gut hurt and I couldn't cry. All I felt was a hollow place in my chest and a sense of panic and a need to get as far away as I could as fast as I could. I didn't want to leave my sister but I couldn't take her with me. Besides, she wasn't as ready to go as I was. She still had high school to finish and her virginity to lose and her loves and passions to discover. Part of me felt that my presence, in some ways, prevented her from going out on her own and doing these things. As I lay there, on my side, listening to her breathing and the water slapping the hull and the small fish and shrimp clicking and snapping against the fiberglass I wondered how many other people were hurt or harmed by my mere presence. And how many, in the future, would be.

Michelle came and got me the next day, as soon as I called her. I could have called Cole but he was back in Annapolis, and I was afraid that if I called him I would be making a decision more permanent than any I had made before. I packed enough for a couple of weeks, and left *Chez Nous* thinking that, this time, I may not go back. The cowboy bars and discount grocery stores of Orange Avenue flashed past us as Michelle and I raced out of town in her Chrysler LeBaron.

The Jehovah's Witnesses tried to chase Michelle and me out of Indiantown. They sent a group of "Elders" down to *Summer Wind* one morning to roust us. "Shhh, stay down below and let me deal with them," Michelle said.

She climbed out the companionway and I heard her talking in low tones to the men on the dock. I peered out the porthole, straining my ears and eyes. All I could see were three pairs of practical shoes underneath long pants. I couldn't believe anyone would wear long pants in Florida in the middle of May.

"Okay," I heard Michelle say. "Thank you for your concern." She tumbled down the hatch, her face red. "Whew," she said. "Holy crap. They just said that they came by because they wanted to warn me not to hang out with you. They think you're 'worldly.'"

"Is that what they said?"

"Yeah. Worldly. What the heck is that supposed to mean?"

"I don't know. I guess they just mean 'not a Jehovah's Witness,'" I said.

We tried to figure it out but didn't get anywhere. I wondered if they meant to say that I was a slut. I was almost starting to believe it. My period had come the day before, so I knew I wasn't pregnant, but the thought that I *could* have been lingered. I was an adult and the realities of adulthood were inescapable. But these people didn't know me, and they didn't know my family. There was no way my dad could have talked to them. They just knew that I wasn't from Indiantown and that I wasn't a Witness.

Michelle's real mom, Kathy, flew into town to help us drive up to her home in Racine, WI, where Michelle would stay with her for a couple of weeks before moving to Newport. Michelle had just met Zak, the son of one of her mom's friends, and one of the reasons she was going to Wisconsin was to spend some time with him and get to know him better. He was a marine who had just been honorably discharged. He wasn't a Jehovah's Witness either.

Gary came down to *Summer Wind* to see us off. Kathy said later that he came just to see her, but Michelle and I knew better. Kathy and Gary had been divorced since Michelle was a baby, and Gary had been remarried for more than half that time, but Kathy still swore that they were in love with each other. The probably were, in the way that you never fall out of love with some people even though you can't live with them. Gary stood with one leg on *Summer Wind* and one leg on the dock. "Well, I guess you won't be coming back to Indiantown ever again, Seashell," he said. "You're going to let your old dad rot away here with all the Guatemalans at the car lot." He laughed and looked around to see whether anybody was within earshot, but the marina was dead in the foggy, hot morning.

"That's crazy, Dad." Michelle was trying not to cry, and even I had a hard time keeping the lump down in my throat. I wondered if Gary ever thought the things about Michelle that my dad had said to me. I wished I could be like them—a father and daughter who seemed to move in each other's orbits gracefully. They didn't battle constantly.

Indian Summer, the boat that Gary and Michelle had cruised aboard and that we had taken across the harbor to get cheeseburgers at Frida's, was destroyed in Hurricane Andrew back in 1992, when the new owners moored it at Dinner Key in Biscayne Bay for the storm. *Summer Wind* was still charred in places by the fire in 1994. *Chez Nous* was up for sale. I felt like Michelle and I would somehow be able to make things right by starting over on a smaller boat.

We drove out of Indiantown with the top down in Michelle's black Chrysler LeBaron, the trunk full of all her belongings and my duffel bag. The fog lifted off of Route 710 and rose over cow pastures and orange groves, and Kathy leaned back and yelled goodbye to Indiantown, even though she had never lived there. Michelle glanced in the rearview only long enough to catch my eye as a tiny smile flickered across her face. Our fathers, *Summer Wind* and *Chez Nous* were far behind us.

Tribe Disbanded

Newport, Rhode Island • Summer 1998

Age 18

Before I knew it, I was back on *Chez Nous*.

I flew into Charleston, SC, because I was convinced that my family needed help taking the boat north. I'd enjoyed myself in Wisconsin, but waking up in a strange bed that far away from the ocean had made me dizzy. I'd wandered outside and hadn't been able to tell which way was south. I sat on the rocks beside Lake Michigan with Michelle and Zak, talking about how we wanted to see the world before we were too old.

Zak took me for a ride on his motorcycle, and we flew into Milwaukee at 120 miles per hour, Michelle falling behind us in the LeBaron. I thought I was going to die.

I didn't talk to my dad when I got home, and none of us said much of anything. It felt like coming home after Baltimore, when I'd gone to see Cole, except this time I'd been gone longer. The trip up the East Coast to Newport was hot and monotonous, and we dropped the anchor off Ida Lewis Yacht Club in early June. Michelle drove out a few days after we got there.

Newport was ripe with tourists, and Michelle and I made good tips when we worked together. On foggy days, I sat out on Adirondack's bow, looking for other boats and buoys and land, while Michelle relayed messages to the captain. I never thought, while I was watching shadows and silhouette sailboats coast through the fog, that I would be the first to fall off or be crushed if Adirondack hit anything.

Michelle moved into an apartment on Anne Street. It was right in the middle of downtown Newport, a block uphill from Thames Street. It was small and old, and the kitchen had a crooked floor. When I was there, I slept on a mattress in the living room. The rest of the time, I stayed aboard *Chez Nous*, drifting back and forth between land and sea.

The first boat we looked at was a Seafarer 31. It was sitting in someone's backyard just over the state line in Connecticut, and looked like it had been sitting for years. Michelle and I drove out in the LeBaron, and met with the owner in the back of a machine shop. He showed us the sails—clean and spread out across the parking lot, ready for our inspection—and drove over to the boat with us following.

"I don't think he's taking us seriously," I said, as we took a sharp turn down a tree-lined street.

"Well, that's his problem, isn't it?" Michelle's oversized Calvin Klein sunglasses slid down her nose.

We parked behind the owner's truck, in an overgrown lot with several rusted cars sitting on blocks placed at odd positions around the perimeter. The boat was in the middle, mast off, sitting proud and full keeled on jack stands. Her hull was streaked green with mildew.

"Well, here she is," the owner said. "I'll let you ladies take your time looking." He threw the key to Michelle.

"Thanks," she said. "Is there a ladder?"

"Oh, sure." He pointed to an aluminum ladder propped against one of the cars. "Use that one. I'm going to go back to the shop, so just bring the key on back when you're done."

"Okay." Michelle struck out for the ladder, and I walked around the hull, looking for the telltale lumps that would show blistering or delamination. I knew that if fiberglass isn't laid up properly, the polyester resin separates from the glass and forms weak patches in the hull. The Seafarer's hull looked solid. I stepped back and admired the slender stern overhang, and thought about how pretty she would look in the water.

Michelle planted the ladder against the stern, and climbed into the cockpit. "This boat needs a lot of cleaning," she said.

"We can handle that." I followed her up the ladder.

Inside, the boat was bare and tiny, with a V-berth that didn't look like it was big enough for one person, let alone two. There was a small alcohol stove in the galley, a fold-down table, and an unfinished head. The sacrifice of space for lines was obvious—on a boat with delicate overhangs like this one had, most of the length was wasted.

We spent the afternoon crawling around the boat, even though we both knew it wasn't the right one. We spent more afternoons over the next few weeks looking at other boats—Ericsons and Catalinas, Morgans and Pearsons, anything over twenty years old and under ten grand.

Nothing seemed to fit. "It's like we're looking at all the wrong boats," Michelle said. We were standing on the bow of Adirondack with Tim, coming in from an evening sail. The tourists were seated in the cockpit, drinking champagne and beer, basking in the summer air and the scenery.

"You'll know when you find the right one," Tim said. The warmth of his presence and the comfort I had knowing that he was part of my tribe washed over me as I opened a cold beer from the cooler. (I didn't drink during the day, while I was working, but the owners of Adirondack didn't mind it if I swiped a beer or two in the evenings.) Tim and Michelle and Cole were ocean people, people who couldn't live without the feeling of water moving under the hull of a well-chosen and well-loved sailboat. We understood each other, and when I looked at Michelle's face, tilted into the sunset with her eyes half-closed, the lines around her mouth rippling into a smile, and Tim's smile surging against his skin in the same way, I felt like I was home.

Tim's eyes were fixed on me. "Don't you think you just need to spend some more time looking?" he asked. Sometimes, his voice wavered when he asked questions like this, as if by my getting a boat and living out my dream it would somehow make up for the fact that he hadn't yet.

"You're right." I rubbed a fingerprint off Adirondack's varnish with the hem of my shirt. "We won't be able to look at anything next week, because I'll be in the Bahamas on that stupid charter with my parents." We were going to lead a group of charter boats around the Abacos the next week—Dad had been hired by the charter company to teach sailing and cruising seminars on a week-long sail. We, his family, were part of the package.

"Oh, you'll have fun," Michelle said.

"No I won't," I said. "We're going to be sailing on a Clorox Bottle."

"Oh." Michelle wrinkled her nose, and I noticed a few lines on her face that were deeper than they should have been.

"I take it you'll never be buying a brand new boat," Tim said. We laughed. Ever since Cole and his dad had delivered one of the mass-produced new breed of fiberglass sailboat from the Abacos to Maryland the previous winter, surviving a near-dismasting when two of the shrouds broke in heavy weather, I'd thought of most newer models as fiberglass deathtraps. "Clorox Bottle" was a term we used to refer to any of these vessels.

I jumped onto the dock as Adirondack slid into her slip. It was my favorite part of the daily sailing trips—taking that flying leap from as far out as I dared, watching the gap between boat and concrete dock narrow under my feet. If I missed, I would be crushed between them.

I never missed. My knees bent to absorb the shock, and I hit the dock running to catch the spring line that Michelle threw to me. The tourists gasped, delightfully aware of the risk I was taking. They started digging in their pockets and purses for tip money. Tim stood back and grinned.

My family spent a week leading starry-eyed sailors around, teaching them how to navigate the Bahamian shallows and how to move aboard and raise a family if, of course, they were willing to make the sacrifices.

Standing on the pier one evening, surrounded by wide-eyed future liveaboards,

I pounded a hole in the whorls of a queen conch that we had collected. I used one of the cheap steak knives we'd found aboard the charter boat to reach in and cut the muscle, feeling the creature go slack against my thumb which was jammed up inside the lip. I grabbed the operculum and pulled the conch out, holding it up for the group to see. "Now you have to cut its head off," I said. "That makes it less slimy." I picked up a sharper fillet knife and slivered through the meat just under the protruding eyes. The chunk of meat fell to the pier and I nudged it away with a toe. "Good bait, if anyone wants it," I said.

The group watched as I skinned the creature and trimmed its orange mantle back, and in the final act of cutting off the operculum I waved the fillet knife with a flair. "Who's next? I'll walk you through it," I said, holding up another conch that needed cleaning. But nobody in the group wanted to give it a try. It was cocktail hour and they were drifting off to the marina bar. Not a bad idea, I thought as I rushed through the remaining conch. The act of killing for food was something that was so natural to me—I never stopped to think about the fact that I was destroying a living creature as I pounded holes through the shells and severed the lifeline between snail and shell with my knife.

Once finished, I washed the slime from my hands and headed to the bar. I ordered Bacardi and diet cola and closed my eyes as I felt the sweet rum slide down the back of my throat. I was old enough to drink legally in the Bahamas, where the drinking age was eighteen. But it didn't really matter, since Bahamian bartenders were famous for giving American girls of any age whatever they wanted from the bar. I joined Carolyn off to the side of the bar and we drank together in silence, watching the crowd get rowdy. Our parents drank and moved from table to table, socializing and selling the dream.

We flew back to Rhode Island when the trip was over, tanned and tired, and piled into Michelle's LeBaron—three of us in the back and Dad and Michelle up front. Once we'd cleared the airport traffic, Michelle started talking. I was sitting right behind her, so I watched the back of her head. "I've been talking to some people about what to do this winter," she said. "Most of the crew here head down to the Virgin Islands. I guess it's really easy to find work down there, and you can make a lot of money."

I was having trouble hearing her in the backseat. Carolyn was squeezed in beside me, and her elbow poked my ribs when I tried to lean forward.

"You know, most of those jobs sound a lot more glamorous than they really are," Dad said, always the cynic. "All you'd be doing is cleaning up puke after the tourists get seasick."

"That's what we do now on Adirondack, Dad," I said. I wanted him to be quiet so I could listen to Michelle.

Her voice stayed flat and level as she spoke. "Zak is coming out here in a couple weeks," she said. "I think he's going to stay."

"For the summer?" I couldn't imagine Zak wanting to move onto a small sailboat with us for the trip south.

"No, for good. I think we're going to try to find a boat that we can help deliver to St. Thomas."

"What, as crew?"

"Yeah, then we've talked about living down there and trying to save some money." Michelle rolled down her window and let the wet Rhode Island air into the car. It smelled like it had blown across miles of tangled seaweed.

"I thought the two of you were going to get a boat," Carolyn said.

"I thought so too." I may have spoken or I may have just thought the words, but nobody responded. Michelle was quiet until she dropped us off at the dinghy dock. *Chez Nous* rested at anchor out in the harbor, floating in a layer of fog. As I watched, the fog became so thick that the boat disappeared and then reappeared only to fade again, as if it was some sort of ghost. New England fog is cold and wet and it hit my bones with a chill that was just as otherworldly as the ghost-like appearance of *Chez Nous*. I thought so too…my mouth was dry even though the air was so, so moist, and I tried to make sense of this new information that I'd been given. I told Michelle I'd see her tomorrow, at work, and went to the boat with my family. Riding through the fog in the dinghy, I wondered what had just happened and what was next.

At the end of the summer, I had turned nineteen and upgraded my Captain's license to a 50 Ton Master's simply because I could. I'd looked through every Boat Trader Magazine that came out, saved up a little more money, and applied to another college. A family friend told me about Eckerd College, a small private school in Southwest Florida that was located right on the water. I filled out the paperwork without giving it a second thought. I made a little bit of progress in my yacht design classes, but didn't think about them much either.

Zak took Michelle away as soon as he got there. He swore he'd learn to sail, so he got a job on one of the 12 Meter boats, an old America's Cup contender. I saw less and less of them.

Cole came to visit. "Why don't you just start looking for your own boat?" he said. "You're perfectly capable of doing it by yourself." We shared a lobster dinner at one of the wharf-side restaurants for my nineteenth birthday. We'd both dressed up to the point where we felt uncomfortable. Earlier that day, we'd rented a moped and flown across the streets of Newport like happy tourists.

"I guess," I said. "I haven't really decided what I'm going to do."

"Well, you know you can't stay on that boat with your parents." Cole dipped a plump piece of lobster into melted butter, and I watched a trail of it glisten on his chin while he talked. "I know you love the boat, but aren't they trying to sell it?"

"Yeah. They're talking about it."

"Well, you could always move in with me. We can head south for the winter, maybe even all the way down to the Virgins." Cole leaned over the table and held my hand between both of his. His fingers were thick and short, and his knuckles were scarred from working on boats. I loved his hands and loved what he stood for, but was beginning to realize that I didn't love him enough to make the sacrifices that being with him required. I was beginning to realize that I would not be satisfied settling for a life of casual drifting, as appealing as that life seemed to be. Moving in with him would be temporary, and temporary wasn't what he wanted. Later that night, I told him that things would never work between us. I had no idea what my plans were, but I was determined to figure them out and carry them through on my own. We broke up that night for the first time in a series of small breakups and heartbreaks that lasted about six months. When it was all said and done and we'd asked each other for that final release of *do not contact me again* I couldn't help wondering which one of us had been taken advantage of more.

At the beginning of September, I drove Tim back to shore in the dinghy after he'd eaten dinner aboard *Chez Nous*. The moon was full, hanging over Newport Harbor like a paper lantern. It left a trail of silver on the water, the trail parting only for the silhouettes of the sloops and yawls that hadn't been hauled out for the season yet.

"What do you think of that moon?" Tim leaned back, his hands clasped around his knees.

"Beautiful," I said. I wanted to cut the outboard motor off and row, so we wouldn't wreck the peace and quiet. And so I could make the short trip take as long as possible.

"Melanie, I have to tell you something," Tim said. "Nobody else knows yet, but I want to tell you." He unclasped his hands and leaned forward. "I'm going to be a dad," he said.

"Oh. Wow." I gripped the handle on the outboard so tight I could feel the bones in my hand rattle. Time slowed down and his words hung suspended in the night air. This wasn't what I had expected. Maybe I thought he was about to tell me he was getting a boat and taking off, finally. Getting away from Newport and the dreary office at *Cruising World*. Deep in my stomach, and only for a moment, I felt a small flutter of hope that he was going to ask me to come with him. I would not have gone with Cole, but I would have gone with Tim.

"Marina just told me she's pregnant," he said. He'd been seeing a woman in Boston named Marina for awhile, but I hadn't thought it was that serious. She didn't seem interested in sailing. I didn't know much about her. I hadn't tried to learn much about her. I wondered how someone like Tim could make it work with a woman who wasn't interested in sailing.

"Were you trying?"

"No. But I guess it just happened anyway." He stared at a Hinkley yawl that slipped past us.

"Well, congratulations." I didn't know what else to say. I knew that things couldn't stay the way they were forever—in all likelihood, this was my last summer in Newport. And while I was good at keeping in touch with people, it now felt like Tim was just as lost to me as the rest of my tribe.

"I'm also getting a boat," Tim said. "A Vineyard Vixen. It's a gorgeous little double ender, about twenty years old. I just want to have something I can take for day-sails around the bay," he said.

"You're not going to have much time for sailing with a baby," I said.

"I know. But wait until you see it. It's a sweet boat. I'm picking it up next weekend. And how great will it be to teach the baby how to sail?"

"What are you going to name the boat?"

"*Ave Marina*," he said.

I dropped him off at the wharf and hugged him goodnight. As I backed the dinghy out into the harbor, a black cormorant shook its head and dove off a piling, ducking underwater. I wondered how I'd managed to say goodbye to the three people I cared about the most, all in one summer.

Dodge Shadow

Fort Lauderdale, Florida • Winter 1999

Age 19

In Annapolis, I made an offer on a Seafarer 27. The broker accepted it and I backed out, saying that the boat needed too much work. It really didn't, but something wasn't right. A few weeks later, I flew to Fort Lauderdale to help my dad deliver the new *Chez Nous* to Wilmington, NC, where we would meet up with the old *Chez Nous* and move everything from one boat to the other.

The new *Chez Nous* was a Gulfstar 53 motorsailor. It was big and bulky, and had a shallow draft and three staterooms. I didn't understand why my parents liked it so much—it didn't sail as well as the old *Chez Nous*. It wasn't as seaworthy. It wasn't as pretty. On New Years Day, 1999, the same day the rest of my family moved onto the new *Chez Nous*, I packed most of my stuff and took a taxi to the airport at Wilmington. I didn't know what I was going to end up doing, but I knew I had to leave. I'd picked the only place that felt remotely like home and booked a one-way flight to Fort Lauderdale. Carolyn didn't ask me why I was leaving and I didn't try to tell her. I didn't really know why, except that it was time. Mom and Dad and Carolyn followed me up to the gate of Wilmington Marine Center, and none of us said anything when I got into the taxi. Mom cried and Dad gave me fifty dollars.

In Fort Lauderdale, it was sixty degrees warmer. A boating friend who I'd met in the Bahamas a few years before picked me up and took me back to the sailboat that she and her sister were living aboard. It was an Endeavour named *Neverland*. I got a job as a cashier in a nautical bookstore, and worked in a restaurant at night. I was a terrible waitress and quit before they fired me. I had a drivers license but I didn't have a car, so I bought a bicycle and rode it everywhere.

My parents arrived in town aboard the new *Chez Nous*, and anchored in Lake Sylvia for a few days. I found an ad in the paper for a used Dodge Shadow convertible for $3,500. I didn't know anything about cars, but in the small photo it looked a lot like Michelle's Chrysler LeBaron, and I'd liked the LeBaron. My dad and I drove in my parents' rental car to a house in Pembroke Pines located just off the Florida Turnpike to negotiate a deal.

"What do you know about the car?" Dad asked, as we searched for the street address.

"Not much. Ice-cold air. About 80,000 miles on it, I guess."

"That's a lot." Dad's hands gripped the wheel of the rental car. As comfortable as my dad was driving a boat, neither he nor my mom were the best automobile operators. He drove well below the speed limit and cursed the South Florida drivers.

"I don't have enough money to buy anything newer." I flipped through the wad of bills in my purse. Earlier that day, I'd had my bank in Virginia wire me $3,000. Cash was power when negotiating. This was something I'd learned from bartering for produce and trinkets with the Bahamian ladies at the straw markets in Nassau and George Town.

"Well, let's check it out carefully," Dad said.

Driving through the South Florida streets in the twilight, we shared a comfortable silence as we each made mental checklists of things to look at on the car. I had learned about engines because I knew I'd be buying a boat someday and I knew it would come in handy, and I had learned about engines because I knew that it would make my dad proud of me.

The seller had half a dozen used cars sitting in his front yard. The Shadow was waxed and pretty, freshly sprayed with new-car-smell. I drove it around the block with my dad in the passenger seat. We couldn't find anything wrong with it, and the four-cylinder engine was incredibly simple and looked like it would be easy to work on. In the seller's living room, I pulled most of the cash out of my purse.

"You're asking $3,500, but we discussed $3,000 on the phone," I said.

"Well, yes. The car is in perfect condition," the seller said.

"It also has a lot of miles on it." I moved the cash from one hand to the other.

"You'll love driving along the beach with the top down," the seller said.

"True, but I saw some of the stitching coming out of the vinyl," I said. "Look, I have cash, and I'm willing to pay $2,500. Will that work for you?"

"How about $2,750?"

"Okay," I said. "Let's do it."

My dad covered his mouth with his hand to hide the tiny smile that flashed across his face. I wondered if he could possibly be proud of me. There were so many things I had done to break his heart, but deep inside I felt like he might be starting to see me for what I was becoming: a scrappy and resourceful survivor-type, just as stubborn as him. The seller signed the title over to me and gave me a temporary tag and I took off in my new car, scared shitless. I wasn't much better of a driver than my parents.

Jalousie

Fort Lauderdale, Florida • Winter and Spring 1999

Age 19

I rented a studio apartment in a triplex that was so close to I-95 that you could hear the sirens and horns and the general hum of traffic if you left the windows open. My salary from the bookstore barely covered the rent. The apartment came furnished with a twin bed and a hotel dresser and a plastic table and chairs. I covered the table with a dollar-store tablecloth and bought brightly colored linens for the bed. The jalousie window over my bed opened to a bougainvillea, and small brown lizards jumped from the plant to the window and tried to slip inside. The neighborhood was mixed: white, black, Cuban, Haitian, gay party boys and straight ones, old folks, kids like me out on their own for the first time in a completely unsheltered and nonconventional environment. The woman who lived by herself next door to me claimed to be an aerobics instructor but I was convinced she was a stripper.

Michelle wrote me a few letters from St. Thomas, where she and Zak were living. They were crewing on tourist catamarans and saving money, just as they'd planned. Tim sent me a letter, which was short and accompanied a book of mythology. He wrote something about a hero's journey that I didn't really understand. He was eloquent and poetic, and wrote that he was excited about being a father. Sitting on my twin bed with the window open and the bougainvillea scratching at the jalousie I thought about writing him back and telling him I'd been a little bit in love with him but that I was over it now. I decided against the lie.

I dated a wiry redneck from the Eastern Shore of Maryland named Carey. He was nine years older than me, and loyal to a fault. He drove a privately-owned sport fishing boat that was sometimes chartered out to wealthy Palm Beach folks to catch sailfish and marlin. On the days when he wasn't fishing, he maintained the boat and played rent-a-buddy to the owner, a millionaire from Maryland who liked to golf and bring his mistresses to the boat. Carey and I had actually met in Wilmington, NC, where his boat was being repaired at the same marina where we were moving everything from the old *Chez Nous* to the new *Chez Nous*.

I had flirted with him out of boredom, but had started to like him when we went out to lunch and he regaled me with stories of big game fishing. When I'd moved to Fort Lauderdale, I'd called him and told him that I'd made the big move and asked if he wanted to hang out.

Carey called me one day as I sat on my twin bed with Tim's card and book. "Hey," I said, holding my oversized PrimeCo cellular to my ear. I'd purchased it right after my move. I'd had to pay an exorbitant fee to get it set up, since I didn't have any credit established.

"Hey. There's something I need to tell you," he said.

"What?"

"Well, I should have told you this before…" His voice drifted off and he took a deep breath. I pictured him drawing on his Marlboro and taking his glasses off as he wiped the back of his hand across his forehead.

"What should you have told me?"

"Well, I'm actually married," he said. "I have a wife up in Maryland. And kids."

"What the hell?" I slammed Tim's book down on the bed.

There was silence on the other end. Then a raucous laugh that got louder and louder until I had to hold the phone away from my head. "I'm fucking with you," he said. "I got you, didn't I?" He sucked in his breath and let it out, obviously pleased with himself.

"Um, I guess you did," I said. "That's not really funny though."

"Yes it is." He laughed some more and I waited for him to finish. Later, he would tell me that the joke had been his way of figuring out how to tell me he loved me. I told him that he had a pretty fucked up way of saying things.

With Carey, I learned how to thread a long needle through live goggle-eyes and twist a hook through the twine just the right way so that a sailfish would see the bait and not the hook. I learned how to fish with a kite, using it to lift the bait and carry it far, far away from the boat. I learned the names for the different brands of gold and silver reels that cost thousands and thousands of dollars. One night, Carey and I drank with the Chief of Police of Palm Beach County, who knew I was nineteen but didn't care.

And with Carey, I became a regular at the Singer Island and Palm Beach fishing bars. The boats would come into the marinas in the later afternoon and the captains and crew would stumble off and find their way to a barstool, where they talked about engines and chicks and fish and passed small bags of cocaine back and forth to each other in the bathrooms. Once I found a bag on the floor of the ladies room at the Buccaneer Club, a small bar that was a favorite of ours. I ran out, terrified that just by seeing it I would be somehow guilty of partaking. Drugs, at this point, still scared me. Nothing good ever came out of them.

Somewhere during the madness of my nineteenth year, my acceptance letter from Eckerd College came in the mail along with offers of scholarships and information about room and board. Since I wasn't making much money at the bookstore, I decided that college would be a good idea. I called them and signed up for the fall semester.

In April, Carey convinced me to spend the summer with him in Ocean City, Maryland. Carey's life was as seasonally inclined as my life had been—during the winter, he kept the boss's boat docked in Palm Beach with the occasional trip over to the Bahamas. Summers, he took it up to Ocean City, where the fishing routine went from lighter tackle to the heavy gear used to catch tuna and white and blue marlins. "You can work cleaning boats," he said, as we drank margaritas at the Buccaneer Club. "Those girls clean up. You can charge a dollar a foot, and if you clean three fifty-footers in one evening you've made $150. All you have to do is wear a bikini and work it a little bit."

"Ha," I said, swirling the ice in my margarita. "I'm sure I don't have what those girls do." I didn't love my body—I was in pretty good shape, but my breasts were still small and my ass still large.

"Trust me. You'll be fine. And you don't really have to wear a bikini. The guys just want their boats cleaned," Carey said.

Later that month, Carolyn and I sat on the stern of a catamaran off Marina Cay in the British Virgin Islands. It was another charter expedition, similar to the one we'd done in the Abacos the year before, except this time there were no conch-cleaning demonstrations and no sessions on how to raise your kids aboard a boat. This time, my dad was writing an article on how to plan a charter, so we'd been set up with a nice family vacation. Tarpon schooled underneath our boat, and I had thrown in a fishing line to see if I could hook one. We passed a bottle of Bailey's Irish Cream back and forth, each swigging the syrupy liquid like nobody's business. Carolyn had become just as good a drinker as me.

The mercurial tarpon grew darker as the sun set, and later that night the moonlight bounced off their scales. *Such beautiful fish*, I thought. Carey had shown me how to reel in a sailfish as it danced across the water, its tail skimming the surface and its slick muscled body glistening. Every fish had its own personality. The shadowy tarpon that circled below us were much more mysterious and ethereal.

"So are you thinking about college?" I passed the bottle to Carolyn, who downed the last of it.

"Yeah. I'm not sure what else to do," she said. "There's good surf in Florida. And Flagler College in St. Augustine is a decent enough school."

"Don't really know anything about it," I said. Then, "You learning to surf?"

"Yeah. Don't you remember? I started last summer in Newport."

Yeah…she had. Had I been too preoccupied to notice? Probably. "Is someone teaching you?"

"Guy named Scooter. He lives on a little sailboat and we've been hanging out with him a lot." My parents and Carolyn had gone on to the Bahamas without me that winter, and they'd sailed to islands that they had never visited while I was aboard—places like Andros and Rum Cay. I was jealous that Carolyn was getting to see those places and I wasn't. For the charter, they'd left the new *Chez Nous* in the Exumas and flown to meet me in Miami, where we all took a plane to San Juan and then to Tortola.

"What kind of name is Scooter?" I swirled my toe in the calm water over the tarpon.

"I don't know. Not his real name, I'm sure." Carolyn leaned back on the swim platform, empty bottle of Bailey's beside her. She had outgrown her awkwardness and become beautiful. She couldn't have been a model because she was short like Mom and I were, but she was thin and brown and had huge blue eyes and sun streaked hair.

"Sounds like a burnout," I said.

"Yeah. He keeps following us. You know, showing up in the same places."

"Sketchy."

We didn't catch a tarpon. We stumbled to our cabins and the next morning I woke up and found my parents sitting out on the swim platform drinking coffee. The empty Bailey's bottle was gone and the sun was already burning water droplets off the deck of the boat, leaving little specks of salt. I grabbed some coffee and went to sit with my parents.

"So did you set up everything with Eckerd College?" Dad asked.

"Yep. I'm starting in August. International Business."

"International Business? Where did that come from?" Mom squinted at me through the glare from the boat's white deck.

"I figure that's the best way to make money, right?" I had picked the major at random, thinking that it sounded like something a smart person would choose.

"Good," Dad said.

We sat in silence for a few minutes, listening to the water lapping on the twin hulls and drinking our coffee. "I guess Carolyn is thinking about college too," I said.

"Yeah. We stopped in St. Augustine on the way down this year so she could see Flagler." Mom bent over her coffee, peering into her cup as if to hide from the sun that she'd been staring into her whole life. She had fine lines around her eyes and her skin was slackening around her jaw. My parents had been older than average when they had Carolyn and me, and now it was showing.

"Good for her. Hey, I am going to go to Ocean City this summer," I said.

"With that Carey?" Dad's face darkened.

"Yeah. He says there's lots of money to be made detailing boats up there. It will be a good way to save for the school year."

"I guess you're planning to live with him then?" Dad's voice cracked the way it did when his anger was rising, and the vein in his neck started to throb. That anger—the same dark anger that I carried, that sometimes reared itself with sudden outbursts or random acts of violence. I threw things or broke things, but only when nobody was looking.

"It's not living with him," I said. "It's just for a couple of months."

"Living with him for a couple of months then," Dad said. He and Mom looked at each other and then we all looked out at the horizon—the rolling hills of Tortola and the slack water.

Not far away, in St. Thomas, Michelle and Zak were planning their return to the States, with money saved up to move to Wisconsin and to eventually move out to California, where they would buy into a yacht brokerage that would thrive in the boom of the mid 2000's and fall apart in the Great Recession that ended the decade. Somewhere on that same ocean, Cole was biding his time on the *Gypsy Lady*, doing who knew what. Tim's boat was winterized up in Rhode Island, and he was learning how to be a father and learning what it meant to be truly tied down and truly in love. And in the British Virgin Islands, I fought the same battle with my Dad that had been fought over and over again except by now we were tired of fighting it. It was a war neither of us could win.

"Why are you so worried about me living with Carey? I'm on my own now anyway," I said.

"Haven't you thought about what it will look like? He's nine years older than you are," Dad said.

"Age is relative. And who's looking?" I'd convinced myself that age was simply a number. After all, growing up on the boat and hanging out with whatever kids came along flying the "Kids Aboard" flag, I'd had friends who were older than me and friends who were younger. Most of my friends now were in their twenties and thirties. I would keep the philosophy moving forward, and tend to see people for who they were to me and not for how old they were.

"Carey's immature for 28 and I'm mature for 19," I said. "So it works."

"Just don't do it," Dad said.

Graveyard

Indiantown, Florida • Spring 1999

Age 19

Michelle and Zak flew in from St. Thomas a few weeks before my planned departure for Ocean City. They were deeply tanned and physically fit, wearing that glow of a couple during the honeymoon phase of their relationship. I met them at the gate and hugged them both, happy to see them and excited to show them my new life in Fort Lauderdale. And I secretly wondered if maybe Michelle was going to be tired of Zak now that they had spent their winter together and if maybe she would leave him and we could go and get our boat now. My money had all been spent, but I figured that we could find a way to rebuild our dream if we wanted to.

As soon as we'd hugged our hellos, Michelle held up her left hand. "Look at this," she said.

A gold band shaped like a small dolphin curved around her ring finger. A diamond sparkled from the center. I took her hand and sighed over the ring the way one woman is supposed to sigh over another's engagement ring, and congratulated them both. Marriage was something that at nineteen I hadn't thought much about. Even in talking to Cole about moving aboard his boat, the subject had never come up. And Carey and I were just biding our time and having fun. I realized later that perhaps our relationship had meant more to Carey than this, but at the time he was simply someone who could show me a different life and teach me how to fish for big game. Tim hadn't spoken much of marriage except to talk about his divorce, although he did marry Marina after their daughter was born. Now, Michelle stood before me with Zak and beamed over her ring. I bristled inside, part of me wanting to tell her that she was too young, but the more rational side of me asking myself what it really meant to be too young. But what really got me was that Zak wasn't a sailor. Even though he had made every effort to learn and had read all the books and had learned how to sail just as well as anyone, he was still an outsider. This was his final act in the play that had begun a year before. He was stealing Michelle away from me. I wondered how she could marry someone who didn't understand her as much as

I did. Michelle could not marry someone who wasn't a sailor.

These were my thoughts, but I stood and smiled and resolved to learn more about the man Michelle was choosing to spend her life with. Years later, on a camping trip in Death Valley, Zak asked me why I didn't like him when we first met. "I didn't know you, Zak," I said. Zak and Michelle and I sat on the back of their truck, the sun sinking over the mountains and coyotes yipping in the distance. "I like you plenty now," I said. "And I'm sorry I didn't give you a fair chance. You were stealing Michelle from me."

But in South Florida in 1999, we sat in the Dodge Shadow and talked about their plans and my plans. They were going to buy a car from her dad's lot and move up to Wisconsin for a while. We ended up later that night in Palm Beach aboard the boat that Carey captained. Carey, drunk, pulled an M16 out of one of the lockers and showed it to Zak, and the two of them compared notes on automatic and semi-automatic weapons while Michelle and I sat on the stern of the boat and talked. I drank a beer and Michelle drank water.

"What do you think of this fishing thing?" Michelle gazed up at the bridge where the stainless-steel and white fiberglass glistened in the humid night.

"I like it," I said. "It's all boating. Whether you're sailing or fishing. It's the being on the water that I like." This was true. Traveling at high speeds on a brand new sport fishing boat thrilled me. The sight of a sailfish spinning on the water behind the boat while being reeled in and the smell of fish blood from the dolphin and mackerel that we caught and kept were magical and made me feel alive.

"I'm ready for a little bit of a break," Michelle said. "All those tourists in St. Thomas can get to you. And the crew—they just party and drink at night and don't save any of their money. You can make a fortune down there if you don't spend it all, but they don't seem to realize that."

"I guess you guys managed to save up," I said.

"Yeah." She twirled the ring on her finger. I wondered what she thought of me now—my drinking and partying and excessive spending that far outweighed my minimum wage salary.

"Is Zak going to get to meet your dad while you're here?" I nodded towards the lit salon cabin, where the silhouettes of Carey and Zak and the M16 rippled across the canvas blinds.

"Dad still won't meet him," Michelle said.

"Because he's not a Witness?"

"I guess. I don't know. I'm officially disfellowshipped now," she said. "I don't even think my dad is supposed to see me."

"That's not right," I said.

"Well, I guess my dad really believes in the religion." Over the years, the Jehovah's Witnesses had tightened their grip on Gary and his family, who attended the weekly meetings at the Kingdom Hall and socialized only with other Witnesses.

The next day, I dropped Michelle off in Port St. Lucie, on the coast, to spend the day on the beach with her dad and the kids. It turned out that family ties were stronger than religion, and Gary wanted to see his daughter after all. Zak and I took off towards Indiantown, wondering if we were going to pass the family going in the opposite direction. Gary wanted to see Michelle, but still wasn't ready for a face-to-face meeting with the man who had stolen her away.

I told Zak about Indiantown and about central Florida while we drove, the Shadow's top down and the heat oppressive. (The "ice-cold air" on my car had stopped working a month after I bought it, so the fact that it was a convertible was a blessing.) I told Zak about the orange groves and about how Florida was second only to Texas in raising beef cattle, and how Lake Okeechobee fed the Everglades and how the middle of the state was a close match to continental Africa in terms of flora and fauna. And, of course, I told Zak about the adventures that Michelle and I had growing up—the sailing dinghies and the beaches and meeting up in random harbors throughout the years. Zak was a good conversationalist, and despite the grudge that I carried against him I found that I enjoyed talking to him. He asked hard-hitting questions for which I didn't have answers, like: "Why do you think Michelle's Dad doesn't like me?" and "What do you think made you and Michelle grow apart?"

To his second question, I wanted to respond: "We didn't grow apart, you asshole. You ripped us apart." But I didn't. I liked Zak in spite of myself.

We drove through Indiantown, past the car lot, which was just a small lot with about two dozen old cars sitting in the overgrown weeds and an air-conditioned trailer for an office. "That's it?" Zak's eyes followed it as we rolled past. We turned at the road that led past the post office and to the marina, driving gradually downhill until we reached the water and turned right to weave through the fiberglass jungle of the dry-storage area. Sailboats of all shapes and sizes sat on jack-stands, and I read the names on their sterns as we navigated through them. The names were all familiar—all of these were boats I had seen in the Bahamas at some point in my childhood. All of them had owners that lived somewhere north of Indiantown and who had either put them in storage for the season or had stored them permanently or semi-permanently while trying to make a few more bucks to fund the dream. Maybe it was as simple as that, I thought. As simple as finding the means.

My dad had been smart enough, worked hard enough and been lucky enough to land and win the big case that paid for our early years of cruising. And he'd been gifted with the art of storytelling and known how to use it to fund the dream in our later years. But what very few of the cruising how-to books ever told you was how to pay for a lifestyle that didn't allow for regular jobs in regular offices. People on boats were either rich, lucky, or strapped for cash and living on a shoestring. Usually, they saved up money to cruise for a year and then went back to shore or settled when the money ran out. A very few, like my father, found ways to sustain themselves afloat.

The boats in Indiantown were empty vessels, each having carried dreams and each having been left or abandoned. Even those that were temporarily stored seemed sad to me. I'd seen these boats poised on aquamarine water, swaying on their anchor lines, or cutting across the banks under full sail, the proverbial "bone in their teeth" of a white wake spreading out from the bow. Names like *Voyager*, *Wandering Spirit*, *Southern Cross*, and *North Star* were written across their sterns in various fonts and colors. Finally, somewhere in the middle of the jungle, we reached *Summer Wind*.

Michelle had told us where to find the key, hidden under the "Welcome Aboard" mat. We propped a paint-covered boatyard ladder up against the hull and climbed aboard, me leading the way and securing the ladder once I reached the top. Zak followed tentatively and stepped aboard, looking around and taking it all in—the tattered Bimini top and the unvarnished teak and the scuffed fiberglass deck. Since Michelle had been gone, nobody had really cared for *Summer Wind*.

Inside the cabin where I had spent so many happy moments, the air was damp and musty. We ventured into the forward cabin, where Michelle had instructed us to look for bags of clothes, letters, books and a few other things that she didn't want to be without on her move to Wisconsin. I listened for the knocking on the hull of someone from the marina or a curious boater, and wondered what I would tell them if we were discovered. After all, we were both trespassing and stealing.

Zak walked through the boat in a trance, feeling the sides of the cabin and sitting down at the settee for a moment before moving to the aft cabin. I knew what must be going through his mind—in his less-than-a-year of yachting, he had crewed aboard a former America's Cup racer, delivered a multi-million-dollar sailing yacht to the Virgin Islands, and then crewed aboard a utilitarian tourist boat. He had been aboard *Chez Nous* briefly, after he first arrived in Newport, but that memory had faded and been replaced by all the boats and places that came next. This boat, the boat that Michelle grew up aboard and the boat from which she called him, night after night, when their relationship was beginning, was nothing like what he had imagined. It was humble and dirty, stout and unglamorous. It was as real as real gets.

I let him think his thoughts as I foraged through Michelle's stuff. We didn't have a whole lot of room in the Shadow, and they would have even less on their drive to Wisconsin, so I placed what I thought would be important to her in bags and set them by the companionway. In a Ziploc, under a pile of clothes, I found a stack of letters that I had written to Michelle. I opened them and dumped them on the V-berth, spreading them out across the cushion and looking for dates or clues as to when I might have written them. My handwriting on the letters was neat and slanted, the cursive practiced, and I thought about how quickly it had gone to shit. Some of the letters were written on yellowing composition paper, and some were on brightly-colored stationary, the kind that preteen girls in the early nineties bought and plastered with stickers of unicorns and dolphins. In one of the letters, written in 1995, I read a paragraph I had written about a Seafarer 26 that I admired. *It's docked at Narrows Marina and the owners never do anything with it,* I wrote. *It's so sad—such a waste of a boat—to see it just sitting there uncared-for. I would never treat a boat that way, and I know you wouldn't either. When we get ours, we'll take such good care of it.*

I folded the letter back up and placed all the letters in the bag, stashing it with the pile of things that Zak and I planned to heist from Indiantown.

We drove away that afternoon, both silent, both craning our necks to get a last look at *Summer Wind*, wishing her farewell for Michelle.

Commercial Fishing

Ocean City, Maryland • 1999

I broke the lease on my studio apartment and packed everything into the Dodge Shadow. My mom helped me drive north to West Ocean City, MD, where we stayed in Carey's marsh side cottage for two nights before driving Mom to the Baltimore airport where she flew back to reconnect with Dad and Carolyn aboard *Chez Nous*.

I convinced a friend of Carey's to let me use the address of her doublewide as my residence. The doublewide had a spare room and I put a few things there in case my parents ever showed up and I needed to pretend to be living someplace other than Carey's house. The doublewide's owner bartended at a small bar that faced the narrow commercial harbor where the longliners docked between trips. The bar served a specialty drink of orange-flavored vodka mixed with Sprite and fresh-squeezed orange juice, and late at night the fishermen would get into fistfights that sometimes landed them in jail. I cleaned boats in the evenings, as Carey and I had planned, and during the day I detailed and waxed them with a local woman who drove a violet pickup truck and owned a boat detailing and fish cleaning business. I got a third job running a water taxi for a waterfront bar in Ocean City proper. The bar was called Seacrets and was Jamaican-themed, with loud reggae music playing over the outdoor speakers and frozen drink specials that brought in the Pennsylvanian tourists by the hundreds.

All three jobs were lucrative and kept me busy enough to not get irritated by the constant drinking, smoking and partying of Carey and his buddies. I loved West Ocean City—the smell of fish, both fresh and rotting, the seaweed that clung to the pilings and the bulkheads, the bait and tackle shop at the mouth of the harbor that sold minnows and live peeler crabs out of fiberglass basins. I got a job there on my second summer with Carey, and learned how to measure out pints and quarts of the squirming minnows to sell to sunburned fishermen and their eager crew.

I loved the fishing and loved the booze and the money. I loved that I was oh-so-much-cooler than the bimbos that typically hung out at the bars and marinas there. I could clean a fish and hold my liquor, and my captain's license allowed me to drive bigger boats than most of the men in the harbor were allowed to drive. I loved the brutal honesty of the place. One summer the girlfriend of one of the longliners fell into the harbor and drowned, and they found her body floating between the boat and the dock on a Sunday morning. The official story was that she had fallen off the boat and hit her head, but the night before we had all seen her lover in the bar, swinging his fists at anything that moved. So naturally we all wondered what had really happened. Another summer a small Cessna crashed offshore and Carey and a SCUBA diver friend of his were hired to retrieve the bodies from the plane. Carey described the crabs that covered the bodies and how they made the bodies look like they were alive in the murky water. West Ocean City was to me like Florida was to Elizabeth Bishop—a place so alive with the poetry of life that I wanted to throw myself down into the marsh and writhe around like a minnow until my body was just part of the landscape.

College

St. Petersburg, Florida • 1999 to 2002

Ages 19 to 22

Eckerd College was perfect for me. It was near the base of the Sunshine Skyway Bridge, an impressive suspension bridge over the mouth of Tampa Bay that I, during my first semester, drove across and back in the Shadow with the top down just for the hell of it. The college was small, expensive, and right on the water. It had a waterfront program with its own search and rescue team and kayaks that you could take out whenever you wanted to. Glossy mangroves lined the shore where I ran in the mornings and white ibises clustered in the grass after the rain.

I was awarded the maximum scholarship that the school offered (there was no such thing as a full ride at Eckerd), took out loans, and my parents paid the balance of my tuition, room and board. I had a work-study job repairing the boats owned by the college's waterfront program, and spent three afternoons a week upside down in their bilges doing electrical work, diagnosing engine problems and sanding, painting and varnishing. I moved into a small dorm room built in the seventies with a quiet and shy girl who was only two years younger than me but seemed to be ten years younger. We were both weird so we got along fine—she was a bookworm and I was the Boat Girl. Whenever someone asked me where I was from, I had to explain how I grew up and how I was from a lot of places. If I liked the person, and cared enough to tell my story, I told it. If I didn't, I just said that I was from Virginia and left it at that.

I signed up for general education classes so I could get them out of the way. I came close to failing pre-calculus until I sought out a tutor and ended up with a B. It was one of the few B's that I would earn in my academic career. I partied some, but not with the urgency of my peers. I drove to Palm Beach on the weekends, where Carey and I continued the lifestyle of the service class. I was driven and motivated, and instead of enjoying my new freedom and partying it up like the other freshmen I dove into my books and did what I'd come to college to do. I learned like crazy. I spoke in class when some new piece of knowledge burned inside me and argued when arguing was appropriate, and was silent when

I didn't have anything to say. I stayed ahead on my homework, since I already knew how to study on my own. Other kids put their essays and assignments off until the night before they were due. I turned mine in early if at all possible.

On the first week of my freshman year, I met a beautiful girl named Celia, who was from Pennsylvania. I corrupted her with margaritas and fell softly in love with her the night I met her, and she would act as a sort of muse to me for the remainder of my time in college. She was a sweet hippie girl with a classic goddess body and eyebrows that curved dramatically over the biggest indigo eyes I had ever seen. Celia was one of those women who everyone fell in love with, male or female. She made bad choices in men and she defended her choices fiercely. She was an artist and a little bit of a witch, and I wrote poem after poem for her. I didn't show her the poems for years.

I went to see the movie "American Beauty" with some dorm mates. The rat-race, normal lives of the family in the movie scared me. I wondered if I, with a degree in International Business, would end up desperately driven to succeed financially like the realtor mother, losing sight of all other things in my life. Looking back, this doesn't make a whole lot of sense, since a degree in International Business and a profession in real estate have very little to do with each other, but something about the movie spoke to me and I knew that I didn't want to end up like those poor suckers. The next day, I went to the registrar's office and submitted the proper paperwork to change my major to creative writing. Writing was what I loved, so I decided it was what I would study. And even if I didn't make a career out of it, at least I would enjoy my college experience more if I spent it writing and analyzing poetry and short stories and reading great works of literature.

I met a lot of girls, and in my sophomore/junior year I lived in an on-campus apartment with seven of them. Communal living appealed to me, because, in a lot of ways, it was like being in a marina. There was always something going on, and if you needed a ride home from the bar or someone to give you a second opinion on an essay question there was always a cheerful girl around to help. One girl had a prosthetic leg and lured the drunken college boys to her room with promises of sex only to remove the leg at the last minute, which either terrified them or coaxed them even further into their infatuation. One was from Minnesota and one from California. The California girl and I shared a room and became close friends. My college life really wasn't that spectacular or unusual. I drank a fair amount but no more than before, pulled all-nighters writing screenplays and novellas, tried pot and ecstasy, founded a club for the creative writing students and convinced the school to give us money to fund an alcohol-infused trip to Key West that involved a drag show and a visit to the Hemingway House. Our club met weekly in my dorm, where we drank cheap wine from a jug and read each other's poetry and short stories and talked about how different and fantastic we were. The smells of oleander and burning citrus wafted in through the dorm room windows and blanketed us with their headiness.

Ecstasy was the drug of choice at expensive private colleges in those days. We'd all heard the story about the student who jumped off the Sunshine Skyway Bridge because his serotonin was so depleted after he came down from a hard "roll," as we called it. And we'd heard other stories about other students who jumped from windows or drowned themselves. Ecstasy was the suicide drug, but everyone I knew was willing to take the risk. Once, Celia and the girl with the prosthetic leg and I drove the seven hours to Key West coming down from an ecstasy trip, the blue water and the low palm scrum flashing by us and shimmering. We drank rum once the E wore off and went to a strip club and stuffed dollar bills into the dancers' garters. Later we fell asleep in the back of the station wagon, the three of us pinned against each other. In the morning, we snuck into a campground to shower, and giggled and smiled as we emerged from the shower stalls clean and brand new.

Celia said that ecstasy made her feel sparkly and erotic, and other people said it made you experience everything with a new level of awareness. I liked the idea of it, but the experience was different for me. I could never let go enough. Sheer physical enjoyment and sexual abandon were things I longed for but things that I somehow could never quite reach. Inside, I was still Boat Girl and Buffalo Butt and Thunder Thighs. I was still a Fighter Slut and still worthless and harmful, and if my body and sexuality had caused me so much trouble over the years then they certainly weren't things worth enjoying.

Carey and I camped in the Florida Keys one weekend and fished for tarpon while rolling on ecstasy that was from Palm Beach and was supposed to be much purer than what I had tried at Eckerd. Carey was like that—if I had an experience in college, he tried to find some way to be a part of it, even if the experience was so far removed from his life that he had to reinvent himself for it. This ecstasy was strong and good, and we sat in a small boat underneath a bridge and watched the tarpon turn on their flashy steel-colored sides and take the sunlight and throw it back at us. We hooked a small one and it floated above the water when it leapt and its scales seemed to disengage and shower us. *If I am going to do drugs*, I thought, *this is how it should be. On the water, with nature, and not at a crowded college party.* But my drug days came and went, and either through luck or through my own willpower I never permanently damaged myself.

The Small Wedding

Racine, Wisconsin • Fall 1999

Age 19

Michelle called me one night on my dorm room phone to invite me to her wedding.

"Oh," I said. "Where are you going to have the wedding?"

"Wisconsin. We found a lighthouse by the lake that we like. It's going to be a really small wedding. I'm not even getting a real dress or anything," she said. "Just wear something black and sleeveless."

"Is your dad going to be there?"

"No," she said.

I wrote down the rest of the details and booked a flight and a hotel room using the thousand-dollar-credit-limit card that my bank in Virginia had issued me in order to start building my own credit. Carey met me in Tampa and we flew into Chicago and rented a car. It was fall and the weather was perfect. Michelle's mom hugged us hello at the Holiday Inn. Michelle was in the room adjacent to ours. Her mom had chilled champagne, even though Michelle still didn't drink, and Carey and I didn't hesitate to pour glasses for ourselves. Michelle changed into her dress—a white sundress that Carey remarked later looked more like something you'd wear underneath a wedding dress than an actual wedding dress. She sat in the cheap hotel chair, looking uncomfortable, while everyone else chatted. It was the night before the wedding, and Zak was off with his family. Michelle's mismatched family consisted of us, her mother and her mother's long-time boyfriend, her aunt and a few cousins. We opened more champagne in the hotel room and talked about everything except for the pending wedding.

When the champagne was gone we switched to the airplane bottles of liquor that Kathy had brought with her so that we wouldn't have to raid the hotel's minibar. Michelle's aunt practiced the thick French braid that Michelle planned to wear the next day, piling and weaving Michelle's dark hair and tucking the end up underneath the braid at the nape of her neck.

Somewhere in the haze of too many airplane bottles of different types of liquor, tears, and congratulations, Kathy and I decided that we should call up

Michelle's ex-boyfriend. "He's a sailboat guy," I said. He was the one who she'd dated when she was fourteen and he was eighteen, and he'd cruised the Bahamas with his parents for several years. Now, their boat sat rotting in Indiantown with all the others and he lived in Ohio, which, we calculated, was close enough that he could drive to Wisconsin that night and show up at the wedding the next day.

"You should at least invite him," Kathy said to Michelle.

"Why? I haven't talked to him in years." Michelle kicked her small feet against the chair and pulled at the hem of her dress.

"He was so much better for you than Zak," I said. "He's a boat guy...he understands you better." I squeezed one of the cheap plastic cups in my hand until the plastic cracked into shards, which I pulled apart one by one and tossed into the trash. I didn't know how much I'd had to drink at this point. Carey and Kathy's boyfriend exchanged uneasy glances, and simultaneously stood and excused themselves to the hotel bar downstairs.

"I don't know why you're bringing this up now," Michelle said. "I'm getting married to Zak. Tomorrow. I know what I'm doing."

"I have his phone number somewhere in my purse." Kathy dug through her oversized bag. I had his number too, in the old-fashioned address book that I carried, but I let Kathy do the digging while I searched for something else to drink. I caught a glimpse of myself in the hotel mirror, which had been so poorly cleaned that the corners were thick with dust. I'd changed just as much as Michelle had. I'd cut my hair short and gotten a perm, and the style didn't suit me. I'd done it just for the heck of it, walking into a Hair Cuttery in Ocean City that summer just after one of my daytime boat-detailing shifts and telling them that I wanted them to make me look dramatically different.

"Found it!" Kathy held up an address book similar to mine. We all had cell phones, but storing numbers permanently in them was still something that people didn't do with the regularity that they do now. Kathy picked up her cell phone and dialed.

"What are you doing?" Michelle jumped out of her chair and tried to grab the phone from her mother.

I had the idea to run into the bathroom and Kathy followed, shutting the door and locking Michelle out. In the bleach-smelling Holiday Inn bathroom, I could hear the phone ringing in Kathy's ear and then a far-away voice answering, "Hello?"

"It's Michelle's mom." Kathy hissed it more than she whispered it into the phone. "And Melanie is here with me. Michelle is getting married tomorrow and we want you to come."

There was silence on the other end and then a dramatic sigh. "Does Michelle want me to come?"

"She doesn't know it, but she does...we don't like Zak and we think she's making a mistake," Kathy said. "Let me let you talk to Melanie."

She handed the phone to me and I took it and held I to my ear, not sure what I was feeling. I liked this guy—we'd done a lot of growing up together and he'd taken me sailing in his Hobie Cat, ripping across the harbor in George Town on the face of the cold fronts that had most sane people rushing back to their boats to make sure their anchors were secure. He'd supported the idea of Michelle and me getting our boat. "Hi," I said. Michelle pounded on the door.

"What's going on there?" The ex-boyfriend's voice was friendly and familiar.

"I think maybe you should talk to Michelle," I said, reaching to unlock the door. She stood there red-faced, the French braid unraveling and falling down her shoulders. I handed her the phone and she stormed past me and motioned for her mother and me to leave. She locked the bathroom door behind us and this time we were left on the outside, pressing our ears to the wall and door to hear what was being said.

Michelle murmured into the phone, catching the ex up on her life since meeting Zak and on their plans, and assuring him that he didn't need to come to the wedding. After about ten minutes of Kathy and me looking at each other, letting the gravity of what we'd just done sink in, Michelle opened the door and handed the phone back to her mom. "He's not coming," she said. "And this is my wedding, so if you don't like what I'm doing you don't have to come either. I'm calling Zak to come and get me."

Nobody spoke and time went by and Zak came and got Michelle. Carey came back from the bar and we all went to sleep, and the next morning Michelle and Zak were married under the lighthouse, Michelle in her white sundress and me in my black cocktail dress, mismatched and uncoordinated, with my perm blowing across my cheeks and scratching my face.

Conch Farm

Bahamas • Winter 2001

Age 21

Occasionally, I crewed on the boat Carey captained either up the coast or over to the Bahamas. We made a Bahamas trip in 2001, and I skipped a week of classes to go. Since the owner and his family were staying aboard and were too cheap to pay for rooms ashore for Carey and me, we slept on the flybridge in sleeping bags, the hard fiberglass hurting our backs. We woke in the morning as soon as the sun rose, sweating and scratching mosquito and no-see-'um bites from the night before and nursing hangovers. On these mornings, my dad's anger crept into me and I had to fight the urge to curse at Carey or curse at his cheap-ass boss for not getting us a room.

I stood on the bridge the third day of our trip and guided Carey into the marina at Staniel Cay. Reading the water was a natural skill, and I had trouble understanding why someone wouldn't be able to do it. It was simple—lighter aquamarine meant shallower water, deep purple signaled coral heads, brown meant rocky shoals that could hole a boat if they were hit under any kind of speed. Carey nodded and drove the million-and-a-half dollar boat where I told him.

In a rented Boston Whaler, I took Carey's boss's wife and kids to Compass Cay, where we explored the winding mangrove creek that had been my secret place as a kid. I showed the kids how to spot conch from the surface and dive in after them, and how to tell the fully grown and legally harvestable ones from the small rollers with the spiky shells. We collected enough conch for me to make fritters for all of us that night, and back at the marina at Staniel I cleaned the conch while the Bahamians and the Americans watched me. The Bahamians chuckled at the white girl who cut away the skin with clumsy slices using a dull fillet knife, and the Americans cringed at the slime and crud that caked my nails.

The fritters were a hit, and later that night in the bar I sat and drank a Bailey's on the rocks and listened to the banter of the crowd. Carey's boss was discussing drugs with the locals and the locals schooled around him. I tuned it out and breathed in the smell of oleander and salt and mangroves and buttonwood and marijuana smoke that wrapped around me like home.

Another boat from Palm Beach whose captain Carey vaguely knew had arrived at Staniel that afternoon, and Carey and the captain huddled over their Kalik Gold beers and bitched to each other about their bosses. I was in a sunburned and sleep-deprived daze, half listening to them and half not, when I heard Carey say, "I'll tell you where to get some conch, if you want."

"That would be great," the other captain said.

"You know where Pipe Creek is, right?" Carey drew on the bar's surface as if creating a map.

"Sure."

"Okay. You have to go all the way to the north end, where Compass Cay is," Carey said. "There's a mangrove creek in the harbor there."

I didn't want to listen to the rest of the conversation. I left my drink on the bar and walked out into the night. At the end of the dock, the boat rocked on the gentle waves coming in off the Bahama Banks. I climbed aboard and found my sleeping bag up on the bridge and tried to get to sleep as I played over what had just happened in my mind. One betrayal leads to another... The conch farm that my family had so carefully populated with rollers many years ago, and from which I had harvested on many occasions, was no longer a secret. I had led Carey and his boss's family there for my own selfish reasons—I had wanted to show them what I knew and prove my worth. And I had made the sacred a little bit less so.

Graduation

St. Petersburg, Florida • Spring 2002

Age 22

I graduated college in three years instead of four, because the advanced classes I had taken through BYU were able to transfer and because I took the maximum amount of classes that could be taken. Despite my partying and weekend trips to Palm Beach, I was a good and focused scholar. For my graduation, my parents rented a Cadillac and drove over to St. Petersburg from St. Augustine, where they were staying aboard *Chez Nous* for a short while and visiting Carolyn, who was in her second year at Flagler College.

The Cadillac embarrassed me, as it contradicted the lower-to-middle-class identity that I'd tried to build among my peers. As I often explained to them, "Growing up on a boat didn't mean that we just sailed around to deserted tropical islands and drank pina coladas all day…we washed our own clothes by hand, caught all our own fish, and fixed everything ourselves." My parents parked that Cadillac right in front of my dorm and picked me up the day of graduation to drive me to Tropicana Field, where the ceremony was to be held. My dad combed his hair, even the hair underneath the matted top layer that never got combed, and my mom wore a dress. They sat in the bleachers and yelled and whistled as I walked up to get my diploma, terrified that I would trip in the high heels that I still wasn't used to wearing. They beamed when my name was listed as one of those graduating with high honors, and they ardently shook hands with my favorite professors. They hosted a dinner that night at my favorite beachside restaurant and picked up the bar tab. They were proud—I had almost become a normal, successful contributor to society.

Almost.

BOOK 3

Hurricane Trash

Short Story

The Eastern Shore of Maryland • Summer 2002

Age 22

The bombs were going off in Tangier Sound. At first, they sounded like thunder, but the only clouds were in the opposite direction, hanging over the Delmarva Peninsula, dark and heavy, dumping rain on the chicken farms. The bomb sound was unnerving—the military was testing some kind of explosives in the shallow water west of Crisfield, MD, reminding me how close I was to Washington, DC. I wondered how many blue crabs and rockfish were being killed with each boom.

I looked up from scrubbing the deck of my sailboat, shaded my eyes with my hand, and stared down the dock. I was waiting for my parents.

A month ago, I'd graduated from Eckerd College with a degree in Creative Writing, and three weeks ago I'd gotten my own sailboat. She was a twenty-eight foot Columbia sloop, built in 1969. I was 22 and on my way to Florida International University in Miami for grad school.

Carey and I had driven out from West Ocean City on a Monday afternoon to look at her. We parked his pickup truck in a tow-away zone, not expecting to be there long, and walked down the dock, peering at the name on each sailboat's stern. Most of the boats were old, from the days when their hulls were built with long overhangs and graceful lines. They bobbed as the wake of a crabber rolled beneath them and clapped their rigging against their masts.

My boat was all the way down at the end, looking proud and bigger than her 28 feet. There was a loud crashing sound and a flurry of movement, and a short gray-haired man popped out the companionway hatch. He gave us the look I was used to getting by now: *You're way too young to buy a boat…and you're a girl!* I'd seen it on every face of every man in every marina where I had looked, all up and down the East Coast. I'd been looking for a long time.

The hatch squeaked as he slid it back. "Shit," the man said. He shook his hand and held up his thumb. "Slammed in the hatch," he said.

I introduced myself.

"Marlin," he said, holding out the hand that wasn't hurt. I found out later his name was spelled like the fish and not the actor. People tended to care more about fish than they did about famous people on Maryland's Eastern Shore.

Marlin showed us the boat, told us how he'd lived aboard it for a year in Salisbury. "Had a little heater to keep me warm in the winter," he said. "You can have it if you want."

"I'm taking the boat to Florida if I buy it," I said.

"Florida," he said, rolling the syllables over on his tongue as if they tasted like pineapple. "I don't think she's ever been out of the Chesapeake. Someday my lady and I are going to take our new boat to Florida." He pointed across the dock to a sleek 35-foot Pearson sloop. "I own two boats now," he said. "That's why I really need to get rid of this one."

I didn't need to bargain with him. He dropped the price two thousand dollars before I even made an offer.

Marlin was a welder, and he worked on a chicken farm in Delaware. "I welded these," he said, showing us the two stainless-steel fuel tanks that sandwiched the Honda outboard.

He told us about his new wife, and about how lucky he was to have found someone who loved boats. "It's hard to find someone who wants to be cramped up in such a small space with you," he said. "You guys are lucky."

I didn't say anything. Carey and I would never make it living aboard a sailboat. We weren't planning on it. We'd talked about marriage a few times, casually and only while drinking, but I didn't think that it was in the cards for us. Marlin went on. "We had some good times on this boat. You see the V-berth? I made it into a queen-sized bed. Yup. Had some good times up there." He peered down the hatch at the little V-shaped bed up in the bow of the boat, and his eyes misted over. "You guys are young. You know what I mean."

I tried not to picture Marlin and his wife naked in the V-berth. I was already thinking of it as mine. A few minutes later, I wrote a deposit check for five hundred dollars, pending survey and sea trial.

Short Story was the name I'd chosen for her.

In 2002, the Chesapeake felt familiar to me, but still not like home. Crisfield is one of the many towns on the Bay that depends completely on the water, which might be why the bombing in Tangier Sound irked me so much. The ratio of commercial boats to pleasure boats there was about ten to one. The crabbers and charter fishermen showed up early in the morning, before first light, and they headed out the harbor in a rumble of diesel engines. Everything there was geared to them—the three hardware stores along the main road, the tackle shops, the Captain's Galley restaurant.

I was in the coffin-sized quarter-berth under the cockpit with a spray bottle of X-14 Mildew Remover when my parents arrived. I'd spent the morning cleaning. Marlin had apparently stopped cleaning the boat when he put it up for sale, and it was covered with mildew, inside and out.

I scooted out backwards through the quarter-berth, coughing, threw a long T-shirt dress on over my bikini and climbed out the companionway hatch. They were standing on the dock, my mom loaded down with cameras and my dad with a clipboard, three legal pads, and a canvas bag full of tools and flashlights and whatever he might need in case the boat started to sink right there in its slip. Years of self-sufficiency had taught them to be prepared for anything.

"Well," I said, "here she is." I climbed onto the dock to hug them and stand with them. I wondered what they saw when they looked at my boat, which they had generously paid for as a college graduation gift. I hadn't expected them to pay for the boat, and they surprised me when, after I found the boat I wanted, they asked me where to send a check. This hadn't been discussed and I hadn't asked for it, but in the fashion of my parents they gave unexpectedly and unceremoniously. Perhaps the underlying message was: *now that you have gone to college and are bound for grad school, we feel like you have finally made something of your life and so we'll give you what you have always wanted.* I wondered whether they saw a trap, a leaky little ship into which I would end up sinking every penny I made, or whether they saw her the way I did: a smaller version of *Chez Nous*, something that felt more familiar to me than any house or apartment or town ever would.

There was still a lot more cleaning to do, but the ugly green mildew spots were gone. The wake from a crabber made my boat jump a little in her slip, like she was ready to go, and her white hull reflected the Crisfield water in zigzag ripples. The blue boot stripe and the toe rail framed the slender overhangs at the bow and stern. She looked like a combination of all the boats I had dreamed about while I was growing up—classy but practical, slender but roomy. Beautiful.

"It looks big," my mom finally said. "Are you sure it's only 28 feet?"

"It's a big 28," I said.

"I remember these boats," my dad said, after going over it with his eyes, walking around to look at it from different angles. One of his best friends had worked for the Columbia yard in Virginia in the seventies, right after my boat was built, and my parents had even thought about getting a bigger Columbia when they bought the Gulfstar 47.

"It's amazing nobody's gotten electrocuted," Dad said, when he lifted one of the hatches to expose the batteries and the back of the electrical panel. He pointed his flashlight into the rat's nest of wires. I swallowed a small lump in my throat. There were a lot of things wrong with the boat, and I knew my dad would find them all. Partially out of habit but mostly out of concern for me, he would catalogue everything that could catch fire, leak, or cause the boat to sink, and he would methodically remind me to fix them and help me fix what I needed help fixing.

Eager to show them the things I'd already repaired, I pointed forward to the enclosed head, where I'd installed a new marine toilet. In the past three weeks, I had installed a new bilge pump, replaced most of the plumbing, which involved sending pressurized water up to the sink in the head, and installed a shore-power plug. I was still working summers at the bait and tackle shop in West Ocean City, MD, and driving to Crisfield every time I had a day or an evening off.

Back out on the dock, Dad made a list of some of the things that needed to be done. *Install 12-volt refrigeration. Fix wiring. Replace rigging.* All of this would have to be done by the middle of August, when the boat was scheduled to be trucked to South Florida.

Dad promised to help me sail across the Chesapeake in a couple of weeks to Narrows Marina, where the new *Chez Nous* was docked. Even though their boat was twenty-five years old and they had owned it for four years, I still thought of it as new.

After my parents left, I made myself busy working on the boat. I worked best by myself. Carey had helped me with some of the projects, which I appreciated, but without anyone around I was faster and more efficient. I liked walking from hardware store to hardware store on Crisfield's main street, looking for the right part or fitting, and wondering what the crabbers and fishermen thought when they saw me carrying old fuel hose over my shoulder. Had I been a man, they wouldn't have paid me any attention, and sometimes I envied men for the freedom that they had to move through the world. I enjoyed my femininity. I liked to wear make-up and dresses, and I was vain about my thick hair. But men could eat alone at restaurants and sit alone at bars without receiving stares or unwanted advances. And men who slept around weren't called sluts.

I was silent while I was there, talking only as much as necessary to make a purchase, content to live entirely within myself while I was on my boat. I fit inside her perfectly, my five-foot body with its sturdy curves resting on the settee or ducking under the boom. Sometimes while I was in Crisfield I felt like I was watching myself from somewhere overhead: a young girl with her blond hair chopped at her shoulders and sweat running down her neck and between her breasts. I felt like I was watching myself become the person I wanted to be.

Carey came out to the boat with me a few times, and we wrestled with hoses in the bilge, ran wires up and down the length of the boat, and drank beer and tried to figure out the boat's systems. But when he wasn't there I was happy to be alone.

That night, after my parents went home, I lay in *Short Story's* V-berth and listened to the bombs go off in Tangier Sound. It sounded like the end of the world, but I felt like it was the beginning.

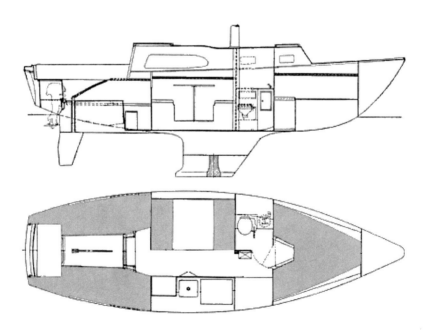

Maiden Voyages

Virginia and Florida • Summer 2002

Age 22

When Dad met me in Crisfield to help take the boat over to Narrows, it was a hot morning and flies buzzed and gathered on the dock where someone had left a piece of bait or landed a fish. The seagulls were quiet and the water was still, and by 7 AM it was already close to ninety degrees. Mom dropped him off and helped him carry his tools down the dock. I had the Honda engine running to warm up and had gotten the boat as ready as I could. The sailcovers were off, which, I thought, was probably a little optimistic considering that there wasn't any wind, and I'd chilled iced tea and Gatorade in a cooler and prepared turkey sandwiches ahead of time. It would be a full day's trip, even under power, and I wanted to be sure I had thought of everything.

As we left the harbor and glided into Tangier Sound, it occurred to me that this was the first time since my dad and I had taken delivery of the new *Chez Nous* that we had been alone together on a boat. And this boat was much smaller. I wondered what he thought of me now. I had finished college, which seemed to be the thing that he had wanted for me most and the thing that makes most parents forgive their kids for all the stupid or self-destructive shit they've done in the past. I'd been accepted into every graduate Creative Writing program that I applied to (most likely because I had applied to the ones that I thought were attainable), and had decided on Florida International University's Master of Fine Arts program because it had famous Florida mystery writers, whose work I admired, as faculty. I'm sure Dad would have rather me have gone to law school or medical school, but since he'd had a successful second career as a writer he couldn't very easily advise me not to make writing my first career.

An hour out, the outboard sputtered and died. We drifted in the wide open stretch of water as I searched the outboard's carburetor for the small screws that would adjust the air flow and therefore the amount of gas that was pulled through the contraption. "Dirty jets," Dad said, as I started the engine back up and kept the choke engaged longer than I normally would.

"Yup. Easy enough to fix, right? We just need to get to Narrows."

"You've fixed an engine or two before." Dad smiled and sat back in the comfortable cockpit, and I noticed for the first time what a small man he was— thin spindly legs and arms, graying hair where the matted brown used to be, shorter than average height. He seemed perfectly content, even on a 28-foot sailboat with engine problems in the middle of Tangier Sound. "Did I ever tell you about the time I got stuck on Tangier?" he asked.

He had, but we talked about it again anyway. As a boy, he'd taken his skiff out from West Point and somehow found his way out the York River and all the way across the Chesapeake, where he'd broken down on Tangier Island. He'd had to stay a few days until the part for his outboard was shipped in. His mother was frantic.

The outboard sputtered and cut off a few more times, but finally whatever dirt was blocking the carburetor seemed to push through and it ran smoothly. When we reached the Bay the wind picked up just enough to put the mainsail up, and I had Dad hold the boat into the wind as I stood on top of the cabin and pulled on the halyard to raise the sail. It was easy work, and I was learning that most things that required physical labor were easier on a small boat than a large one like *Chez Nous*. After motorsailing for an hour, we put the jib up and cut the motor and cruised along under sail. With very little wind, the handheld GPS that Dad had brought clocked us at 2.5 knots.

It would have been a good time for us to talk about the ugly things that stood between us, but we didn't. The part of me that wanted closure and acceptance wasn't as strong as the part of me that just wanted everything to be okay, and I was beginning to realize that maybe you never really got closure. It was better to live in harmony and to love and appreciate my father for the work that he'd done and the story he had told about our lives.

Short Story was picked up by truck in the middle of August and Mom and I followed the truck down to Florida in my station wagon (the Shadow's replacement). I would have liked to have made the trip down the Intracoastal, but my jobs in Ocean City were too lucrative to justify taking the month off. Plus I was afraid that the trip would take longer than planned and that I would miss my first week of classes at FIU.

The truck pulled into a boatyard in a residential section of Fort Lauderdale and Mom and I parked and watched as the truckers, a husband and wife team who did an excellent job, inspected the boat and transitioned her into the boatyard's travel lift, a large piece of industrial machinery that lifts vessels by positioning straps underneath them and then wheels them to the launch where they are dropped into the water. *Short Story* was covered in road dirt and stripped of all her rigging, and everything was tied and strapped down to endure the hurricane-force winds of the interstate.

Fort Lauderdale was hot, but the tropical smells and the humid Gulf Stream air made me feel alive as I watched my sailboat being placed into the New River. I hopped aboard and started the engine to move the boat over to the slip where she would stay for a couple of days while we put everything back together and got ready for the trip down to Maule Lake Marina in North Miami Beach.

"Let's get the air conditioning on," Mom said, as she stepped aboard and climbed down the companionway. A carpenter friend of my parents had fashioned a brace that fit into the bottom part of the companionway and into which you could fit a small window-unit AC system. As long as it was tilted so that the condensation ran out into the cockpit rather than into the cabin, it cooled the boat perfectly and was one of those genius things that I could never have lived aboard a small boat in South Florida without. We turned it on and relaxed for the first time in days as the cool air filled the cabin. I looked around the inside of the boat and admired it—the small settee was an efficient use of space on the port side of the main salon, and a fully enclosed head was positioned just forward of the settee. The whole starboard side was dedicated to the galley, where the two-burner alcohol stove sat atop a custom cutout where Marlin had installed a microwave, forward of which was a small sink and then an icebox which my parents had converted into a refrigerator for me. Then there was a hanging locker, and then the V-berth—my comfortable, cozy, book-lined V-berth that had an insert placed between the berths making one end into a queen-sized bed while the other end tapered into a V at the anchor locker in the bow. Two brass reading lamps and a small shelf on which sat a CD player completed the room where I would sleep for the next five years.

Short Story's twin quarter-berths were packed with stuff—the books and clothes and belongings that I hadn't quite figured out where to store, and my mom's travel bags. But otherwise, the small boat was uncluttered, clean and comfortable inside. Mom and I cracked open a bottle of warm white wine to celebrate our landing in South Florida. "I'm envious of you," Mom said.

"I'm envious of me too," I said.

Sometime that evening, it occurred to me that I should check the bilge to make sure that it was still dry. Unlike most bilges, *Short Story's* had always been bone-dry, with the keel bolts firmly and solidly attached. I pulled up the floorboard in the main salon and peered in. There was about four inches of water in my boat's bilge. "What the hell?" I grabbed a flashlight off the counter and looked again, dipping my hand into the water and licking my finger just to be sure it was salt water and not the result of a leaky fresh water tank. It tasted salty.

Mom was staring too, and she repeated the dipping-and-licking just to verify my diagnosis. "Could the keel bolts have loosened on the drive?"

"You know, I did see some rust stains that I don't think were there before," I said. I'd seen them and pretended not to—streaks of rusty water that seemed to have appeared out of nowhere on the boat's keel.

"Well, let's pump it out and see what happens," Mom said. So we did, and a few hours later the water level had risen again. We pumped again, and dried the area and the bolts meticulously. I held a flashlight and watched as water pooled in the tiny cracks around the bolts and beaded up from out of nowhere in the bilge.

"It looks like it's just kind of seeping in from everywhere," I said. I sat on the floor and felt my heart sink and my mind start to jump from one scenario to another—my new boat would sink with my mother and me aboard, we'd have to be rescued halfway to Maule Lake, and I'd miss my first week of classes at grad school because I'd be stuck in a boatyard. I was supposed to meet with the faculty member I'd been assigned to for my teaching assistantship the next day, a professor named Dan Wakefield, about whom I knew nothing except that I would be helping him teach a large lecture class on the literature and culture of New York City during the 1950s. I didn't know anything about New York during the 1950s, but the Beats were appealing to me.

Mom and I slept for a few short hours and in the morning the water level had risen to about six inches. She told me that she would take care of things while I went and met with my professor, so I showered in the marina showers while wearing my flip flops and changed into an outfit that I deemed somewhat professional—a skirt and blouse and low heels. I drove to North Miami Beach and stopped at Maule Lake on my way to drop off my check for the first month's dockage. The marina's owner eyed me in a suspicious but bored way, as if he'd seen every type imaginable walk through the office doors to drop off that first month's rent.

At FIU, Dan Wakefield welcomed me into his office and told me how much he'd loved my thesis from undergrad, a novella named "Divers," which I had used as my writing sample for my grad school applications. It was about a married woman who worked at a bait shop in West Ocean City, Maryland, and had an affair with the guy who delivered ice to the shop. It was thick with imagery and the rough details of life in the Commercial Harbor. "It seemed like it was written by someone much older," Professor Wakefield told me. He was in his seventies and the class was based on his personal experience as a writer coming of age in New York City during the fifties. He told me to call him Dan and gave me a pile of books to read and things to photocopy for our first class, which would be next week. I liked him immensely.

Back at the boat, Mom greeted me with an encouraging smile. "I talked to Dad," she said. "He's heard of this kind of thing before, in another cruising boat. He hired a friend to come out tomorrow morning and help us with the fix. We have a list of things we need to buy first though."

She explained the fix—we'd be taking automotive grease fittings and tapping them into the fiberglass around the keel bolts. Then, with a grease gun, we'd inject heavy duty marine caulking into the glass through the grease fittings. Theoretically, it would seep in through the cracks in the fiberglass and fill the spaces through which the water was leaking. The boatyard had suggested that we haul the boat and have the keel dropped and new bolts embedded into the fiberglass, a fix that would cost, they estimated, $5,000. On a boat that had cost $6,000, this didn't seem like a good idea. I was already paying the yard a fortune to step the mast, and had just spent $2,000 having the boat shipped, so my cash supply was dwindling.

Mom and I drove around Fort Lauderdale, visiting the same marine supply and automotive shops where Dad and I had searched for parts for the old generator we had rebuilt years ago. We were greeted with the typical condescending offers of help that women who enter such establishments usually receive: "Do you know what you're looking for?" and "Are you sure that's what you want?"

The heat was thick and we sucked down large iced coffees from Dunkin Donuts, loaded with sugar and cream. We drove up and down State Road 84, walking through Boat Owner's Warehouse and Sailorman in our cutoffs and flip flops, speaking easily together about small projects that still needed to be done to the boat.

The next day, we had already screwed the grease fittings into the bilge when my dad's friend showed up to help us. The three of us crouched on the cabin sole of *Short Story* and took turns squeezing the thick caulking into the fittings, watching as beads of it popped up from small cracks in the fiberglass inches away from where it had entered.

"It's doing what it's supposed to do," Mom said. We shot more and more in through the fittings until we'd emptied three large tubes of caulking into *Short Story's* bilge.

The leaking stopped, and Mom and I left the boatyard for Maule Lake early in the morning, before the heat was too oppressive. I drove, navigating the winding path of the New River, passing through drawbridges that opened on the hour and half hour and staying out of the way of the megayachts and tugs and working vessels that made up the everyday traffic on the New River. We crossed the inlet at Port Everglades, which we had passed through many times before aboard *Chez Nous*, and it felt strange to me not to turn and head out to sea. Because one of the bridges in Miami was too short for our mast, we had never taken *Chez Nous* through the stretch of the Intracoastal between Fort Lauderdale and Miami, so passing Port Everglades and heading on through Dania and Hollywood and Aventura was like going someplace entirely new.

The turn off the Intracoastal into Maule Lake was so small it could have been easily missed. We motored up a small canal between condos, which opened into a wide lake, spotted with anchored boats and lined with mangroves. The white concrete pilings of the marina were easy to spot, and with *Short Story's* bow pointed in their direction Mom and I made the dock lines ready and placed fenders out on either side of the boat. As I took us into the slip on B-dock, idling the motor and coasting most of the way in, I noticed the people gathered in small groups on the dock. They offered to help with the lines, and then they walked away, looking over their shoulders and pondering the mother-daughter team that had just expertly navigated into their world.

Celia in Miami

Miami, Florida • Fall 2002
Age 22

Fuck, it's hot, I thought. The sheets bunched around my feet, up at the end of the V-berth where Celia's feet rested, one on top of the other, touching mine because there was no way to avoid touching in a bed as small as the one on *Short Story*. Her legs were tangled in the sheets, and the full moon coming through the open forward hatch cast a swath of light across the bed and over her breasts. I wished she would cover them up and I wished she wouldn't.

The South Florida September heat barely lifted at night. I flipped onto my back and imagined waking Celia up and taking her out to the cockpit, and going for a night swim in the Oleta River or pouring buckets of salt water over each other until we cooled off. I wondered whether *Short Story's* anchor was holding. It had seemed to set just fine. We'd anchored directly off the Florida International University campus, where the Oleta River fed into Biscayne Bay. We'd had martinis for lunch and wine for dinner.

Celia had driven over from St. Petersburg to see me. She was younger than me and had seemed so naïve when I'd given her shots of tequila in the dorm at Eckerd College. She still had a goddess body.

She was out cold from the wine. She mumbled something I couldn't understand and turned to face me, her breasts spilling onto the sheets and her brown hair softly wrapping around them. I wanted to reach out and touch her and run my hands along her soft and glowing skin. *Short Story* spun on her anchor chain as the current shifted in the anchorage, and a night heron called somewhere in the mangroves. I pulled myself out of bed, careful not to wake her, and climbed out the companionway. I sat in the cockpit and looked at the night sky—too bright with the moon and the city lights of Miami. Ashore, the cars hummed as they rolled by on U.S. 1, just west of the FIU campus. I took a bearing on one of the buildings and a city light behind it and watched for them to move in relation to each other. But they didn't. *Short Story's* anchor was fixed to the bottom.

I could have folded the settee down into a bed and made Celia sleep there.

I could have put her in the quarterberth. But the V-berth was the most comfortable place on the boat. My mother and I had shared it only weeks earlier. However, Celia and my mother were two very different people, and I didn't think I'd be able to get back to sleep up there with her. I drifted off in the cockpit.

I woke up sweating at seven in the morning. Celia was still asleep, so I moved around on the deck as softly as I could. I pulled in the anchor line, hand over hand, coiling it on the bow, until the remaining line met the water at a right angle and the anchor was directly underneath the hull and still buried in the sand below. I slipped back to the stern and started the outboard, idling it as low as it would go without dying, and returned to the bow to pull the anchor the rest of the way up. I leaned back against the weight of the line, expecting to feel the soft pop as the anchor let go of the sand.

Nothing happened. I rested a few seconds and tried again. I'd put the anchor down while the boat was in the slip and pulled it back up, just for practice, and the anchor and chain together weighed no more than 40 pounds. I leaned over the bow and looked at the white nylon line where it disappeared into the murk. I didn't want to have to dive on it.

"Hi," Celia said. She sat on the cabin in her bikini top and gym shorts, brown strings of her hair clinging to her cheeks. "I think I got attacked last night." She smoothed her hands over her thighs, which were red with mosquito bites.

"I'm sorry. We should have stayed at the dock."

"No, I'm glad we got to take the boat out." She cupped her hand over her mouth and yawned. "I feel like I know you a lot better now. I've seen you doing what you do best and what you love to do, and it's beautiful."

"We're stuck," I said. "I can't get the anchor up."

"I'm sure you can."

I braced my legs against the bow pulpit and pulled again, stretching the line so tight I wondered if it would snap. After a few more yanks, it gave a few inches and I could see the chain where it was spliced to the nylon. Celia stood next to me and stared into the water. A dusky angular shape had appeared just beneath the chain.

"What do you think it is?" Celia asked.

"I can't tell." I pulled at the anchor some more and the thing rose a few more inches. "I'm going to get into the dink and see if I can get a better grip on it." I cleated off the line and brought the dinghy around from the stern. Celia watched as I climbed in and kneeled in the bilge, keeping my center of gravity low for stability. I reached into the water, leaning so far that it came up to my shoulders, and grabbed the anchor line. Tiny bubbles formed on my arm hairs and let go, spinning to the surface. I leaned back into the dink and pulled the line in a few more inches. "Can you take in the slack?" I held the line with every muscle in my body and watched Celia wrap the line around *Short Story's* small cleat.

After a few more heaves and wraps, I could see the anchor and the thing it had snagged—a tangle of old lines covered in barnacles and muck, all wrapped neatly around an underwater cable. It looked less ominous near the surface. "What do you think it's from?" Celia handed me the boat hook before I had a chance to ask.

"Probably somebody else caught their anchor on that cable and just cut it loose. Or maybe it's from a sunk boat." I wondered how many boats had been abandoned and sunk or lost in hurricanes in the murky waters of northern Biscayne Bay and Maule Lake as I pried at the cable with my boathook. Celia dropped the anchor a few feet while I held the cable and *Short Story* was free.

We pulled back into the slip at Maule Lake Marina half an hour later, both sweaty and needing showers. Celia handled the dock lines like a pro. I watched her duck beneath the shrouds as she walked one of the spring lines to the cleat on the stern. Thunderclouds hung over the Everglades to the west, rumbling and announcing themselves even though it was still too early in the morning for the storms I'd come to expect every day during the South Florida summer.

A small crowd of men had gathered on the dock in front of *Short Story*. I wondered why they hadn't offered to catch our lines—the standard marina code of conduct—but it didn't bother me.

"Did ya'll have fun?" The oldest one was slightly overweight and had a white Hemingway beard. His jeans were held up with green suspenders, and he smiled as he stepped closer to my boat and did the same thing I always did when I saw a boat I'd never seen before: he looked up at the top of the mast and scanned down, taking in the lines and probably calculating hull speed and the year she was built and all the rest of the specs. "I'm Rob," he said. "That's my boat." He pointed to the beautiful ketch in the slip next to me.

I introduced myself and Celia and told him he had a gorgeous boat.

"Where'd you go?" The second man was younger, but gaunt and unhealthy looking. A mangy black dog sat on the dock next to him and scratched its neck.

"Um, we anchored off FIU for the night," I said, suddenly aware that I had nothing on but a faded bikini top and cutoff jeans. I pulled the jeans down over my thighs where they tended to creep up and stick to my skin when it was hot out.

"That's a pretty anchorage," Rob said. The rest of them, five in all, stood back and nodded.

"We got the anchor caught on a cable, but other than that it was nice." I hopped into the dink to bail it and tie it up properly.

"So are you here for the long run?" The skinny one with the dog sat down and swung his feet over the dock.

"Depends on how long that is," I said.

"Well...I've been here eight years now. Some people have been here for twenty."

"Not that long," I said. "Just until I finish school. A few years."

"What are you studying?" Rob asked.

I decided I would call him Captain Rob. "Creative writing," I said.

"You'll have a lot to write about here," said the skinny one. "See that boat over on A-dock?" He pointed to a weirdly misshapen Catalina 22 that looked like the hull had been chopped in half and then built up for more headroom. "That guy's a male prostitute. I mean, for guys."

"Oh?" I looked at the boat and Celia followed my gaze. I would have to befriend the male prostitute and find out for sure. I'd seen him, a young Latino, climbing on and off his boat late at night, and he seemed friendly enough.

"And the people on that houseboat are the ones who've been here for twenty years. They're nuts," he said. "But most everyone on this dock is okay. This is the high-class neighborhood."

"That's why they stuck you over on C," Captain Rob said.

"As soon as a slip opens up here, we're moving. Right?" The skinny guy rubbed the black dog behind its ears.

They stood there and watched as Celia and I finished stowing everything and hosed the salt and grime off the deck. I wondered how much more they wanted to ask, like what was a 22-year-old woman doing with her own boat, and what had happened between Celia and me out in the anchorage. They'd be disappointed by the truth, I thought. And I was a little disappointed too. Would things have been different if I hadn't fought the urge to touch her?

Celia drove home that afternoon and I sat on the dock and drank a Miller Lite with Captain Rob. "There's a lot of history here," he said. "This place was one of the busiest drug-running spots in the eighties. There used to be high-speed chases out in the lake, and everyone knew Tuna's was the place to go for a party," He pointed at the marina restaurant. "I wasn't here then."

I did more listening than talking, and Maule Lake started to grow on me.

That night, the band at Tuna's was just loud enough so I could hear it from *Short Story's* V-berth, and the lights in the marina parking lot filtered though the hatch, illuminating the cabin. But something was scraping at the bottom of the boat. I tried to close my eyes and ignore it.

It went away for a few minutes and then came back, just below my head. I grabbed the flashlight I kept next to the V-berth and slowly opened the forward hatch and pulled myself through, hooking my arms over the flange and wiggling my body onto the foredeck. Flat on my stomach, I inched to the side of the boat and waited until I heard it again. I swung the beam of my flashlight into the water and leaned out so I could see. A prehistoric looking boxfish, with octagonal scales and tiny fins, stared sideways at me and went back to pecking at the hull. I stared at it for a few minutes, an eerie feeling creeping over me, thinking: *This place is so strange. But it feels right. The people here don't fit in with the rest of the world but they fit here. This place is perfect for me.*

Love Spell

North Miami Beach, Florida • Spring and Summer 2004
Age 24

Life at Maule Lake wasn't defined by the regular patterns that dictate most people lives. My class schedule was irregular. I took classes and taught classes. When I wasn't at FIU, I was working on the boat or sleeping or writing or drinking on the dock. There was always a party, always a grill going on someone's boat, always a bottle of rum or wine. I tried dating from time to time, but there really wasn't anybody who understood my way of life. It was a careless and independent existence.

When a grad school friend of mine explained, at a party, that he had just paid off all his credit card debt and put a down payment on a condo by borrowing the maximum amount of subsidized and unsubsidized Federal student loans that he could ("It's practically free money," he said), I filled out my FAFSA and applied for loans. I'd intended on living just off of the stipend from my teaching assistantship, but $10,000 a year didn't quite cut it. I should have taken on an extra job, and I did take on extra classes, teaching whatever sections of English Composition that I could as an adjunct during summer terms, but the temptation of "practically free money" was more than I could resist. I borrowed the maximum amount from Sallie Mae and never thought twice.

In 2004 I tried online dating and met a man from Rhode Island. We discovered that we'd crossed paths when I was fifteen and he'd been working at a marina where my family had docked. I vaguely remembered having a small crush on him that summer. Buck and his wife were separated and I was certain that the divorce was just around the corner. We spent a long weekend in the ground-floor apartment of a house on a canal in the Keys, and every day we ran out along the reefs in a small Boston Whaler. Buck didn't believe me when I told him I could freedive 50 feet, so he dropped me in 55 feet of water and asked me to return with something from the bottom. When I returned with a small limestone rock, he was waiting for me, gray eyes sparkling. He grabbed me by the waist and pulled me towards him, gently removing my snorkel for a kiss.

Buck speared a hog snapper later that day, and I watched as he swam up through water that was almost as clear as the water in the Bahamas. The fish trailed behind him, dangling on the spear and thrashing as its blood spread ink-like through the water around it. Three barracudas circled underneath Buck, following him to the surface and inching closer to the snapper with each foot of ascension. The water was deep, maybe forty feet, and I had seen Buck follow the snapper under a ledge, his broad back small underneath all that water. I'd watched him aim and release the speargun, a contraption that I had never used as they were illegal in the Bahamas. And, as the barracudas followed him up to the surface and I watched through the hazy blue water, I fell in love.

In the evenings at the house in the Keys, we drank Captain Morgan and Diet Coke with the juice of fresh key limes, and I wrapped whatever fish we had caught that day in foil and cooked it Bahamian-style with peppers and onions. Buck was in his thirties but had the look of a much older man. His skin was weathered and he had a beard that he wore like an old salt. He was reserved by nature but talkative with me, and I was convinced that after all this time I had met the man I was meant to be with.

But the marriage wasn't as close to ending as I thought, and as he made plans to move back to Rhode Island to be with his wife I summoned up all of my mental energy in my yoga and meditation practice to offer out to the universe in an attempt to change his course. Tammy, my best friend from the marina, and I drove to a botanica in Little Haiti where we purchased the various accoutrements of a Santeria love spell. The dark and heavy woman behind the counter stared expressionless at the two white blond women who browsed through the books and charms and figures and oils.

Sitting in *Short Story's* small cabin with candles, a photograph, oils, a small fish figurine and a piece of Buck's hair laid out on the table in front of me, I drank Captain Morgan and Diet Coke and considered what I was doing. Didn't I have just as much a right as the next person to practice a religion that wasn't mine? My sister and I had been raised to respect other peoples' religions, and on several Easter Sundays we'd attended service at the Baptist Church on Staniel Cay. But religion had never been a consistent thing in our lives, so as far as I was concerned all religion was fair game. I believed in some kind of higher power, but would never have called it God.

The spell didn't work, and the meditation didn't work. Buck and his wife stayed together and I was miserable. I fell while jogging in the Oleta River State Park and fractured a bone in my elbow shortly afterwards, and I couldn't help wondering if karma was getting back at me for giving away so much of myself to try to win the love of this man who was never mine to begin with. Or maybe this was my payback for fooling around with a religion I knew little about. Cursing and holding my elbow close to my body, I drove myself, one-handed, to the FIU clinic where they sent me off to the emergency room. I finished my final papers for the semester typing with my left hand and high on painkillers. That summer, I taught a few classes and tried to work on my thesis. I drank boxed wine at lunch every day and moved to rum in the evening. It was a rough time and I hardly remember that summer.

Fall came, and I got a paid internship for the Miami Book Fair. I woke up at seven every morning to drive to downtown Miami and sit in a cubicle at Miami Dade College. This was my second real office experience, and it wasn't as dreary as the office of *Cruising World* had seemed when I was fifteen. The people around me talked about books and art, sometimes in English and sometimes in Spanish. I started to pick up a few words and phrases in Spanish and started to feel more comfortable with the city of Miami. The office was right downtown, in the Wolfson building of what was then Miami Dade Community College, and the Latin kids on their way to and from classes were fresh-faced and smart. They wore trendy shoes and glowed with the hope of boom-time in South Florida. They were future businessmen and businesswomen who dreamt of condos overlooking Biscayne Bay and luxury hybrid vehicles. Café con leche and empanadas were the fuel of choice for us all, and I brimmed over with awe as I made travel arrangements for famous (although sometimes finicky) writers. It was an election year, and I attended a John Kerry rally with my classmates in Bayfront Park. Miami was all optimism in 2004.

On the last day of the book fair, Buck called me to tell me he was passing through town and wanted to know if I cared to meet up for dinner. I braced myself and pretended to be over him and I told him no. I sat on a bench as dark fell on downtown Miami and wondered what would have happened if I had said yes.

Hurricanes Frances and Jeanne

Fort Pierce, Florida • Summer and Fall 2004

Age 25

It was September, 2004, in the short weeks between hurricanes Frances and Jeanne, and my body was on autopilot. I took the Orange Avenue exit off I-95, slowing my small Mazda (my third car, since the Shadow had been rear-ended and totaled and the station wagon had blown a head gasket) to twenty miles per hour above the posted speed limit on the exit ramp. I didn't think about what I was doing there. I was following some kind of gut instinct, the kind that people try to forget that they have.

The marinas around Fort Pierce had reportedly lost over forty boats in Frances. People were without electricity and water for weeks. Roofs had blown off of houses and businesses. None of the gas stations had any fuel left. The green road signs along I-95 were warped and twisted. I could read some of them; most of them I couldn't.

Hurricane Ivan was making its way towards the U.S., having already swept over parts of the Caribbean. It was projected to hit Cuba, then take a slight turn west into the Gulf of Mexico, but the different models showed it making landfall anywhere between the Gulf Coast of Alabama and Miami.

I had taken the sails off of *Short Story* for Frances, tied extra dock lines to pilings two slips away, and hauled my dinghy out of the water and set it ashore. (It was promptly stolen after the storm.) I had removed my computer, my Coast Guard license, a few unfinished writing projects, insurance papers, some photo albums, Grandmom June's engagement ring (the only nice piece of jewelry I owned), and my dog. I went to a friend's apartment in Hollywood and waited for the storm to be over. Now that Ivan was on the way, I had decided to get out of South Florida.

I hadn't planned on stopping in Fort Pierce. I was headed to St. Augustine, to stay with Carolyn for a few days. She was getting close to graduating from Flagler College, and had taken root in the small, historic city. I left Miami around noon, and by two I was trying to find my way to downtown Fort Pierce. I felt guilty for being there. The people I passed stared straight ahead with blank, shocked faces, and I thought they looked like they were waiting for nature to reverse itself somehow, for the winds to come back and blow their roofs back on, to fix their windows and unflood their houses.

I stopped across from the City Marina, not wanting to park too close. I wasn't sure why—maybe because I didn't want anybody to see me. This was about me, and I didn't feel like running into my parents' friends or friends of mine from my days with Carey in the sport fishing circuit. I unloaded Stella, the beagle I had ended up with one year into grad school the same the summer I broke up with Carey, and shuffled over to the marina.

Chez Nous was supposed to be here somewhere. The new owners had emailed my dad after Frances, telling him that *Chez Nous* (now *Sea Fox*) had been damaged in the storm and that they were waiting until the marina cleared the other damaged boats out of the way so they could move it into a yard for repairs. I hadn't seen the boat since New Years Day 1999. I wasn't sure if I wanted to see it now, but something had made me turn off at Orange Avenue and drive down to the water.

Stella and I made our way across the marina. The air was oppressive and sweet with dead fish. I felt the dust lodging behind my contact lenses, and my legs itched. Stella started coughing violently, bracing her paws on the dock. A small group of people from the tiki bar stared.

"It's okay," I said. "She's asthmatic." She wasn't, but this was an easy explanation that seemed to work whenever her trachea collapsed in public. You learn how to make excuses very quickly when you own a beagle.

There was yellow tape strung across the entrance to the dock office, and beyond the office more yellow tape blocked off the dock. I wondered whether the police thought the tape would really be enough to keep boat owners away. I ducked under it and listened for an alarm or siren or somebody to yell at me and tell me that it was unsafe to proceed.

Right after hurricane Andrew, my family had docked at Chub Cay in the Berry Islands. Andrew had passed over the Bahamas before it ripped into South Florida, doing as much or more damage to the unprotected islands as it did to Homestead. At Chub, dogs and cats lay dead all over the marina, electrocuted from walking into puddles of water charged with electricity from the live wires that stuck out of the ground, sometimes as invisible as blades of grass. The marina had smelled worse than rotting fish. It smelled like people's dead pets. We stayed aboard *Chez Nous*, my parents assuring my sister and me that it would be just as easy for one of us to be electrocuted and killed as it had been for the rotting dogs and cats.

I thought about this as I stepped over a huge gap in the concrete dock and around a puddle, leading Stella on a short leash. *Chez Nous* was right on the other side of the dock, with her bow to the marina office. I couldn't think of her as *Sea Fox*, for some reason. There was nothing wrong with the new name, and the new owners had lived aboard and treated her well, but a new name couldn't erase the nineteen years of history between this boat and me.

Behind her, boats were piled on top of each other. A large motoryacht, maybe 65 feet long, sat with her whale-like belly and one of her props on the neighboring dock. A few of the floating docks had broken up, and wedges of concrete filled the spaces between hulls as snugly as if they belonged there. The scene was like a puzzle, with fiberglass and concrete and twisted metal wrapped intricately together. In the middle of the puzzle, *Chez Nous* held her proud bow over the dock.

Her mast was crooked, because the whole boat had been pushed sideways by a piece of dock, but she was the most intact piece of fiberglass there.

I braced myself, wondering what it feels like to be electrocuted, then reached for *Chez Nous'* stainless-steel bow rail. I couldn't see any live wires, but you can never be sure. I figured if it was my time to go, then I would have to accept my fate, and I hoped that, if I got electrocuted, somebody would rescue Stella.

Nothing happened. The rail was cold and smooth, but not charged. I tied Stella's leash to it and stepped aboard, over the anchor windlass and around the roller furling gear.

I made my way back to the cockpit, and checked to see whether the companionway hatch was locked. I knew that going inside would be officially considered breaking and entering, but I was ready to go to jail if necessary. It was locked. I rattled the padlock and looked around for a key, but gave up when a sudden wave of guilt swept over me. This wasn't my boat. I had no right to be here.

I left the cockpit and went back to the stern, where the worst of the damage was. The stern rail was twisted off, and the starboard davit had been ripped out of the hull. It had been attached with bolts to a heavy backing plate, but the plate had been pulled straight through the fiberglass, leaving a jagged hole almost a foot across. My dad had installed the davits the second year we went south, to hold the Boston Whaler skiff that we later replaced with an ugly-as-hell but practical and tough aluminum dinghy.

Still, the damage wasn't too bad. Every other boat in the marina seemed to be worse. The boat right behind *Chez Nous* had a smaller boat on top of it, the bow pulpit of one rammed into the cabin windows of the other. The damage on *Chez Nous* was cosmetic—nothing that couldn't be repaired. I wondered if it would be feasible for me to buy the boat, dirt cheap, and spend a few years fixing it up. But I only had about a hundred dollars in the bank, and I had at least two more years of school ahead of me. Stella howled from the bow, and I made my way back to her.

Back in my car, on the way to St. Augustine, I called my parents to tell them about the boat, and about how the damage wasn't too bad.

Ivan hit the Gulf Shore of Alabama, bringing the whole ocean with him, and I drove home to Miami only to prepare for the next hurricane. I didn't know that, in Grenada, Cole and his family were surveying the damage to their boats, washed ashore by Ivan. I learned this later, when I found a website they had created to show the damage to the boats.

Jeanne hit the Bahamas and then, when everyone thought she was heading out to sea where she would lose steam and die, she made an unprecedented loop, crossed back over her original path, and hit Fort Pierce in the middle of the night. I slept through the storm in my friend's apartment in Hollywood.

Chez Nous was one of the last boats to be pulled out of the marina between Frances and Jeanne. She, along with several others, was towed out and anchored in the river the day before Jeanne hit. There wasn't enough time to get her to the boatyard.

In the morning after Jeanne hit, the only thing visible was a mast sticking out of the river, snapped in half. *Chez Nous* had sunk, her hull breaking in two as hurricane force winds pounded against her. She had finally been given more than she could handle.

I'll never understand how a boat could live for twenty-five years, take one family thousands and thousands of miles, go through so much weather, and then sink that easily and completely. I must have somehow known that this would happen. Why else would I have stopped in Fort Pierce to see a boat that I hadn't seen in over five years? I always thought that, since the boat was built the year I was born, we had a spiritual connection.

Short Story and I were close, but we didn't have the same history. We still had to build one.

Misfits of Maule Lake

North Miami Beach, Florida • 2005

Age 25

The lights of Sunny Isles Beach cast a trail across Maule Lake, broken only by the masts and hulking wrecks of the boats that had met their fate in the 2004 hurricanes. The boats anchored in Maule Lake had been mostly abandoned, with no working bilge pumps and nobody to care for them, so a little extra rain had sent them to the bottom. If I was in the right mood, I could look out over Maule Lake and see a graveyard for boats, fenced in by the condos of Sunny Isles. Sailing the lake was treacherous—you had to keep a careful eye out for the wrecks where they inched above the surface like warm-water icebergs.

We sat on the stern of Tammy's trawler, the *Lady T*, like we did almost every night, drinking Captain Morgan rum and listening to Jake run his mouth about whatever bullshit he had on his mind. Jake was loud and volatile, a citizen of Maule Lake. "Look at those fuckers over on A-dock," he said, waving his drink around and splashing some onto the deck. Tammy, his girlfriend, shrieked and grabbed a paper towel. "I mean, they got stuck over there for a reason. It's just a bunch of freaks and rejects. They don't even have cable!"

Captain Rob scratched his beard. "Actually, there are some nice folks over there," he said.

"Traitor. Maybe you should ask the marina to move you." Jake sat on top of a cooler with a thud.

"I like my cable TV." Rob sipped from the thermos he kept full of bloody Mary mix and vodka. Somehow, B-dock was the only one with cable. The previous dockmaster, who lived on C, had strung an underwater cable between the docks to her hulking ferrocement ketch, which had since been abandoned in the lake. When I'd moved to the marina in 2002, she'd told me I was getting put in the best slip around. She'd been evicted in early 2004, when the Loggerhead Club, a fancy marina chain that bought up run-down marinas all over South Florida, moved in.

"Seriously, Rob," Jake said. "Look at what you've got over there. You've got Grant and Betty rotting on that houseboat with those mangy dogs. You've got that boat with no mast. I heard it ran into a bridge in Palm Beach over a year ago and they haven't fixed it yet. Now you've got those hippies on that little sailboat. I mean, how can they live like that? I bet they don't even have a toilet."

"Hippies?" I scanned A-dock, its pilings and boats shadows in the Miami night.

"He's talking about that couple on the little Ericson that just moved in. Boat's about the size of yours," Rob said.

"Are they living aboard?"

"Seems that way."

"Good for them." I'd have to go over and introduce myself. They couldn't be half bad, living on a little sailboat like that. I never got around to it though. A-dock, in many ways, was a world away from B-dock, and unless you had a reason to go over there, well, you just didn't. I'd gone over once before, to see the male prostitute's boat, more because I was curious about what the inside of a terribly-modified Catalina 22 looked like than because I wanted to hang out with him. I never found out whether he was, indeed, a male prostitute, but it was likely, since the park right next to the marina was a known meet-up place for the gay underworld in North Miami. Now, the boat sat abandoned and derelict, like so many others, up in the mangroves.

There was an extra pair of flip-flops on Aaron's back deck the next morning. Aaron was a Coast Guard pilot who'd just gotten divorced and moved into the slip next to mine. "What do you think?" Jake asked. "Size six?" He coughed and tossed his cigarette butt into the lake, which was dirty as sin from all the construction. It was eleven in the morning on Saturday and we were standing on the dock behind Aaron's boat.

"I dunno," I said. "They look about the right size for Texas." Texas was the married chick that Aaron had over every once in a while. Her name wasn't really Texas, but none of us were very good with names so we just said whatever came to mind. She was from Texas, and the last time I saw her she had a T-shirt on with Texas stretched across her boobs. I thought it looked good on her.

"Shit, he's done with her," Jake said. "It can't be Texas." Jake's voice boomed, and people always told him he should hire it out: do voice overs for the movies. It was deep and scratchy, like an old man's who's been smoking all his life, except Jake was one of the youngest people on the dock. He was thirty-six. Tammy had a great voice too. She was from Tennessee, and she had this little kid's high-pitched drawl. She looked like Leanne Rimes (the gorgeous grown-up Leanne, not the child star one) so when she and I went out we told everyone that she was Leanne and I was Leanne's manager or best friend, depending on what kind of attention we were trying to attract. Most people in Miami didn't know who we were talking about.

"Does Texas know he's done with her?" I asked.

"Who the fuck knows."

There was movement on Aaron's boat and Jake and I pretended to be looking at something else. Aaron's boat was a twenty-six foot Regal speedboat, one of those pieces of disposable fiberglass that people buy and forget about in a few months. Jake's term for a boat like that was an "add-a-dick-to-me." Aaron drove a Corvette too. He was a good looking guy, but he had bad taste in boats. I jumped aboard *Short Story*.

"Where are you going?" Jake asked. There was no room for privacy on B-dock. I didn't feel obligated to answer, so I shrugged and swung myself through the companionway. I grabbed Stella by her harness and tossed her out onto the deck so she could stretch her legs.

Tammy stood on the dock next to Jake when I returned. She wore a baggy T-shirt that said *Captain Morgan* on it, and her platinum hair was bed-messy. "How are you feeling?" I asked.

"Oh, I'm all right, hon," she said. "Are you?"

"Sure."

"You've got age on your side," Tammy said. I don't know why she always brought this up, because I wasn't that much younger than her. "I wish I could still drink like that. Right, Jake?" She put her arms around Jake's waist and I tried to not laugh at them, because last night they'd been fighting like it was all over. I guess that's just how some relationships work. Jake was like a big balding kid, and Tammy made a good mom.

The fiberglass door on Aaron's boat slid open, and we tried to look like we're busy playing with Stella, who stood on the bow of my boat howling at Tammy. Tammy howled back.

The flip-flops weren't from Texas. They belonged to the new bartender from Tuna's, the marina restaurant. Tammy rolled her eyes at me and I said, under my breath so the bartender wouldn't hear, "Next..." The bartender saw us all standing on the dock and fluttered her hand at us in a half-hearted wave. She was dark-haired and beautiful, but she looked like she didn't ever get enough sleep. Aaron followed her out the door wearing mirrored sunglasses, and he shook his head when he saw us but I couldn't tell what he was thinking through the sunglasses. The bartender slid on her flip-flops and Aaron helped her off the boat and we all watched her walk down the dock, hips swaying as she made her way across the parking lot to Tuna's.

"She needed a place to stay last night," Aaron said. "I wasn't going to send her home."

"Right, buddy. That's our Coastie, looking out for everyone," Jake said, coughing.

"Aaron, I think they need to start warning the bartenders up there about you," I said. Tuna's had lost at least three bartenders in the past month. They left out of embarrassment or pride or who knows what.

"Yeah?" Aaron yawned. "I'm not that bad, am I?"

"You're all right," I said.

It was almost noon so Aaron and Jake cracked the first beer of the day and sat on the dock box behind Aaron's boat. Tammy and I headed for the air conditioned cabin of *Lady T*, Tammy's forty-foot trawler.

"You're s'posed to know about this stuff, Mel," Tammy said. She was pulling off the settee cushions inside *Lady T*, and she pointed at a spot of water damage on the teak.

"You can't refinish a spot like this without recoating the whole wall."

"Damn," she said. She wanted to fix the boat up so she could sell it. "You know, I asked my shaman what to do about the boat, and he said it's going to sell really fast." Tammy called a shaman in Tennessee at least once a week. She's told me that I should call him too, that he'll tell me everything that was going to happen in my life. I wasn't sure I wanted to know.

"Have you put the boat up for sale yet?" I asked.

"No. I don't want to pay for the ad in *Boat Trader*." Tammy clenched her eyes shut and swept her hand across her forehead. "Migraine," she said.

The Loggerhead Club and a company called Boca Developers had plans to build two twenty-four story condominium towers in our parking lot. The construction had already started on the other side of the marina, where the boatyard used to be, and a coat of gray dust clung to the dock and the boats and our skin, reminding us that we were living on borrowed time. The marina would be torn up and privatized as soon as the condos started selling. In the mid 2000s in South Florida, condos were being bought and sold before they were even built.

Jake slid the cabin door open and he and Aaron came inside. He pulled a bottle of rum out from one of the cabinets.

"You all are going to start drinking *that*?" Tammy said.

"Damn right." Jake poured a shot from the bottle straight into his mouth. "I know Melanie wants some," he said.

"Not really."

A few minutes later, we were all on *Lady T*'s sun deck and Aaron was lounging back in the deck chair, sitting as far away from me as he could get. Aaron and I didn't really know what to do about each other in small spaces, being the only people single and under thirty in the marina.

Jake had a stack of magazines spread out on the chart table. He picked up the latest issue of a boating magazine called *Latitudes and Attitudes*. "Mel, how come that isn't your picture on the cover?" he said. He flipped through the magazine, letting the glossy photos of sailors in Fiji and Bora Bora spill across the table. "Look," he said. "I don't see your name in here. When are you going to get off your ass and do some real writing?"

"Jake," Tammy said. "Give her a break. She's in school. She's writing a *thesis*."

"Well I don't see why she can't write for a real magazine," Jake said. "Fuck all that literary bullshit."

"Leave her alone, Jake," Adam said. "Why don't you write for *Lats and Atts*?"

"Maybe I will," Jake said.

Tammy laughed. "You can barely even write your own name," she said. This may have been true, but he could drive a boat better than almost anybody I knew.

"I'll be right back, guys." I let myself out through the cabin door and headed down the dock to *Short Story*. I was planning on just grabbing a Diet Coke from my icebox, but when I reached the boat there were too many cords running from my boat to the dock. One of my professors, when she'd visited the marina, had said, "So it's just like the books—boat people really do sit around and drink and hit on women all day." She was so right and yet so wrong at the same time.

The cable TV came off, then my phone line. I climbed below and turned off the A.C. and my computer, and I unplugged the 30 amp master power cable and coiled it on the dock. My fresh water hose was next, and by the time I'd finished unplugging things I was laughing. Four separate umbilical cords had been connecting my boat to the dock. No wonder I never went sailing anymore.

The Honda outboard started and I shifted into reverse and then forward to make sure the linkage was okay. I let it run while I untied the dock lines and removed my canvas sail cover. I worked as quietly as I could. I didn't want help casting off. I didn't want a big show when I left the slip. I backed out, trying hard not to overwork the tiller. Stella ran up and down the deck, so excited she forgot to bark. Captain Rob popped his head out the hatch of his boat and waved at me, grinning.

Jake and Tammy and Aaron didn't see me slide past the end of B-dock. Once I was clear of the marina, I pointed into the wind and climbed up on deck to raise my mainsail. I cut the motor off and fell into a nice beam reach. *Short Story's* bow cut though the water, and I eased off on the main sheet as I weaved through the derelict boats in the anchorage.

The only sounds were the water against my hull and the hum of the wind scooping around my mast and into the sail and sliding across the rigging. As I made another pass by the marina, I heard Jake's voice booming over the water and Tammy yelling something and laughing. Aaron's voice was quieter than theirs, but I knew he was still there, laughing at Jake's jokes and telling them all about the chick he had aboard last night. At that moment, it was nice to be alone with my beautiful boat. I rested my hand on the warm fiberglass and felt the vibrations of sail and water and life move up through my arm. I loved this boat. Loved her. *Boatlove*, I whispered. *I have you and I am where I want to be.*

Love on A-Dock

North Miami Beach, Florida • Spring 2005

Age 25

One morning, in early 2005, I walked in on a beautiful raven-haired girl with a towel wrapped around her waist in the marina bathroom behind Tuna's. Her mouth made an O and she pulled the towel up over her breasts. Her hair spilled over her thin shoulders.

"I'm sorry," I said, backing out of the bathroom door. I stood in the bright light outside and waited for her. There were four showers, but, since I was one of the few women who lived at the marina, I usually had the bathroom to myself. It was run-down and moldy, and only two of the showers worked. The tile was chipped off across most of the floor, and cockroaches the size of rodents waved their antennae at me while I showered. I'd gotten pretty good at ignoring them. I didn't mind showering at Maule Lake. It was a worthwhile sacrifice for the cheap dockage and the odd family life of B-dock which I had come to love so much. I'd set my blow-dryer up on the shelf, and left it, along with a tube of cheap hair gel, for anyone to use. I knew some of the working girls who hung out at Tuna's probably used my stuff, but this didn't bother me.

The dark-haired girl came out of the bathroom and lowered her eyes as she walked past me. "I'm sorry," I said again. "I'm not used to there being anybody else in there this time of day."

"That's okay," she said, and she smiled. It made her eyes crinkle. I thought she must have been one of Aaron's women, but she looked too natural.

I saw her a few days later at the laundry room. I'd been cleaning out my bookshelf, and she held the door open for me as I stumbled in with an armful of paperbacks. "Thanks," I said. I set the books on the wooden bench that served as the marina's giveaway table. Book swaps were a common thing at marinas, and even a scrappy and run-down place like Maule Lake had one.

I waited for her to take her clothes out of the one working dryer so I could put mine in. "I'll have to tell Dave to come up and go through those books," she said.

I figured she must live here, and felt my heart flutter. She was, I thought, close to my age! I introduced myself and she told me her name was Laura and she lived on the Ericson 27 out on A-dock. I remembered Jake talking about the new couple—the hippies—the other night. I'd meant to go introduce myself.

"That's a great boat," I said. "Does it have an Atomic 4?"

"Um, yeah." She looked up from the laundry she was folding. "It does. How did you know that?" Her eyes were deep and black, and I had trouble looking into them.

I felt my cheeks redden. "Um, I've spent a lot of time researching boats. I live on the Columbia 28 on B-dock. *Short Story*."

"Are you a writer? I mean, is that why you research boats?"

"Sort of." It was hard to explain that researching boats was a lifelong obsession for me.

"You should meet Dave," she said. "He's interning at *The Miami Herald* right now. And he's studying journalism at FIU."

"No kidding," I said, and told her I was going to FIU for creative writing. They'd just gotten back from a month in the Bahamas, she said, and they were planning on living here until Dave finished school and they could save up enough money to take off cruising.

"That's awesome. I wish there were more young people out here living on boats," I said. I meant it. I wanted to hug her, to welcome her to my world, to jump up and down.

She smiled at me again. "You should come sailing with us sometime."

"I'd love to," I said.

I couldn't wait.

I never saw Dave, except for a few times late at night when he'd pull his red pickup truck into the marina and park next to Laura's car. I figured he worked journalist's hours. Once I saw them standing in the parking lot, arguing. I watched it the way you watch a bad car accident, before I grew ashamed of myself and turned away.

I showered next to Laura nearly every morning. Usually she'd be in the shower when I arrived, and she'd finish and leave the bathroom before I got out so we never had to deal with the awkwardness of standing naked next to each other. We talked occasionally—about the marina, about their trip to Michigan for Christmas. "Dave's from Michigan," she said.

I saw her walking back and forth to A-dock with laundry and groceries. I got used to looking for her car when I came home. I told her, a few times, that they should come over and hang out on B-dock some night when we were all having cocktails, but they never came. In the mornings, she sat in her car with the air conditioning on and put on her makeup before she went to work. She was a teacher.

I envied them. As much as I loved living on my own, I wanted to share my life with someone. But most men were the same: they were turned on by the fact that I lived on a sailboat and freaked out by it at the same time. They wondered what was wrong with me, and whether I would ever be a normal girl they could introduce to their mothers. I was sure their fathers would like me, anyway. I usually got impatient with mothers. On most dates, I drank heavily to make them bearable.

"I don't know what's wrong with all these guys," Tammy said. We sat on the stern of the *Lady T* drinking white wine, like we did most evenings. "I think you're too independent. You must scare them or something. They don't want a girl who knows more about engines than they do."

"I'm not going to worry about it," I said.

"Yeah, but you shouldn't be alone. You're beautiful, and intelligent, and good."

"You're a good friend," I said, and we clinked glasses and cringed as Jake and Aaron stepped aboard.

"Hey," Jake said. "Aren't you supposed to be doing homework or something?"

"It'll get done."

"That's the right attitude. Hell yeah," Aaron said. He poured me another glass of wine and slid onto the settee so close to me our legs touched.

Jake lit a cigarette and Tammy shooed him out onto the deck. I passed by him on my way back to *Short Story*. "Another shitty day in paradise, huh Mel?" he said.

"Guess so."

Dave and I crashed into each other in the marina parking lot at 2:30 in the morning on a Saturday in April. He approached me as I was getting out of my car. I'd driven home from a party when I probably shouldn't have, and could still taste the salt from the night's martinis. The party had been an awkward gathering of grad students at a piano bar north of Fort Lauderdale, and I'd been there to say goodbye to two of my closest friends who were moving away. I'd taken them sailing earlier that day, and we'd anchored off the FIU campus and grilled dolphin and drank beer all afternoon. I didn't want them to leave but it seemed like the natural thing. I'd gotten used to people coming and going, so I did what boat people do—grilled and had some last beers with my friends.

"Hi, I'm Dave...newly single." The bearded hippie boy who I had only seen from the distance of B-dock to A-dock held his hand out to me across the parking lot. "It's Melanie, right?"

"Oh, hi," I said. "Right."

"I have some beer over on my boat. I'm just getting home and I'm really not ready to turn in yet. Do you want to come over?"

"Okay. I'll be right there. Just let me put my stuff on the boat." I let the gate of B-dock slam behind me and climbed aboard *Short Story*, holding the lifeline with one hand and reaching the other out into the air for balance in the way I'd become accustomed. I let Stella out of her crate for a few minutes while I sat at the settee and collected my thoughts. It didn't seem very smart to go over to his boat, but then again it was practically next door. And I was curious.

The water was flat and the fecund smell of the mangroves hung over the marina as I made my way down A-dock. When I got to his boat, Dave looked at me like he hadn't expected me to come or had forgotten he'd invited me. It would take me a few years to realize that it had probably been the latter. I climbed aboard and followed him into the small cabin. It was a lot like mine, but with the galley aft. Inside, the gasoline smell from the Atomic 4 engine overwhelmed the mangroves. There was something comfortable about it, like it was a smell I'd known all my life. It reminded me of gasoline outboard motors and of Cole's boat and of the dozens of small sailboats I'd looked at with Michelle. Dave opened a Guiness for me and I sat next to the small table and tucked my legs underneath, leaning back and fitting into the boat so as to take up as little space as possible.

"So," he said. "It's sure a lot easier living on a boat when you're just one person."

"What happened?"

"Laura moved out a while ago."

"I thought maybe she had. I haven't seen her car lately."

"You've been looking for it?"

"No. But I'm a people-watcher."

"Oh. Well, it's a big fucking mess," he said.

"How's that?"

"She just couldn't get used to living on the boat. We bought it together and we were going to take off someday. But it just didn't work."

"I'm sorry," I said.

"What are you sorry for? It's not your fault." He sat across from me and packed a glass pipe with pot. I enjoyed the smell when he lit it—combined with the gasoline and the mangroves, it seemed homey and comforting. It reminded me of all the times I'd smelled it at parties and cookouts in the Bahamas. "You don't smoke, huh?"

"No. I just drink a lot."

"Cheers to that," he said. We sat in silence and I breathed in the smoke as it wafted through the boat's small cabin. A dreamcatcher hung in the porthole by the V-berth and a selection of herbal teas sat on the galley counter by the sink. A photo of Laura and Dave standing in the snow was tucked into a magazine rack above the table. I guessed that the tea and the dreamcatcher were her leftovers. I studied their faces in the photo—her big smile like a moon hanging over her winter scarf, crouched on skis, Dave next to her clowning for the camera.

"Is that in Michigan?" I asked.

"How did you know?" His voice cracked as he spoke and held his breath at the same time, pulling the smoke deep into his lungs.

"Laura told me that's where you were from. She said you guys went up there last Christmas."

He looked at me for a long time before speaking. "I didn't know she knew you."

"Well, we just talked in the bathroom and laundry room a few times. I always told her you guys should come over to B dock and hang out."

"She didn't want to," Dave said. "I did."

"Then why didn't you?"

"Because she didn't want me to."

"Oh." I left it at that and relaxed even more into the boat's cushions. I wasn't tired, even though it was past three in the morning.

Dave told me about himself, about how he'd grown up in the Upper Peninsula of Michigan, sailed on Lake Superior with his parents, traveled to New Zealand as a kid, gone to college for the first time at the University of Michigan, dropped out and drove a taxi around Ann Arbor, worked as a journalist for a small paper in Houghton, MI, quit and come down to Key West because he wanted to be where it was warm and to eventually buy a sailboat. He'd lived in his car in Key West until he had his credit cards paid off and could afford a place.

We moved over to my boat when we ran out of beer on his, and we sat inside *Short Story's* cabin while I listened to him talk. "You must be a good writer," he said, looking at me over his glasses.

"Why's that?"

"Because you're a good listener."

"I guess I just like stories," I said.

We put on a Grateful Dead CD that I hadn't listened to in years and danced inside the tiny cabin to "Uncle John's Band," hitting our elbows against the bulkheads and laughing. We fell asleep later on in the V-berth, fully clothed, just because we didn't feel like breaking off the evening yet. When I woke up, Dave was sitting next to me, reading a Tennessee Williams play he'd pulled from my bookshelf. "Arghhh, she has salt water in her veins," he said when he saw me move. "You're a pretty unique individual, you know that?"

I fought off sleep and a headache and pieced together the night before. I remembered all of it, from coming home from the party and meeting him in the parking lot to winding up on his boat and then mine. It had been innocent and wholesome, despite the drinking and pot, and he'd slept next to me without trying a thing. I briefly wondered what the rest of B-dock would think when they saw him get off my boat, but didn't really care.

For the rest of the week, and the rest of the month, we did everything together. He cooked for me on the alcohol stove on his boat, or showed up at mine with a bottle of wine or a papaya. We drove around Little Haiti and North Miami Beach, exploring the back roads and all the places I'd never been in my three years of living there. We slept together without ever touching

I called my sister and told her that my life was different now but I wasn't sure why. I started my first "adult" job out of grad school, one with benefits and a salary, on May 5, 2005, at Bluewater Books & Charts, a nautical bookstore in Fort Lauderdale. My position there was new and undefined. I was to be the editor of their online newsletter, book buyer, event planner, and anything else that was needed. That night, Dave and I celebrated my job by drinking martinis at Tuna's and sleeping together in *Short Story's* V-berth.

I dropped anchor off *The Miami Herald* Building on a Friday night in June. The water was flat and the lights of the Miami skyline floated both over and under the oily waterline where Biscayne Bay pulled at the grit and limestone that held the city together. The Herald Building was low and squat, the big neon blue letters looking oddly like a beer sign in a bar window: *The Miami Herald* and *El Nuevo Herald*. *Short Story* was the only boat resting under the letters.

I'd come from Maule Lake by myself, navigating the busy ICW and timing the bridges just right. I'd motored the whole way, with the Honda 4-stoke chugging and spitting and Dave's inflatable dinghy trailing in the wake. The sun set behind the city and I thought about how much nicer it was to be out on the water than sitting in traffic on I-95, and about how much like home Miami had become. It was one of my many homes.

Dave wasn't due to get off work for another two hours, so I sat in the cockpit and caught up on a few phone calls. I kept an eye on the Herald Building to make sure the anchor wasn't dragging. It had taken me four tries to get it to set.

The last call I made was to Michelle. I hadn't talked to her in a few months, which was normal for us. She was busy running the yacht brokerage that she and Zak had purchased in California and I was busy finishing school. Something felt right about talking to her that night, about sitting on my boat and telling her about Dave, about the Miami skyline that she and I had seen from the water so many times when we were growing up, about the way the current pulled *Short Story* at an awkward angle causing her to roll gently even though there were no waves. Michelle would be out in Florida in a few weeks, and I made plans to pick her up at the airport.

Later, I rowed the inflatable in to shore to pick up Dave. The outboard worked just fine, but I felt like rowing. The slick water curled around the oars and a tarpon flashed its silver scales a few feet away. I passed a small homeless camp under the bridge, and edged the bow up to the dark rocks underneath the Herald sign. Dave stood hunched under a backpack heavy with books and papers, and he made his way across the rocks to the dinghy. A spotlight swept across his face and we both turned to see a police chopper hovering over *Short Story* and fanning the water out in circles.

"What do you think they want?" Dave threw the backpack into the dink.

"I have no idea. Maybe I'm not supposed to be anchored there?"

"It makes me kind of uncomfortable," he said.

"No kidding. Let's get back out there." I pushed away from the rocks with an oar and rowed towards my boat. The chopper dropped lower, then, as fast as it had appeared, swerved around and headed out towards Government Cut and the lights of South Beach. "Weird," I said.

We sailed *Short Story* through the rest of the bridges and hit the open water past the Rickenbacker Causeway on a beam reach, watching the skyline get smaller behind us. I loved Miami so much more from this vantage point. Night sailing in Biscayne Bay reminded me of those evenings so long ago on *Chez Nous* when we sat at anchor and looked at the city lights of Miami, my talking about how lucky we were to be heading out across the Gulf Stream in the morning and away from the madness of civilization.

Hurricane Wilma

North Miami Beach, Florida • Fall 2005

Age 25

The wind shook me awake around 3 AM. It took hold of *Short Story's* mast and rattled the small sailboat as if it were playing God. I didn't believe in God, but I believed in hurricanes. I rolled onto my side and looked at Dave. He was sweating and floating somewhere between asleep and awake. I'd gone to sleep hours before he had, and I didn't want to disturb him. I knew he was thinking about his boat, which was anchored no more than 200 yards off the marina where we slept aboard mine.

Rain came over us in waves, spitting against the deck. Inside, the boat was shaped like a cave. We slept in the V-berth. My books lined both sides of the berth—Hemingway, Robert Stone, Elizabeth Bishop. The 3:00 AM light that filtered through the overhead hatch made Dave's skin look pale. Stella, the beagle, rested her head on Dave's shoulder and gazed at me. Her brown eyes were calm. Her body trembled.

We'd spent the day getting *Short Story* and *Dreamcatcher* (Dave's boat) ready for Hurricane Wilma. It was a process I'd been through dozens of times: sealing the hatches with duct tape, lashing the mainsail to the boom, stretching long spring lines from the boat to the dock, checking each line for chafe, diving on the anchors that held Dave's boat out in the lake. We'd done everything we could do.

Dave rolled in his sleep and turned his back to me. An electric transformer popped somewhere outside and blue light filled the cabin. I rolled onto my back. It was useless to try to get back to sleep. Another transformer exploded, with a sound like a backfired engine, and the blue light illuminated the rivers of rainwater that flowed over the portholes. The air conditioner clicked off and the bedside clock went blank. *We're in it for the long haul now...*I sat up and swung my feet onto the cabin sole.

It took two steps to get to the center of the boat. I checked the air pressure reading on the brass barometer that my mom had mounted to the bulkhead when I'd gotten *Short Story*, but I could already feel the change somewhere in my inner ears. It was a lightness, and high-pitched ringing that I could have been imagining but could have been real too.

At a break in the rain, I stood on the settee and slid open the companionway hatch. North Miami Beach and Aventura glowed in the pale green light, an urban jungle under a thick sky descending from the air over the Everglades. Blue lights glowed like flares and faded as electric transformers went out across the city and condo lights and street lights gave way to darkness. The center of Wilma was still far from us, approaching from the west, and I wondered what the conditions were like across the state in Naples.

"Hey." Dave stepped onto the settee behind me so he could see out the hatch. "Where do you think the center is?"

"Maybe Naples," I said.

We stood there until the rain picked up again, watching the blue lights and the darkening sky. East of us, the anchored boats in Maule Lake shivered on the black water and pulled at their anchor chains and lines. A man on a 34' Hunter woke and stepped onto his deck to check his anchor. Another man on a 22' MacGregor peered out his companionway at the mangroves and nodded before going back to sleep, certain he was in a safe place and no hurricane could shatter his quiet, solitary world. The people in the low houses between Maule Lake and the Intracoastal Waterway tossed and turned and wondered how their hurricane shutters were holding up. The jagged line of condominiums between the Intracoastal and the Atlantic rose like teeth in the eastern sky, where the sun would have been pushing into the world on any other day.

The National Hurricane Center said, "The center of Hurricane Wilma is now located at 25.1 N and 82.8 W, moving to the northeast near 20 MPH. Maximum sustained winds are 120 MPH, and minimum central pressure is 954 MB."

Stella was wedged in between us on the settee. She had her nose in Dave's armpit and her front paw on my face. The pads of her feet were like sandpaper. I tried to push her away but she wouldn't budge. "Let her stay," Dave said. "She's scared."

By 9:00 AM we stopped trying to get back to sleep. The wind moaned through *Short Story's* rigging, and the dock lines squeaked as they chafed against her cleats and stretched against the boat's weight.

The National Hurricane Center said, "Wilma is centered over the southern Florida peninsula..." Stella tried to bury herself under a blanket, and Dave stretched out and closed his eyes. "Are you Okay?" I asked.

"I'll be fine."

"Are you worried about your boat?"

"A little. I just want to go down there and take a look at her," he said.

"Don't go outside now."

At 10:00, I talked to my mother on the phone and she said the eye should be over us soon. We'd been listening to a news broadcast on a battery-powered FM radio. The newscaster said the eye should be over northeast Miami-Dade County in about twenty minutes. "Good," I said to Dave. "We can go out during the eye and check on your boat and check our lines." We waited, but the eye didn't come.

I pushed aside the curtains I'd made from bamboo placemats a few years before and peered out the salon window. One of *Short Story's* spring lines was hanging by a strand of frayed nylon. Another gust of wind hit us from the southwest, and I fell back onto the settee as the boat heeled over and pulled at all of her lines. "We've got a line about to snap," I said.

We suited up in yellow foul-weather gear and slid the hatch open. The shrieking sound cut through my skull. On deck, we walked with our knees bent, hanging onto the stainless-steel shrouds. Captain Rob hurried over to help with the lines.

"I'm going to check on my boat." Dave jumped onto the dock from the bow. The gate at the head of the dock slammed shut behind him. I couldn't see him through the swirl of rain and wind-driven spray, but I wasn't going to go below until he was back. I squatted on the bow and held onto the rail and waited. The rain clouded my glasses and stung where it hit my face.

When Dave came back, we both climbed through the companionway and fell onto the settee, dripping. "Well?" I said.

"She's moved," he said. "She's about halfway across the lake. I hope she's just dragging anchor and she'll catch on something. None of the boats out there are doing well."

"I hope nobody stayed aboard any of them," I said.

"I think someone was on that Hunter 34," he said. "The houseboat broke one of its lines and it's grinding into the dock. I'm going back over there to help secure it." The houseboat belonged to Grant and Betty, an eccentric couple in their late seventies who had lived at Maule Lake possibly since before Dave and I were born. It was a large and flimsy piece of fiberglass with a broad hull that caught the winds like a sail. They, along with most of the other liveaboards at the marina, were riding out the storm in a friend's condo. (I usually did too, but the storm wasn't supposed to be this bad). Dave's cell phone rang. He looked at the caller ID and hesitated before answering.

"No, Grant, don't come down here." Dave paced the boat's narrow cabin like he always did when he was on the phone. "We'll see what we can do." He hung up and looked at me.

"Well?"

"Grant thinks someone can jump onto the boat, start the engine, and back her around into the slip again," Dave said.

"And that someone is supposed to be you?"

"I guess."

"Then we're both going." I put Stella in her crate. She howled louder than the wind.

We hung onto the fence as we made our way out to A-dock. We couldn't see any of the boats anchored in the lake. The air was white with spray, and there was only about 100 yards of visibility. The gate on A-dock took both of us leaning against it with our shoulders to budge. We squeezed through, but a gust hit the gate and slammed it back. It hit my right side and I tried to hold it as it pushed me towards the water. The rain stung my face and my heart pounded and then there was no more dock under my feet and I was in the water, reaching for the dock and the gate and Dave.

I went under, and everything was still and quiet. I opened my eyes. The waves on the surface were inverted and bumpy, and brown light filtered down from them. The peace underneath the water was eerie compared to the madness of the storm above, and for a moment I wanted to stay there. I held my breath until I couldn't anymore, then moved my arms and kicked and reached for the surface. I came up right next to the dock. The wind and waves pushed me away, and I wondered what would happen if I couldn't grab something. Dave was on his stomach reaching for me, and I grabbed his arm with one hand and the dock with another. His glasses were crooked and water ran down his face and through the coarse hair on his chin. For a second I thought I would just stay there until the storm was over.

He pulled me out but there was no time to think about what was happening. "God," he said. "Are you Okay? Don't do that."

"I didn't mean to."

At the end of A-dock, a man wearing a flannel shirt stood with his back to the wind. He looked at us and then stared out at the lake. Somehow I was ashamed that he saw me go in the water. When we got down to where he stood, he spoke through the wind. "Have you all seen that Hunter 34? The one that was next to your boat?"

"Not since yesterday," Dave said.

"My brother stayed aboard." The wind took the rest of his words out of his mouth and across the lake before I could hear them. We didn't know him very well, even though he'd been living on A-dock for almost a year. His boat stayed in the slip next to where Dave's used to be before we moved it out to the anchorage.

The man in the flannel followed us to the houseboat, where another man tried to pull in one of the lines. But the boat was too big, and the four of us couldn't budge it. A jagged hole gaped at the waterline where the fiberglass was rubbing against the concrete pier.

Grant had said he wanted someone to jump aboard and start the engine, but the only place to board the boat was from the concrete finger pier, which had begun crumbling under our feet. The big houseboat was going to sink.

Back at *Short Story*, another line was about to chafe through. We removed one of the spring lines to replace it. We were down to the last line.

Dave's phone rang as soon as we were back aboard. "Grant, nobody can get aboard her now." Dave paced. "It's not safe…sure, you can come down here, but you're not going to be able to do anything…do you really want to be on the road right now?"

I peered through the windows at the line we'd just replaced, praying under my breath that it wouldn't break.

"Someone called him and told him his boat was holed," Dave said as soon as he got off the phone. "And he's coming down here. He thinks he's going to get on the boat and set everything straight."

"He's going to kill himself."

"That's why I need to help. So he doesn't."

"Did he ask you to help?"

"Yes."

There was nothing I could do but hope that Grant didn't show up. I knew that Dave was going to help him no matter what I said. Dave wasn't as cautious as me.

The storm should have been letting up by now, but it didn't seem like it had lost any strength. The eye had never come. We learned later that it had passed just north of us. We sat on the settee and I thought about the serene brown light underneath the lake.

A pair of headlights flashed in the parking lot next to *Short Story*, sweeping through the windows and blinking off. "Shit," I said. A horn blared, intermittent, against the shrieking wind. Dave's phone rang again. I looked out the porthole and saw Grant climbing out of his white Escalade, white hair plastered to his head. He wasn't wearing foul weather gear, and his shirt clung to his skinny body. He opened the gate to B-dock and I couldn't see him out the porthole any more because he was standing on the finger pier next to my boat, calling for Dave.

Dave climbed out the companionway and I followed. I didn't go all the way, just enough so that I knew Grant could see me and hear me. I started yelling. "Grant, you're a fucking idiot. There's nothing you can do right now. Go home and wait until the storm's over." I couldn't believe I was standing on my boat in the middle of a hurricane, yelling at a man old enough to be my grandfather. But I kept yelling until my voice cracked. "You're going to kill yourself and kill everyone else along with you. Get the hell out of here and go back to the condo." I yelled until Dave kissed me on the cheek and he and Grant disappeared though the spray to A-dock.

Then I lost it.

I sat on the settee and hyperventilated. I tried to slow my breathing, but the boat rolled with a gust and I imagined the rest of the lines snapping, and *Short Story* slamming into the concrete seawall. I thought about how thin the hull really was, and how much time it would take for the concrete to rub though the fiberglass. My dad and I had drilled through it with a hole saw once to install a through-hull fitting, and we'd both been surprised to find that it was maybe half an inch thick. I picked up my cell and called my mom. I knew I shouldn't. I didn't want my parents to know how scared I was. I didn't want anybody to know. I hadn't even told Dave. I was the one who was supposed to be strong, who had my captain's license at 18, who had spent my whole life on boats. Dave joked that I was really an old gray-bearded man trapped in a blond girl's body. I was the Old Salt. I wasn't supposed to be afraid of a storm.

"Can you tell me where it is?" I choked and sucked in my breath, trying not to let my mother know that I was crying. She was a thousand miles away in Virginia, watching the storm's track on cable. I told her about Grant's boat, about falling in the water, about the wind. She told me to call her when Dave got back and not to leave the boat. It was almost over, and the eye had moved offshore.

I got off the phone and realized I hadn't eaten anything all day, so I opened a box of crackers and ate three, but they hurt the back of my throat. I call a friend in Fort Lauderdale, thinking maybe she needed someone to talk to. She didn't answer.

Then, just like my mom said it would, the wind started to die. It died fast, and I could see all the way to the other side of the lake when I climbed outside. I jumped off the boat and headed to A-dock. I could finally walk without hunching down and bracing myself against the wind. The sky was slate-gray overhead, but it was lightening in the west. I wondered if it was clear over the Everglades.

Dave's boat rested ashore on the north end of the lake. The jib was tattered and she was on her side against the concrete seawall. There were six other boats washed ashore with her, with broken masts and broken backs and frayed canvas. My stomach turned and I started crying again, but stopped as soon as I was close enough for Grant and Dave and the other guys to see me. The man in the flannel shirt had left Grant's boat, and he walked past me down the dock, staring at the jumble of boats on the seawall. There was no sign of the Hunter 34.

Grant rushed inside his boat and started carrying piles of his wife's expensive clothing up the ramp as the boat settled lower into the water. A pile of clothes was strewn on the dock. Dave jumped into Grant's inflatable dinghy and tried to get a line to one of the outside pilings. The boat was sinking faster every second, and Grant was still inside.

"What the hell is he doing?" My voice cracked and I remembered yelling at Grant. I felt bad about it, but I was still angry. And now he was inside his own sinking boat, trying to rescue his wife's shoes. The water was halfway up the big windows.

"Grant, get out of there." Dave reached for the line that held the dinghy to the sinking boat and slashed at it with a pocket knife.

The water was almost above the windows, and Grant was still inside. His wife and daughter came down the dock, sprinting, hand in hand.

Finally, Grant came out of the aft cabin. The water was up to his chest as he waded toward the bow. His daughter and I reached down and pulled him up onto the dock as his boat lurched and settled on the bottom of Maule Lake. Grant opened his mouth to say something but nothing came out. Dave and I carried Grant's belongings down the dock. I wanted to tell Grant I was sorry, but I couldn't look him in the eye. Not yet.

I was sorry about his boat. I wasn't sorry I yelled at him.

An hour later, the wind was still blowing about thirty-five miles per hour, and the cold air from the front that had steered Wilma to us was moving in. Maule Lake sparkled and the sky was sapphire. Dave and I drove over to Point East, the condo development where his boat had washed ashore. We took his truck so we'd be able to go through puddles and newly-formed potholes in the road. All the lights on Biscayne Boulevard were down, and a few cars crept though intersections. Branches and trees looked like they'd been twisted off by a thousand tornados, and trash and roofing tile littered the road.

We parked a little ways down from the boat and walked through the community's previously manicured lawn, stepping over twisted aluminum and broken glass. We both wore boots.

People trickled out of the buildings, walked down to the water and stared at the boats. I recognized most of the boats from the anchorage. They sat in odd positions on the seawall. Most of these boats had been cared for and loved—few were derelicts. Wilma seemed to have left the derelicts in the lake and moved the nicer boats ashore. A woman wearing too much makeup for right after a hurricane craned her neck at Dave's boat and I wanted to slap her. I didn't know what had gotten into me—first yelling at Grant and then feeling violent towards this woman who I didn't even know. All I wanted to do now was survive and move on. Niceties were insignificant. Dave and I walked the length of his boat.

There was a hole in the bow, just under the waterline, about a foot long, running up the stem. "She's a tough boat," I said. "It took a lot to hole her."

Dave didn't saying anything. He felt the rudder to see whether the post was bent. It wouldn't budge. The forward hatch, which was bolted down, had been ripped off. He climbed aboard and began to flake the loose mainsail. "I just want to keep it from getting any worse," he said.

I stood on shore, because I didn't know how stable the boat was and I didn't want it to move or slide back into the water. Dave carefully folded the sail over onto itself, an act of routine maintenance that seemed odd and somehow right.

While Dave was inside the cabin, the flannel-shirted man from A-dock appeared on the seawall. He walked fast, pushing past the onlookers the same way we had. There was something feral in his eyes. He walked straight to me, as if we were the only other people alive at the Point East Condos, and shook his head at the boat, but didn't say anything about it. He touched the hole in the bow.

"Any sign of your brother?" Dave came out of the companionway, holding a stack of books.

"No," the man said. "Are there more boats down there?" He pointed to the northeast end of the lake, where a canal flowed out to the Intracoastal.

"We haven't been down that far yet," I said.

"Ok. I'm going to keep going until I find him," he said. He wrapped the shirt around his chest as if he felt a chill that nobody else could feel. "I'm sorry, man," he said to Dave as he patted the hull.

"Can we help you look?" Dave said.

"No. Take care of your own boat right now," he said. "Maybe later, when you're done." He continued east, walking with his head down, scanning the murky water along the edge of Maule Lake.

We stayed at Dave's boat for about an hour. He called BoatUS to file an insurance claim. They said they'd get to it in a few days—they had a lot of work to do. We taped a garbage bag over the hole where the forward hatch should have been. Dave went below again. "I just want to get a few more books," he said. The books he piled in the cockpit were soaked and spotted with mildew. While he was below, a van marked "Police Divers" drove past us through the condos. For half a second, I wondered whether the van had anything to do with the missing man from the Hunter.

We carried a few things to the truck, not sure what to take and what to leave on the boat for the insurance people. In the end, we just took the VHF radio, an expensive pair of binoculars, and the books. "Are you sure you want these? I have most of them on my boat," I said, my arms full of wet Faulkner and Tennessee Williams. When we'd met, Dave had been reading *Cat on a Hot Tin Roof,* and he'd walked around the marina, barefoot, with the book sticking out the pocket of his cutoff shorts. I'd known right away that he was going to play a significant role in my life.

"I can't get rid of books," he said. "I'm not as unattached to my stuff as you are."

Dave was right. The only things I'd ever really been attached to were boats.

That evening, the marina filled up again. People had been arriving all afternoon, gazing around in shock at the damage before picking through the crumbled concrete and garbage to their own vessels, where they combed the decks for damage. The air was crisp, and a small group of liveaboards gathered at the foot of B-dock in front of *Short Story*. Dave and I turned down glasses of wine because we couldn't drink as fast as it was being offered. As the sun set over the Everglades, the silhouettes of trees in West Greynolds Park, where the gay underground and the homeless wandered the mangroves and coexisted on any normal day, stretched into the orange sky. Usually the trees were gray and washed out by streetlights, but now they were black and skeletal. Halloween was only a week away, and they looked well suited.

The marina still had water pressure, so I headed up to the marina showers. I carried a heavy flashlight with me so I could see in the dark while I let the cold water run over my body and wash away the salt and sweat of Hurricane Wilma. In the beam of my flashlight, the bathroom took on an eerie glow. It was all concrete and mildew, with broken tile and palmetto bugs that seemed unnaturally large haunting the corners and drains. Sometimes I wondered why I chose to put up with them. I could have rented a nice apartment when I'd moved to South Florida. I would have had to get a roommate to afford one, but I wouldn't have had to shower each day in a campground-style bathroom. Instead, I'd bought a thirty-something-year-old fiberglass sailboat. I'd chosen to live aboard during grad school because it seemed like the natural thing for me to do. I'd chosen to prepare for each hurricane like my life depended on it, and to live among the derelict boats and characters at Maule Lake Marina. I'd chosen to be that girl who's a little tougher than most of the guys, who scares them off when she curses and drinks too much rum, who, because she's blond-haired and twenty-five, looks halfway good sanding the teak and scrubbing the decks in her shorts and bikini top. I'd chosen, by default, to have an old age of skin cancer and wrinkles. I dressed in a hurry and switched off my flashlight as I pushed open the bathroom door and headed back into moonlit Miami.

Dave and the man in the flannel shirt stood in a tight circle near the marina entrance, talking to a woman I didn't recognize. Dave broke away from the two, who huddled over something in the woman's hand, and walked to B-dock with me.

"What's going on?" I opened the gate and my mind flashed to the gate on A-dock, slamming into me in the middle of the storm and knocking me overboard.

"That woman lives at the Point East condos," Dave said. "She had pictures of the guy's brother. His Hunter's broken into pieces over there, and he washed up naked on the seawall. She saw a body and snapped a bunch of pictures."

"I guess maybe that makes it seem less real. Like CSI or something."

Dave just looked at me. "The police divers showed up pretty fast," he said.

"She thought the pictures would help identify the body."

"Did you see them?" I glanced over at *Short Story*, where the soft glow of 12-volt lighting illuminated the portholes. The power was out in the rest of South Florida, but we had light aboard my boat.

"Yeah."

We sat on the dock for awhile later that night, drinking more wine with our neighbors, huddled in sweatshirts and jeans. The air had turned cold, and the night was perfect and dark. All around, where North Miami Beach and Aventura and Sunny Isles were usually lit, darkness blanketed us. I hadn't seen stars in Miami until that night.

Back inside *Short Story*, I opened a can of clam chowder and fixed grilled cheese sandwiches on the alcohol stove, while Dave sat on the settee with Stella on his lap. Light from two candles played across the cabin. I was ready to eat dinner and go to sleep for a week. Stella eyed the food on the galley counter.

"That's a comforting smell," Dave said.

"What, Stella's breath?"

He laughed. "No. Stove alcohol. We can cook, and all those people living in condos and apartments can't right now."

We both knew that the power could be out for weeks. *Short Story's* batteries wouldn't last that long, but one of our neighbors had a generator and we could plug the battery charger into his boat so we'd be able to run the 12V refrigerator and the lights.

On the last of my cell-phone battery, I called my parents again. They had seen the images on the news of boats tangled along the shore and roofs blown off and homes destroyed. The death toll in Florida was rising as people emerged from their homes to be electrocuted by loose wires. The man on the Hunter 34 in Maule Lake was one of the first reported deaths in Miami, and news crews showed the row of boats washed ashore at the Point East Condos and interviewed condo owners, who said they'd feared for their lives when they'd looked out their windows and saw the boats being tossed ashore like toys.

"The important thing is that you're okay." I could hear my dad breathing into the phone.

"Yeah," I said. I was almost too tired to talk.

"It may take awhile for the insurance company to get to Dave's boat," he said.

"I know. They're dealing with a lot of claims."

"They still haven't cleared all the boats out of Fort Pierce from the hurricanes last year," he said. "The old *Chez Nous* is still there."

"Really?"

"Yeah, it's sitting beside the ICW, up in the marsh. You know the hull is cracked, right? So I guess it's almost impossible for it to be moved."

I tried to picture *Chez Nous* sitting abandoned in the marsh in Fort Pierce.

My childhood home was now just another piece of hurricane trash. I'd spent almost nineteen years aboard *Chez Nous*, trying to live a normal life with my parents and sister and all our pets, trying to be a regular kid and then a regular teenager. "I'm surprised she cracked," I said. "She had a solid hull. You watched them build her."

"Well, it actually wasn't as solid as you'd think," Dad said.

"What do you mean?"

"The hull was badly delaminated," he said. "When I was installing some electronics about ten years after we bought her, I had to drill out a cross-section of the hull. The layers of fiberglass came apart just like that—there was air in between them where there should have been resin."

"Why didn't you tell me that before?" I sat on the settee and rested my back against *Short Story's* bulkhead.

"I thought you'd worry about it too much," he said. "Sometimes a boat is just a boat. It's a thing. You can't get too attached to it, even if it's your home. There are plenty of other boats." He would know. He'd had four sailboats so far and had no problem trading up.

"Tell Dave that, okay?"

I did, but I don't know if either of us believed it. I went to sleep that night wondering whether it would be worth driving up to Fort Pierce and wading through the marsh to see *Chez Nous*, and to see for myself whether the hull was as badly delaminated as my dad had said it was. The Hunter had probably broken up during Wilma from a poorly constructed hull, and Grant's boat had sunk because the concrete pier had ground through fiberglass with too little resin. I thought about the time my dad and I had drilled out a cross-section of *Short Story's* hull, how it had been thin but solid. My dad had shaken his head and said, "You'd better not be planning on crossing the Gulf Stream on this boat."

A cool wind blew through the overhead hatch, ruffling the hair on my forehead. Dave and Stella breathed in unison next to me, and *Short Story* rocked me to sleep.

Hurricane Trash

Fort Pierce, Florida • Fall 2005

Age 25

A month later, I found myself back in Fort Pierce. This time, I'd traveled to Stuart for work, and Fort Pierce was only a few more miles away. I couldn't find *Chez Nous* at first. I parked just north of Port Petroleum and walked across a sand lot to the edge of a deserted quarry before I saw her, sitting in a yard on the other side. I backtracked to my car and drove around and into the yard.

Her back was broken. Before, the damage had just been cosmetic—a little fiberglass work would have fixed her. Now, there was a jagged tear down the starboard side, and I could look through it into the galley. The streams of rust looked like blood and the old eyelashes that my mom and my sister and I had painted over the running lights made her look human.

Two guys from the yard came over in a rusty pickup truck and looked at me. They didn't say anything—just parked and stared. After all, there were "No Trespassing" signs posted all over the place.

"Um, I used to live on this boat," I said. "I lived on it for 19 years. I just wanted to come over and see it."

"Oh," said the guy behind the wheel. He scratched his head under his baseball cap and looked at the boat, then back at me. "I guess that's pretty hard for you."

"Sort of," I said.

"Well, you don't want to go onboard." He made it sound like seeing what was inside the boat would be too difficult, but I knew what he meant. He meant that it wasn't safe, and that if he saw me try to climb onboard he'd come over and chase me off. Fair enough, I thought. It was his boatyard and I was trespassing.

They drove away, leaving a cloud of dust that settled in my eyes. I walked around to the stern of *Chez Nous* and looked for a way to climb onboard.

The boarding ladder was hanging crooked, attached with one bolt where there should have been four, and I didn't see any other way to board. Searching the yard for a ladder would have been too obvious. I wanted to go inside, to see what she looked like at twenty-six years old, sunk and broken. I wanted to take something with me—a token of a life and a boat that I'd left at nineteen.

I grabbed the ladder and hoisted my leg up, but three years of practicing yoga hadn't made me flexible enough to climb onboard. I circled around to the bow, and saw the guys in the pickup truck watching me.

The gash in the bow showed where she had been driven into one of the barges that she'd been moored with. The fiberglass was thick here, probably the thickest part of the hull, and the most susceptible to storm damage. Dave's Ericson had been holed in the same place in Wilma, right at the stem, a place where patches were almost impossible.

I pried a piece of fiberglass loose from the dry laminate and stuffed it into my pocket. It wasn't much, but it was a tiny bit of *Chez Nous*, enough to satisfy me. I knew that I'd probably forget I had it in a few days, that it would probably come out of my pocket in the laundry or sit in my car for months, but that didn't matter.

Maybe the reason I don't attach myself to material things is because I can keep them alive by writing about them. I hardly ever take pictures, because I trust my mind to remember the details. But this is naïve, isn't it? My memory isn't always going to be good. I took a few photos of the running light eyes, rust streaming down the hull like tears, and I got in my car and sat. Around me, the industrial wasteland of Fort Pierce spread and crumbled into the marsh and I thought about how this was the place of my first big heartbreak, the time I felt the need to run away from my family after my dad had told me that my life would never amount to anything because I had thrown away my virginity, and about how Michelle had come to rescue me only for the two of us to be hounded by the Jehovah's Witnesses all the way out of town. I called Michelle, because I knew she would understand, but she didn't answer. She was probably closing another deal at the yacht brokerage that she and Zak owned in Southern California. As busy as she was these days, I knew she'd call me back when she could.

When my parents arrived in Fort Lauderdale for the season, I showed them the photos. I'd hidden them up to that point like they were from a crime scene that I wasn't supposed to see. The same night, Dad pulled out some old photos of a massive blister repair job we'd completed when the boat and I were only five. No boat, at five, should have had the kind of blisters that she had. But we fixed them, draining and drying and filling in each one, and that boat took us over 3,000 miles each year for the next fourteen years.

Mom and Dad and I looked at the pictures in the light of the new *Chez Nous'* kerosene lamp, passing them around without speaking. I could almost smell the polyester resin and the sweet fumes that leaked out of the blisters in the fiberglass when my dad had popped them like blisters on someone's skin. It's no wonder that I thought the boat had so many human qualities. As much as we tell ourselves that it's just a boat, it never really is.

Selling the Dream

South Florida • Fall 2006

Age 27

Dave and I got our eviction notice on March 10, 2006, along with about 85 other boats at Maule Lake Marina. The boom had finally found its way to our little run-down pocket of South Florida and Boca Developers was ready to break ground on the twin condo buildings that shimmered luxuriously in the architectural renderings on advertising collateral. This was the time of pre-construction investment buying, when condos were being bought faster than they could be built.

A few people had been evicted already over the past year, as the marina's new owners saw fit to do so for one reason or another. One sad man, whose name I'd never known, donated his boat to some nonprofit organization that had to tow it away, oyster shells and all. His boat hadn't run in at least ten years. He sun-baked cans of beef stew all day long in the cockpit before he opened them and ate them standing in his companionway and using the deck for a table. The trimaran at the end of B-Dock, on the deck of which proudly sat an old marine toilet, moved down to Coconut Grove.

The rest of us stayed, knowing that we were living on borrowed time. Dave was writing articles for *The Miami Herald* about imminent domain and the folks who were being ousted from ocean-front trailer parks just so that condos could be built to "better" the community. Their plight was no different from ours.

By the end of March, the marina was alive with the sound of power-tools as everyone shifted into refit mode. Boats that hadn't left the dock in years were finally being fixed up. I bought the $200 worth of outboard parts (a new carburetor, fuel pump, and fuel filter) that I'd needed to get *Short Story's* Honda running properly again. For the first time in four years, I listened to the outboard hum without sputtering. Across the dock from me, Captain Rob stood back and admired the new Awlgrip job on his ketch.

"I didn't buy a boat so that I could stay in one place," said Mike, one of the marina tenants who, along with his wife, Brenda, lived on a nice Island Packet. They'd been at Maule Lake for a little over a year, and were planning to go to the Bahamas before coming back to the States to replenish the cruising fund for another adventure.

Sliding out of Maule Lake on a perfect, sunny April Fool's Day, *Short Story* rounded the end of A-Dock, cutting through the water. There were no crowds waving us off, and, even though I'd arrived at the marina almost four years ago, leaving felt easy. Dave and I were bound for a nicer marina on the Dania Cutoff Canal, and home was right under our feet: a 28' classic sailboat, happy to be on the move.

The marina in Dania was in a nice residential neighborhood behind the Jai-Alai, right across the canal from where small island freighters emptied their cargo and sought repairs on the jungle-like southern edge of Port Everglades. We made friends with the other folks at the marina and grilled out on the community grill on Saturday nights. Dave befriended a homeless man named Billy who sold Haitian mangos and other stuff out of an old pickup truck and we spent weekends on Dania Beach basking in the sun and listening to Billy talk about the price of mangos and his time in the Florida Department of Corrections. Billy used the marina showers, which was how he and Dave had met, and he hung out with a rough group of guys who ran crab traps offshore. Since I was somewhat of an expert on commercial fishing and fish in general, Billy and I had long conversations about the nobility of making a living on the water.

Weekdays, however, were pretty normal. I shared my small office at Bluewater Books & Charts with a tattooed chick who scared the crap out of me for my first two months on the job before becoming one of those unexpected best friends. I made a niche for myself at Bluewater and traveled to boat shows to sell books and charts. Dave worked the night shift as a part-time copyeditor at the *Herald*, so our paths barely crossed during the week. The boat would roll to its side in a violent way at three or four in the morning when he came home and I would wake up for a minute or two and then try to go back to sleep as he sat at the dinette and pounded the keyboard on his laptop.

Living on a boat in South Florida was becoming increasingly more expensive. The high value of waterfront property was driving slip rent up, and in Dania I was paying nearly four times what I had originally paid on monthly dockage at Maule Lake in 2002. The hurricanes in 2004 and 2005 had caused many insurance companies to drop vessel policies in Florida, and *Short Story's* insurance was now triple what it had been. Life, also, was more expensive. I had student loans to pay back and credit card debt, all of which had been the end result of not working enough during grad school. My job came with an office and health insurance, but I was starting to think about things like starting a retirement fund and getting ahead. At twenty-six, it hit me that I hadn't chosen a career in which I would suddenly earn lots of money. Maybe I wasn't ever going to find a way to support myself from the boat while cruising. Life as I had known it was over.

I took on the challenge of selling *Short Story* the way I do every challenge. I sat down at the computer one day and asked myself what I could do to make it happen. I wrote a flowery description of the boat and posted it, along with some photos that made the interior look larger than it actually was, on Craigslist. I priced it at market value, which was slightly less than what my parents had paid for it in 2002. I started getting phone calls right away but none of them were serious.

I went to bed early on a Sunday night at the beginning of December, and at ten the phone rang. I didn't recognize the number. "Hello?" I propped myself up on the pillow so that I could get better reception.

"Are you the person selling the sailboat?" A gruff male voice was on the other end. He sounded like he may have had a cigarette in his mouth.

"Yes," I said, trying to wake myself up enough to go into selling mode.

"My girlfriend and I want to buy it," he said.

"Um, ok. Would you like to come take a look at it?"

"We've already seen it. We were down at the marina today and saw it. If it looks anything on the inside like it looks on the outside, then I am sure it is great shape."

"Well, I would be happy to show you the inside. I work tomorrow but get off at five."

"Listen, we're staying in a weekly rental on Dania Beach. We just moved down from Rhode Island and we'd really like to be able to move aboard at the beginning of next week. So we don't have to pay for another week here." He coughed and just as I was starting to wonder why he was in such a hurry he said: "I can give you cash—half tomorrow evening and the rest on Friday if that gives you enough time to move out."

"Okay—that sounds good." My head spun and my mouth felt dry.

"Can we meet you there tomorrow night at 5:30?"

"Sure. I'll work up a contract tomorrow."

We ended the call and I wondered what in the hell had just happened. This wasn't supposed to be so easy. Most buyers would have asked for a survey and a sea trial, and would have negotiated on the price. But cash was cash, and South Florida was the land of transients who came down from the north loaded with it.

I called Dave, who had moved off the boat into an efficiency in North Miami. I had asked him to leave after an outburst that was just on the wrong side of violent. We were in that awkward not-broken-up-but-not-really-together phase. "I think I just sold the boat," I said.

"What the fuck?" I could hear him in the background throwing something against the wall of his efficiency, which I had never seen.

"Yeah. They are coming tomorrow with cash. Can you be here?"

He stopped throwing whatever it was. "Sure."

I tried to sleep, Stella curled up against my side. I listened to the water rippling against the hull and the pecking sound of the tiny shrimp and fish that fed on algae. I thought about the boxfish at Maule Lake that had kept me awake on that night shortly after my arrival, and about how much like home Maule Lake had felt. This boat had been my home for almost five years, and as long as I was alone it was all the home I needed. But it wasn't big enough for Dave and me (we would learn later that no space was big enough for us) and it didn't make sense economically for me to stay aboard. It was really time to be an adult and make big-girl decisions.

The couple from Rhode Island was waiting on the dock for me when I got home the next night. The man was tall and wore a cowboy hat and the woman was a perky and cute blond who looked about my age. We shook hands and they climbed aboard, eager to see the inside. I sat in the cockpit and listened to them exclaim over the two-burner stove and the spacious berth and the refurbished head. I knew, after listening to them speak quietly to each other, that they were going to stick with their decision.

Dave arrived as the couple and I were signing an as-is purchase agreement that I had drafted while at work that day. He sat on the dock and watched as they handed me the $2,500 deposit in cash and we laughed and shook hands again. They hugged each other and held on to each other's waists as they walked to their car to leave.

Dave and I found ourselves at a waterfront bar in Ft. Lauderdale. Even with all that cash in my pocket, I couldn't bring myself to go crazy at one of the high-end restaurants on Las Olas Boulevard. Slumming it with a cheap carafe of white wine and fried seafood felt much more comfortable. Come to think of it, slumming it had always felt more comfortable than the frantic social climbing and quest for material success that my peers seemed to embrace. I was plenty driven, but didn't care for designer handbags or expensive shoes or top-shelf vodka. I was just as happy drinking boxed wine in the cockpit of my old sailboat as I would have been sipping a twenty-dollar martini at a flashy nightclub.

In a few days, sitting in the cockpit of my sailboat wasn't going to be an option. Panic was starting to swell in my chest and throat, and I stared across the table at Dave and poured myself more wine and twisted my napkin around between my fingers.

"What are you going to do?" Dave wiped his hands on his shorts underneath the table and slouched over a beer.

"Find an apartment, I guess."

"In four days?"

"Guess so."

And by the end of the night, it was decided that Dave and I would find an apartment and move back in together and give things one more shot before parting ways for good (in a year). With four days to look and at the height of tourist season, we found a furnished monthly rental in Hollywood, FL. It was an old and musty triplex less than a block east of U.S. 1, just in from a busy walk-in clinic and a tax preparer's office. The small kitchen had a jalousie door that opened into a swath of bougainvillea and the rooms were cooled by two window-unit air conditioners. Bad hotel artwork hung on the walls and the queen bed sagged in the middle. But it was big and had a bathtub and room to spread out. There was no dishwasher or washer and dryer but there was enough closet space so that everything that I had kept aboard *Short Story*, all my earthly belongings, could easily be stashed away and out of sight. Only the things I needed for my day-to-day life would be left out in the open in this new place.

The buyers met me on Friday night, as planned, at the marina in Dania. The man carried the rest of the $5,000 cash in an envelope in one hand and a brown bag containing a bottle of cheap vodka and plastic cups in the other. He, his girlfriend, and I sat together at *Short Story's* dinette and signed all the appropriate paperwork to make the boat theirs. He poured small portions of the vodka into the plastic cups and we toasted to their new boat and sat in silence. I leaned back for a moment and looked around the boat. All my things were gone. The brass lamp and the books and the few framed photos and my old boxes of letters and magazines and souvenirs from my life had been moved to the Hollywood apartment earlier that day. I could easily have been lulled into believing that this was like any other evening, and that I was sitting inside my boat drinking with new friends and sharing stories in the non-judgmental way that most boaters did when they first met.

Their stares jarred me out of my calm. I realized that they were waiting for me to leave. This was their boat now and I was their guest, and they were eager to relax and start getting used to their new home. I stood and shook their hands again and flew out the companionway, into the cockpit and onto the dock, where I planted my feet for one last look at my boat. Her waterline was high now that all of my belongings had been moved off, and her stern was empty where I had removed the name. I didn't want the new owners keeping the name *Short Story*.

Short Story and I had never been to the Bahamas. We had never been south of Biscayne Bay. But we had lived together with more trust and intimacy than most humans do, both loving each other equally as much and both finding our own ways to show it. I showed my love by taking care of her, waxing and polishing her and keeping her teak sealed, and she showed hers by enveloping me and keeping me safe and rocking me to sleep every night. I wondered if I had made a terrible mistake by letting her go, but my feet moved me forward to my car and I put my head down and kept moving. There was no turning back. This was life and I was an adult and if my childhood dreams didn't fit any longer with my adult reality then what could I do but move forward?

For most of the year, *Short Story* stayed in Dania. I drove down to the marina to look at her some evenings after I left work, in no hurry to get back to the dreary apartment in Hollywood. I kept my visits short and hoped, each time, that the new owners wouldn't see me. I checked to make sure they were keeping her clean and caring for her, and I marveled at how strange she looked with someone else's stuff drying in the cockpit or draped over the lifelines.

One evening she was gone. Haze hung over the Everglade to the west, where the sun was dipping down into the swamp, and a single frigate bird glided above the marina on its way out towards the Gulf Stream. The other boats rested on flat calm water and across the canal the boatyards and island shipping terminals had shut down for the night. I recalled the new owners saying something about taking her to Rhode Island for the summer, and I hoped that they were somewhere offshore, under full sail and cutting through the thick air and water on their way north.

Short Story would enjoy that.

Restless

Florida • 2012

Age 32

I find myself looking at the tiny infant life preservers whenever I walk into a West Marine, although my trips to West Marine or any marine supply store are few and far between these days. I live in a modest house in St. Augustine, Florida, and am married to Will, the boy from Virginia who kissed me in the V-berth of his friend Trey's boat at Narrows Marina when we were thirteen. Will has a successful career in the financial industry and I have a successful career working for an art college, helping recent graduates find work in their fields. I spend approximately ten hours a week commuting to and from Jacksonville in my Honda CRV with my one-year-old, Maryann, sleeping in the back, gently breathing and sighing and occasionally waking and saying, "Dadadadadada bah!" My sister lives in another modest house, just down the road from me. She and her husband have a baby boy, and we fantasize about the perfect and conventional life that the two cousins will have, growing up in the same neighborhood.

Will and I talk constantly about how we ended up here. After I sold *Short Story*, Dave and I moved in and out of a series of small apartments in South Florida. But Dave's ups and downs had finally gotten to be too much for me. I moved into a cockroach-infested efficiency in Fort Lauderdale that reminded me of the apartment I had rented the year I moved off *Chez Nous*.

Will graduated from Virginia Tech in 2001, stuck around Southwest Virginia because of a girl, and married her in 2002. They moved to a town in Central Florida optimistically named Beverly Hills and bought a house with a swimming pool and enjoyed the benefits of boom time as the real estate market bubbled and the value of their house went up and up. In 2007, they got divorced and Will, like many people, ended up with an upside-down house.

Will found me on an online social networking site, and we met up for dinner in Fort Lauderdale. In October, 2008, we were married in Deltaville, VA, a small town at the mouth of the Rappahannock River and very close to Narrows Marina. We would have had the wedding at Narrows, but the marina was in such a state of disrepair that even the idea was depressing. Michelle and both her parents were there, and Tim surprised us by driving down from the Annapolis Boat Show for the occasion. My favorite professor, Dan Wakefield, flew up from Miami, and my dad fought back a tear as he walked me down the dock from the new *Chez Nous* to the chairs and friends and future that were set up on the grass in front of the small marina clubhouse. As cliché as it sounds, the wedding was perfect. And the marriage, as cliché as it sounds, is perfect too. It is a healthy marriage, with its small fights and big ones, but it is still perfect.

Will and I bought a trailerable sailboat right after we got married. It was a Starwind 19, and, in retrospect, a poor choice made out of eagerness to just buy the first boat we could afford that met our criteria of being easily trailered and launched, sailing well, and having enough room in the cabin for us to spend the night. We had some good sailing days in the Florida Keys, off of Fort Lauderdale, and in St. Augustine, but a dismasting and ever-present leaking problem prompted us to sell the boat in 2010. Besides, I was pregnant, and I didn't think that I could possibly spread my love thin enough to include a needy boat, a husband and an infant.

We moved to St. Augustine when we decided we wanted to have kids. It was an easy decision and an easy move. We had originally wanted to sell Will's house and buy a liveaboard sailboat, but as the real estate market tanked it became obvious that selling his house was not going to be an option. We were lucky, after almost a year of having it on the market, to find a renter for a fraction of the monthly mortgage payment. I applied for and received a promotion that would move me to the Jacksonville location of the chain of private art colleges that I worked for, and Will received a transfer a month later. We bought a house just down the road from my sister's, optimistic that real estate, in 2010, was becoming a good investment once again.

Maryann arrived five weeks early, eager to see the world and get on with her life. I couldn't help thinking, in the sleepless and physically exhausted daze that follows giving birth, that she was already a lot like me in her persistence and independence. At one, she is immensely stubborn, always convinced that she is right, and sometimes I think that maybe she is wiser than I am.

I am on the phone with Tim, trying to grasp again at the dream and how it can be defined and redefined. How, as a responsible adult with student loans to pay off over the next twenty-plus years, does one work boatlove into one's life? Is the answer to charter occasionally, when money allows? Is it to buy another trailerable sailboat? Is it simply to keep on moving forward, with abstract goals and plans in mind, like I seem to be doing?

Tim sits in his house in Rhode Island and looks out the window at his graceful *Ave Marina* in the driveway, prepped and ready for springtime launch and sailing. Tim tells me how nice the weather has been in Rhode Island and about how he and his daughter had just applied a fresh coat of bottom paint to *Ave Marina*. He talks about sailing with his daughter and about how she has been his favorite person to sail with and about how much she loves it. "Last summer, the best sailing I had was with her and a 12-year-old pal of hers, sailing to Wickford," he says. He, it seems, is happy.

I am distracted by that happiness and my mind defaults to an image of crystalline Bahamian water running through an inlet on the incoming tide and detaching each individual grain of sand from the limestone islands to carry it out and deposit it on the shallow banks. The incoming tide was always my favorite time to dive, because the water that came in from the deep Exuma Sound was clear and clean. The visibility was good and the underwater horizon stretched on forever. Sometimes I stopped moving my hands and feet and just let the current carry me along with it, keeping pace with the grains of limestone sand and the Sargasso weed and the small fish that didn't fight it. Riding the current like this was the closest thing to flying that I could imagine. When it carried me over the rolling hills of deposited sand where the water became shallower and the current slowed down I watched the underwater landscape change and began kicking my feet again, refusing to slow my pace.

I feel an overwhelming sense of the unstoppable movement of life, pulling us along in its current. I talk about my job and the book I'm finally finishing, this book, and how it makes me want to live aboard again.

"You and I chose passion careers," Tim says. "We chose the types of jobs that we weren't going to make a lot of money at and that weren't necessarily going to fund living at sea."

"Is it that simple?" I look around my office at my framed degree and my institutional furniture, and at the photos of Will and Maryann.

"Maybe," Tim says. "I wanted to be a writer too. I had the dream of living on a boat but the dream of being a writer was just as strong. I knew I had a good career at *Cruising World* and I stayed with it instead of going cruising right away."

"Sometimes I wonder if I should have gone to law school," I say. "You know—worked my ass off like my dad did. Made money while I was young."

"You would have ended up writing anyway."

"Maybe." I let Tim's familiar voice fill my head and it reminds me, like it always has, who I am. I'm a writer just as much as I am a boat girl. And I am a parent and a wife and a friend. I feel guilty because I realize that Tim has given me more in this conversation than I have given him. The simple fact that a person can understand you so well that you are able to call them and ask them something about yourself that you can't understand is so overwhelming that I am afraid for a moment that I am going to cry.

"Do you want to hear more of my story?" Tim asks. It is a story he has hinted at and shared with me in pieces whenever I cared to think less about my own dramas and more about someone else's. It is about what he was going through when he and I first met, and about the life aboard a boat that he intended to have but, as of yet, has not.

I want desperately to hear it but am so caught up in the retelling of my own story that I don't listen to him as well as I should. I regret this the instant our time is up and the empty dial tone is ringing in my ears.

In the background of my relationship with Tim are the questions that I asked him the first day we met. *"I want to know how you felt about growing up aboard,"* I had told him. *"I mean, how do you feel about it now that it's over and you're living ashore?"*

"I wanted to keep doing it," he said. *"I didn't want to go to college or move ashore."*

"Then why did you?"

"Circumstances," he had said. And I understand that now. My circumstances have changed so much from when I left *Chez Nous*. I am nearing the same age that my parents were when they bought her and made the decision to raise a family aboard. I understand how hard it must have been for my father to give up his lucrative career, and for my mother to learn how to bake bread from scratch and teach her kids at home. When people ask me, now, how I feel about having grown up aboard a boat, I tell them that I am happy and thankful that my parents were able to raise my sister and me the way they did. Anything that I missed by not going to a regular school or being a "land kid" seems so insignificant compared to the things we learned and did. If I could find a way to move my family onto a boat, I would do it. But my circumstances are different. I chose a passion career rather than a money career. I went into debt to go to college and grad school. I was born at a different time and under different circumstances. I am not my parents. They don't have the same opportunities that I have now, and I don't have the same ones that they did then.

I wish I could give Maryann a hot night in a marina or anchorage somewhere hundreds of miles away, where she could watch buttonwood fires and listen to her parents talk to people from different places and different backgrounds. I want to open her mind to that different way of life and teach her to treat each friend as if they might sail out of her life permanently at the next weather window. I wish I could teach her how to repair an engine and clean a conch, and show her how to identify different species of shark and how to wash laundry by hand over a cistern on a deserted island. I want to teach her how to enjoy taking it easy and moving slowly through the water on a feminine and shapely sailboat rather than rushing from one thing to the next, and to appreciate the unique, different, and crazy people who come along in life instead of being afraid of them. I want her to question the things that everyone else accepts as "normal" and to think for herself. I want her to be strong and self-sufficient.

Will is optimistic and he thinks that we may be able to find a way to give Maryann some of these things. We just have to make some sacrifices and change our circumstances.

Looking at those infant life preservers, I have to fight the urge to buy one, knowing that by the time I get Maryann out on a boat on any kind of permanent basis she'll have outgrown it by several sizes. It would be more prudent, I think, to save the $30-50 and put it towards the "boat fund" that tends to be more a figment of our imagination than anything else. The conversations Will and I have usually go something like this:

Will: "Remind me, again, why we moved to St. Augustine and didn't just buy a boat and live on it?"

Me: "We were being responsible. We thought it would be a good place to raise kids. Houses are better investments than boats."

Will: "You were trying to be more like me and I wanted to be more like you. I was the responsible one and you were the crazy one."

Me: "We need to find a middle ground."

Will: "We need to get a boat."

Me: "We need to get a boat. But we have too much stuff. Debt. Houses. Furniture."

Will: "We can get rid of it. That's one thing about you and me. If we want to do something, we don't make excuses. We figure out a way and we do it."

Me: "I'll wreck my credit, say 'fuck it all' and move onto a boat if you'll wreck yours."

Will (thinking about it): "We can figure out another way."

And so we go on like that for a little while and always come to the same conclusion: that we are restless and may not be as cut out for the normal life as we thought we were. For a guy who grew up on a farm, writing letters to a boat girl and dreaming about sailing to tropical islands, and a boat girl who grew up sailing to tropical and not-so-tropical islands, the normal life is a little mundane. My dad, when people always said, "Welcome back to the real world," on our return to the States, would reply: "This isn't the real world. The real world is out there." He'd point to the Gulf Stream, whichever direction it was, his arm like a compass's needle.

I remind Will: "Raising a child is a bigger adventure than either of us have ever had," and he agrees with me. And we know, because of who we are and where we've been, that the adventure of normal life will be anything but normal.

Melanie Neale grew up aboard a 47-foot sailboat, exploring the U.S. East Coast and Bahamas. She earned a Bachelor of Fine Arts degree in Creative Writing from Eckerd College in 2002 and a Master of Fine Arts degree in Creative Writing from Florida International University in 2006. She has taught college, detailed boats, captained and crewed on boats, coordinated marketing events, and scooped minnows in a bait shop. Melanie currently works as the Director of Career Services for a private art college in northern Florida, where she lives with her husband and daughter.

Melanie's fiction, poetry and nonfiction have been published in many literary journals and magazines, including *Soundings, Seaworthy, Southwinds, GulfStream, Latitudes & Attitudes, The Miami Herald's Tropical Life Magazine, Balancing the Tides, The Georgetown Review, RumBum.com* and *Florida Humanities*. Her "Short Story" column appeared bimonthly in *Cruising World Magazine* from 2006 to 2009. *Boat Girl: A Memoir of Youth, Love & Fiberglass* is her first book.

CPSIA information can be obtained at www.ICGtesting.com
Printed in the USA
BVOW071918300912

301792BV00003B/2/P